T0303410

AMERICAN HISTORY THROUGH A WHISKEY GLASS

HOW DISTILLED SPIRITS, DOMESTIC CUISINE, AND POPULAR MUSIC HELPED SHAPE A NATION

HARRIS COOPER

Skyhorse Publishing

Skyhorse Publishing books may be purchased in bulk at special discounts for sales promotion, corporate gifts, fund-raising, or educational purposes. Special editions can also be created to specifications. For details, contact the Special Sales Department, Skyhorse Publishing, 307 West 36th Street, 11th Floor, New York, NY 10018 or info@skyhorsepublishing.com.

Skyhorse® and Skyhorse Publishing® are registered trademarks of Skyhorse Publishing, Inc.®, a Delaware corporation.

Visit our website at www.skyhorsepublishing.com.

10 9 8 7 6 5

Library of Congress Cataloging-in-Publication Data is available on file.

Cover design by Brian Peterson
Cover photo credit: Getty Images

Dedication:

Elizabeth Moore Durie Cooper
We are companions for life

CONTENTS

Old Spirits Brought to a New Continent

Way Out West. . .in the Ohio River Valley

The 18th Amendment. . .and the 21st

Home from the War and Ready to Party

It's Hip to Be Square

Whiskey Today: Millennials Who Mash

The Constitution only gives people the right to pursue happiness. You have to catch it yourself.
—Ben Franklin

Chapter 1
PREREQUISITES

The truth of history? A fable agreed upon.
—Napoleon

A SOBERING ASSESSMENT OF HISTORY

How do you fashion trustworthy history when many of the actors, those people recounting events, were inebriated or breaking the law when the events occurred? Or, when history is conveyed on recipe cards and notebooks shared among friends and tinkered with by each? Or, when it is in a song, with "borrowed" lyrics and melodies, heard but rarely written down?

Napoleon's assertion (he wasn't the first to make it) that history is myth is certainly correct in one sense. The reconstruction of past events frequently involves some informed imagination. And more so for the history of popular culture than most other narratives. The episodes involved in whiskey history, for example, often were clandestine, were acts of rebellion, or were carried out by people who were, well, maybe not as mentally sharp as they could be.[1]

But the history of popular culture is much more than tales spun after a sip or two. Good accounts of history are the result of painstaking work, much to be admired. They help us understand today in the context of yesterday. An old proverb declares, "History doesn't repeat itself, but it rhymes." Amen.

And then there was Winston Churchill. He liked to say (again, he certainly was not the first), "History is written by the victors." True, sort of. Churchill was correct in that societies—and American society is

---

1   Even for our personal histories we need to fill in the gaps in our life stories. Sometimes we do this with memories that are real but that our minds have gently shaped to fit a coherent chronicle. Or, we simply make memories up, however truthful they may seem to us. This adds to the challenge for the whiskey historian.

no exception—are filled with individuals, families, clans, work groups, churches, and other assemblages of people. This Matryoshka nesting doll of unique identities means each person will experience the same events in different ways. In Churchill's time, the person who owned the printing press owned history. But there was more than one printing press and more than one voice interpreting events when the presses rolled.

THIS BOOK

American History Through a Whiskey Glass: How Distilled Spirits, Domestic Cuisine, and Popular Music Helped Shape a Nation is a rendition of history told through the lens of our country's most distinctive products: bourbon and rye whiskey. But it is more than that; its purpose is to guide you in *experiencing* the role alcohol, food, and music have played in the lives of common and uncommon Americans. It will do so using an immersive approach. The narrative will focus on American whiskey, but the histories will be followed by suggested tastings of America's own spirits, descriptions of yummy food recipes culled from cookbooks throughout the country's past, and recommended playlists of music evoking the times. If you take up the challenge, this journey through America's past will involve your senses of sight, smell, taste, and hearing.

There are lots of ways you can enjoy the book. You can simply read it cover-to-cover by yourself. Or, you might read it while tasting some of the whiskeys, making use of the recipes, and listening to the music. Or, you might get adventurous and say to a friend or partner, "Hey, let's invite some folks over for a potluck dinner."[2] You can assign each invitee an era and have each bring an appropriate whiskey and dish. Maybe you'll call it a "pot still dinner." If you are really adventurous, you might do most of the preparation yourself, with a little help from friends.

And American humor plays a large role in telling the nation's story as well. If you choose to read in solitude, I promise you will chuckle along while learning about some interesting episodes in American history. If you choose to enjoy the book with others, I assure you that you and your friends will have an evening you will never forget.

One more quotation here, this time from the novelist Julian Barnes. He wrote that history is ". . .that certainty produced at the point where the imperfections of memory meet the inadequacies of documentation."[3]

Let's look at the different sections of the book.

THE HISTORIES

I have divided American history into eight eras. Some eras cover relatively long spans of years, for example colonial times, while others are shorter, like the 1950s. Whiskey history dictated the epochs. Each era is covered by two chapters that look at different aspects of that time.

Also, you will find words and phrases throughout the book that were *slang* and idiomatic expressions that came into common usage around the time the chapter covers. Slang is informal language (perhaps short for "secret language") used more in speech than writing, and it typically originates in a particular subculture. It can then make its way into broader usage, often culminating with an appearance in dictionaries. Carl Sandburg wrote that slang "rolls up its sleeves, spits on its hands, and goes to work." John Moore called it "poor man's poetry." And slang words for alcohol and alcohol consumption compete with sex for top spot on the frequency list.

---

2   Don't try to do all sixteen chapters in one night, please. Pick your favorites and then do it again.

3   The best way to convey a sense of a time is to use the words spoken by the people living in it. In fact, maybe the best history speaks for itself.

THE WHISKEYS

Along with each history, I describe a whiskey that is obtainable today and claims to be a reasonable facsimile of a product available at the point in time being covered.[4] Charles Cowdery has written that "Whiskey makers of all sizes will tell you that a whiskey needs two things to succeed: a good flavor profile and a good story. Does the story have to be true? Not necessarily."

The Tasting Notes

I have provided three tasting notes or flavor profiles for each whiskey. The first note is an excerpt or description from the distillery website and the second is from the webpage of an expert whiskey taster. Any material quoted exactly from the webpage can be identified because it is indented on the page (and used with consent). Each tasting note is accompanied by the web address of the provider so you can visit it yourself and see a fuller description (as well as notes on tastings of lots of other spirits).

The third tasting note is a consensus of three panelists, "The Over a Barrel Gang." First, Watson Fitts who is a Certified Specialist in Spirits. Second, Elizabeth Cooper who is a former third grade teacher who prefers gin over whiskey. Finally, I am the third taster, and I prefer whiskey over gin. We completed the tasting notes separately, then compared our notes and came to consensus.

You will notice a few things about tasting notes. Sometimes the tasters agree on the sensory experience they encountered from each whiskey, sometimes not. Sometimes the profiles are terse, other times they are filled with wonderful and vivid language. But

remember, no one is a better judge than you are of a whiskey's aroma (its "nose," in the biz), taste (sensation on your palate), and finish (how it feels going down your throat). Sharing your impressions with friends, new and old, while you sip whiskey together can be a blast, and enhance your friendship.

Many whiskey tastings follow a presentation order that starts with softer whiskeys (less spice, less alcohol) then move on to more bold expressions. This helps the taster get a more nuanced feel of the later whiskeys because their nose and taste buds are not *burned out*. I don't do this here because whiskey history didn't unfold that way. Not to worry, though. If you are eating dinner while tasting, the evening will take long enough so that your senses should settle down between sippings (and the foods are generally not spicy). Also, it's always best to consume plenty of water between tastings to cleanse your palate (and dilute the alcohol in your body).

I can tell you there isn't a loser whiskey in the bunch, but the whiskeys do differ in cost and availability. Different ones will appeal to different noses and taste buds. Also, the notion of pairing whiskeys and food by their complementary taste or making selections based on the season of the year are both great ways to enjoy whiskey. Pairings of these sorts involving whiskey would have rarely happened in the days of yesteryear.[5]

I finish each tasting note section with a suggested toast, should you be enjoying your trip through history with friends. Most include a quotation from a person relevant to the time.

---

4   Nearly all of the whiskeys listed can be found in multiple expressions, meaning they have been bottled at different ages, selected from different barrels, contain different amounts of alcohol, among other variations in production. I had to choose one, so I picked the one I thought was most appropriate for the brand's place in history.

5   Thomas Jefferson might have held wine tastings at dinners. He was a wine aficionado. Imagine sitting at Monticello with a vast array of food on the table (in colonial times meals often weren't divided into too many courses) coupled with a large selection of wine, mostly imported from France. (British Lieutenant Colonel Banastre Tarleton missed taking Jefferson prisoner when he captured Monticello, but he did capture several bottles of wine from Jefferson's cellar.)

THE RECIPES

The recipes were drawn from cookbooks of the era or from websites that focus on traditional, era-specific, or regional cooking. As with the whiskey tasting notes, most of the recipes contain direct quotations (again signified by being indented on the page) and the source is listed.

The courses for the eras flow roughly from appetizers to desserts. I have kept an eye on a few things when picking recipes: authenticity, or a main ingredient that is true to the time; relative ease in preparation; and dishes that can be served in small portions. Speaking of portions, earlier recipes may not suggest portions; later recipes do say how many they serve. Most recipes suggest the proportions of ingredients are based on serving six to eight people. Adjust accordingly; remember, if you are cooking for or with friends, you may be preparing several small plates.

I stayed away from recipes that included squirrel or raccoon, for obvious reasons. All the recipes can be modified to appeal to modern tastes, and in a few instances, I make suggestions for modification. Obviously, you can do the same. You might even find a source for the entire dish or its main ingredient that prepares the dish for you in advance. If you would like to substitute your own recipes, the key to being true to a particular period is to focus on the main ingredient so the culinary history remains relevant. Main ingredients should be easy to pick out.

I do suggest that you read the recipes even if you don't intend to cook them; many contain a valuable lesson in history, whether through their ingredients, utensils, directions, or even the terminology and dialect in which they are written.

THE MUSIC PLAYLISTS

The music playlists have been constructed to evoke the historical era. The songs are not strictly from each era, though most are. Some songs are about people or events that occurred during the era but the song itself was written later on. Some were recorded by contemporary artists. The songs are also selected to represent different genres of music. I apologize if there are omissions; in the end, it was impossible not to reveal my personal sensibilities through the selections. The main focus is on songs that would have been broadly popular at the time. A good backstory or a well-known composer or artist also helped me pick a song. I also provide the date of recording for all songs, and the year they were penned for some of the older songs. A brief liner note on each number is provided.

LET'S GET STARTED

Are you ready to immerse four of your senses in a trip through American history? Before starting our journey, a few preliminaries will help make sure your experience with the whiskeys is optimal.

The Etymology of "Whisky" and "Whiskey"

The word "whisky" is derived from the Gaelic "uisge baugh" [WEEZ-ga-bochh] or from the Irish "uisge beatha," meaning "water of life" (early distillers—alchemists—believed alcohol could prolong life). Say either quickly and it becomes "WEEZ-ga," anglicized to become "whisky." This origin story has a competitor, though. Oscar Getz wrote that "whisk" (Scottish: "quhiske") means to move away rapidly. A whisk was the name of a small carriage for one or two people used by smugglers to evade the tax man. The smugglers used a whisk, and smaller barrels than the law required, to move their contraband quickly. We still whisk things away today, use a whisk to stir things, and until 2017, *Wisk* laundry detergent made that "ring around your collar" disappear in a flash.

In the United States and Ireland whiskey is spelled with an "e." It is spelled whisky almost every place else, but even some United States distilleries (for example, Maker's Mark, Cascade Hollow, Old Forester) dropped the "e" because of a family connection with Scotland. Where did the "e" come from? It may simply be from different translations of the Scottish and Gaelic-Irish word, or the Scotch and Irish may have used it to distinguish their product from one another.[6]

Bourbon. Bourbon is a type of whiskey. To be called bourbon a whiskey has to be made in the United States from a recipe that contains no less than 51% corn, distilled at not higher than 160 proof alcohol (80% alcohol by volume), put into a new charred oak barrel, and bottled at no more than 125 proof (62.5% alcohol by volume) or less than 80 proof. Canada, Scotland, Ireland, Japan, and lots of start-up countries also produce whiskey but they ain't bourbon because they ain't made in the United States (more on this later).

What Glass to Use

If you are drinking at a bar, you will likely be served whiskey in a tumbler. That's fine, but don't let the large circumference of the glass entice you into sticking your nose in below the rim (see nosing, below). Some antique whiskey tumblers are beautiful, my favorite being a Clear Crystal Tear Drop Pattern from the Duncan & Miller Glass Company of Pennsylvania. It holds

A diagram of the Glencairn whiskey glass.
If your bartender brings your whiskey in this glass, you're in the right place.

about three ounces. You won't see these at bars because the originals were made from the mid-1800s until 1955. The granddaddy of all whisky glasses is the Thistle Whisky Tumbler by *Edinburgh Crystal* from Scotland. These are also collectibles now. But if you want to treat yourself, hunt one down and enhance your experience at home. Don't drink whiskey from a plastic cup; the smell of the plastic will interferes with the aroma of the spirit. If a bar tries to serve you in a plastic cup, leave.

The go-to whisky glass today was developed by Glencairn Crystal Ltd., also from Scotland but widely available. The glass was designed by the managing director of the company. The shape of the glass began with the traditional nosing glass used in whisky labs in Scotland. The glass's final design was settled upon when *Glencairn* invited master blenders from the largest whisky companies in Scotland to improve on the traditional design. The new design went into production in 2001. It holds a bit more than four fluid ounces but should be filled up only about a third of the way, to the point in the glass with the largest circumference. In 2006, the *Glencairn* glass won the Queen's Award for innovation in design and it is endorsed by the Scotch Whisky Association. It is now used by every whisky distillery in Scotland and Ireland and most distilleries in

---

6   I will use both spellings, depending on whether I'm referring to American whiskey or a whiskey distilled in a country or by a distiller that doesn't use the "e."

the United States. It was designed to focus the whisky's aroma. Hold it close to the bottom of the glass.

Now to the backwoods experience. If you're drinking *moonshine* straight from the jug, stick your forefinger in the finger hole, flip the jug onto your shoulder, and drink like the boys in the holler do, and as pastorally stated in the song *Copper Kettle* (see chapter 11), "lay there by the juniper while the moon is bright."

How to Taste Whiskey

Instructions on how to taste whiskey have some generally agreed-upon steps. First, start by holding your glass up in a gentle light and become familiar with its appearance. Is its color dark or light? Amber, brown, or gold (whiskey is sometimes called *liquid gold*)? Color in whiskey comes from lots of aspects of the aging process (unaged whiskey is clear). Generally speaking (and unless a coloring agent has been added, which it can be for Scotch whisky), the deeper the color the longer the whiskey has been aged, or, more precisely, the more interaction it has had with the inside of the barrel in which it rested.

Second, swirl your glass gently and notice whether your whiskey leaves a ring where it reached highest on the glass. Is the whiskey dripping down the insides? This indicates the liquid's viscosity (its "legs") and gives you an indication of the feel the whiskey will have in your mouth. Lotsa legs, creamier.

Third, tilt your head and glass toward each other at about a 45° angle. Gently inhale your whiskey's aroma. This is called "nosing" and the aroma that whiskey gives off is called its "nose." As you do this, leave your lips slightly open, allowing the aroma to get in the back of your mouth and your throat. Approach the glass slowly and don't let your nose get inside the rim. Alcohol is fiery stuff and you don't want to "burn out" your sense of smell. Is the aroma robust (is it strong and does it hit your nose while it is still well above the glass?), delicate, or somewhere between these extremes? Once you've had time to think about

what you're experiencing, back off, take a few breaths, and do it again.

Also, if you are tasting with a person serving as a whiskey guide, now is about when your guide will ask, "What aromas do you smell?" Your guide should never disagree with you. There are hundreds of smell sensors in your nose and different people have different combinations of them. You and your friends can smell different things, some more than others, and all be correct.

Fourth, take a small sip of the whiskey, enough to excite the front of your mouth and then slowly push or let the whiskey wend its way to the back of your tongue. Is the body on your tongue light or heavy (full-bodied)?

Fifth, focus on taste as you take another sip. Your taste buds can pick up any of five flavors—sweet, sour, salty, bitter, and umami (or savory, the experience you get from gravies, mushrooms, broths)—all over the tongue. Taste buds also are a bit more sensitive on the sides of your tongue than in the middle. Your tongue picks up slightly more bitter flavor at its back. If you can sense this happening as the whiskey slowly covers your tongue, you're on your way to being a pro.

Sixth, take a small *swig* and swish it around your mouth. Now you will get the full experience. If you have a tasting guide, she or he will say, "What do you taste?" Again, the guide should never disagree with you. True, there are identifiable chemicals in whiskey that you could use to verify what you are tasting and in what proportion. But what fun is that? Beyond the general experience of sweet and spicy, creamy or watery, along with a few flavor staples (vanilla, maple, caramel), tasting whiskey is a lot like seeing faces in the clouds. If someone says, "Hey, that cloud looks like Santa Claus," we all see the bearded gentleman. Peoples' sensitivities are different too, so smell what you smell and taste what you taste. Enjoy the whiskey that tastes best to you. Remember, the finer differentiations you experience will come mostly from your nose, not your tongue. Other people may try to influence you to like what they like; this will work only to the extent you let them.

Seventh, swallow. Do you feel the spice and alcohol heat in your throat? Is this sensation weak or strong? Some whiskeys, especially ryes, will pepper your throat. Finally, some whiskeys you will feel all the way down your esophagus and others not (long or short in length). This experience will best be predicted by the amount of alcohol in your drink. You can find the alcohol (ethanol) content of your whiskey on the bottle's label expressed as its proof (200 proof is pure ethanol) and its percentage alcohol by volume (ABV).[7] Most American whiskeys range from 80 proof (40% ABV) to about 120 proof (60% ABV; these latter expressions are typically called "barrel strength" but not always, so be careful). Again, how you react and how much you enjoy these sensations are your personal preference.

Before you try your next whiskey, cleanse your mouth with water. Also, put your nose in the bend of your elbow and take a deep breath. That will reset your sense of smell, with a smell familiar to it, before you start nosing the next whiskey.[8]

Neat, Water, or Ice?

Some whiskey drinkers will tell you to never add anything to your drink. They advocate tasting whiskey straight or neat (clean, unadulterated) as it was intended by the distiller. Others will tell you to add water if you want to dilute the alcohol content and prevent burning out your taste buds. You will also experience different flavors because the water will "open up the whiskey." Adding ice (*on the rocks*) may dull some flavors and put your taste buds to sleep, but you may also find the cooler temperature is more refreshing. It will also reduce the alcohol burn.

At a whiskey tasting, if the serving amount permits, consider drinking about a third of your pour neat then adding one or two drops of water or one small piece of ice. If you add ice, taste it after a minute or two then let it sit until the ice is completely gone. Taste it again. You will have three different experiences and know which suits you best when you have that whiskey brand again. You'll like different whiskeys in different ways.

Should you use a large or small cube of ice? Small cubes (the ones with the ends carved out) will cool your drink faster than large cubes as long as the total surface area is the same. After twenty minutes, the cooling will be the same regardless of the size of the cube. A bunch of small cubes will dilute your drink faster. A whiskey stone will reduce the temperature of the drink about ten degrees in five minutes and stay that way for about twenty minutes. No dilution whatsoever.

Now, how did whiskey cross the Atlantic Ocean and get to America?

---

7   How did "proof" come to be? No one knows for sure, but one story says British sailors in the 18th century doused their gunpowder in rum to test the rum's potency. If the wet gunpowder still ignited, it was 100% proof the rum was good. Actually, it was about 57.15% ABV. In the United States, though, proof has been standardized so that 100 proof means 50% ABV.

8   Don't wear perfume or cologne to any tasting. It can interfere with your experience and that of the people seated around you. If you are the host, you can suggest this to your guests; they should be impressed. Also, ensure they have a designated driver, a car to pick them up, or are walking home.

OLD SPIRITS BROUGHT TO A NEW CONTINENT

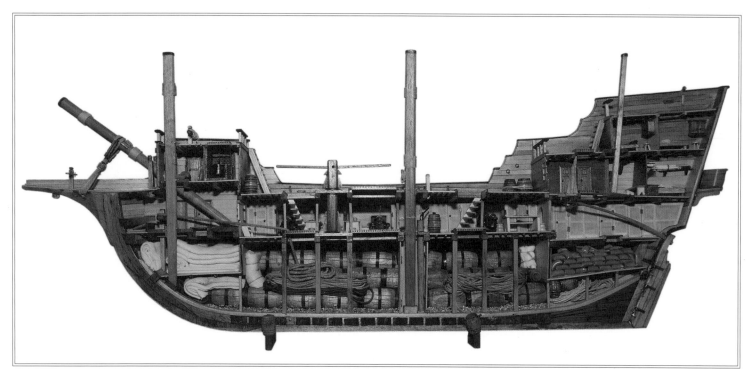

Cross section of a 17th century merchant ship.
The *Mayflower* looked like this (note the barrels).

Chapter 2
A DECIDEDLY AMBIVALENT MEETING OF THE NEW AND OLD WORLD

[Tavern keepers are to sell] not over twopence worth to any one but strangers just arrived.
—Plymouth Colony Law, 1633

WHICH WAY ARE WE HEADED?

Benjamin Franklin is considered by many to be "The First American."[1] Franklin was known for his genius, but also for his love of wine, the company of women, and jovial companions. Yet, Ben disapproved of drinking alcohol in excess. Drunkenness was off limits. So much so that in 1737 Franklin published in his newspaper, the *Pennsylvania Gazette*, a dictionary of over 200 synonyms for drunkenness. We don't know the reason he did this. Perhaps, it was Philadelphian's penchant for alcohol; in 1754, the City of Brotherly Love had twelve churches and fourteen rum distilleries.

The first successful English settlers to North America predated Franklin's birth by nearly a hundred years. They were not big whisky drinkers either, not even malt whisky, though it had been made in Scotland since the 12th or 13th century, first distilled by monks. Beer was the beverage of choice. The Pilgrims on the Mayflower in the fall of 1620 brought with them forty-two tons of beer and fourteen tons of water, with ten thousand

---

1   Of course, this requires you to ignore the Asians who first arrived here in the Ice Age after crossing the Bering Straits. You also must ignore their descendants who numbered in the millions before the first Europeans arrived. The first recorded English birth in North America was Virginia Dare, but she disappeared with the other members of the Lost Colony of Roanoke, VA. Maybe we can consider Franklin the first person to exhibit traits associated with the American character.

SOME OF BEN FRANKLIN'S SYNONYMS FOR DRUNKENNESS
Published in his newspaper, the *Pennsylvania Gazette*, 1737

A: Addled, Casting up his Accounts, Afflicted, In his Airs.

B: Biggy, Block and Block, Boozy, Bowz'd, Piss'd in the Brook, Drunk as a Wheel-Barrow, Head is full of Bees, Been in the Bibbing Plot, Drank more than he has bled, Sees the Bears, Had a Thump over the Head with Sampson's Jawbone.

C: Cagrin'd, Cherry Merry, Half Way to Concord, A Cup too much, In his Cups, Non Compos, Loaded his Cart, Been too free with the Creature, He's Chap-fallen.

D: Disguiz'd, Kill'd his Dog, Took his Drops, Dipp'd his Bill, Dagg'd, Seen the Devil.

E: Wet both Eyes, Got the Pole Evil, Got a brass Eye, Eat a Toad & half for Breakfast.

F: Fishey, Fox'd, Fuddled, Sore Footed, Fears no Man, Crump Footed, Been to France, Flush'd, Froze his Mouth, Fetter'd, His Flag is out, Fuzl'd, Been at an Indian Feast.

G: Gold-headed, Glaiz'd, Booz'd the Gage, As Dizzy as a Goose, Had a Kick in the Guts, Been with Sir John Goa, Globular, Got the Glanders.

H: Top Heavy, Got by the Head, Hiddey, Hammerish, Loose in the Hilts, Knows not the way Home, Has Taken Hippocrates grand Elixir.

J: Jolly, Jagg'd, Jambled, Jocular, Been to Jerico, Juicy.

K: Clips the King's English, Seen the French King, Got Kib'd Heels, Knapt, Het his Kettle.

L: In Liquor, Makes Indentures with his Leggs, Lappy.

M: Sees two Moons, Moon-Ey'd, Muddled, Muddy, Rais'd his Monuments.

N: Nimptopsical, Got the Night Mare.

O: He's Oil'd, Smelt of an Onion, Oxycrocium, Overset.

P: Drank till he gave up his Half-Penny, Pidgeon Ey'd, Has scalt his Head Pan, Wasted his Paunch, Eat a Pudding Bagg.

R: Raddled, Lost his Rudder, Ragged, Been too free with Sir Richard, Like a Rat in Trouble.

S: In the Sudds, As Drunk as David's Sow, Got his Top Gallant Sails out, As Stiff as a Ring-bolt, Staggerish, It is Star-light with him, Carries too much Sail, Stew'd, Soak'd, Been too free with Sir John Strawberry, Has Sold his Senses.

T: Top'd, Tongue-ty'd, Tann'd, Tipium Grove, Double Tongu'd, Topsy Turvey, Tipsey, Swallow'd a Tavern Token, Thaw'd, Trammel'd.

V: Makes Virginia Fence, Valiant, Got the Indian Vapours.

W: The Malt is above the Water, Been to the Salt Water, Water-soaken, Out of the Ways.

gallons of wine thrown in for good measure. The voyagers drank beer in impressive amounts because it was safer to drink than water (which would grow algae on the ship). Regardless, the Mayflower was aiming for Virginia but ended up in New England. Some say it was bad weather, others say they were out of beer or maybe they just needed a designated driver.

Once on land, settlers throughout the colonies brewed beer, brandy from peaches, rum from molasses (imported from the Caribbean Islands), and hard apple cider.

RYE WHISKEY

When the colonists made whiskey, it would most often have been made from rye. Rye is a grain related to barley, the grain of choice back in their land of origin. It was also plentiful in the colonies because it is a hardy grain that can be grown in relatively poor soil. Distillers would make "all rye" whiskey, which was 100% rye, or a mixture of rye and barley grains. In those days, whiskeys were named for the location of the still it came from, not for the distillers themselves. So, whiskey was known as Monongahela, or Pennsylvania, or Maryland.[2]

The origin of the first rye whiskey made in the colonies is lost in time. However, we have a contender for the first corn whiskey made by an Englishman on new world soil.

GEORGE THORPE

Many historians credit George Thorpe with being the first distiller of corn whiskey. Or at least, Thorpe was the first to document it. In a letter to his business partner John Smyth, on December 19, 1620, Thorpe wrote that the colonists had "found a waie to make soe good drinke of Indian corne. . . I haue diuers times refused to drinke good stronge Englishe beare [that is, beer] and chosen to drinke that." Indian Corn, or maize, was a remarkable crop. It had a large yield per acre, was hardy through inclement weather, cultivated without plowing, and obviously, made a fine-tasting beverage.

George arrived in Virginia before the Mayflower. He was an owner of the Berkeley Hundred plantation on the James River (you can still visit the site today: http://www.berkeleyplantation.com/history.html). Thorpe was also an educator. His attempt to establish a college is credited to have started the lineage of The College of William and Mary.

Part of Thorpe's mission in Virginia was to convert the indigenous people of North America to Christianity and save them from *tarnation* (hell). He was less successful at this than his other ventures. He thought well of the natives though, writing they were "of a peaceable & vertuous disposition."

---

2   Today, rye whiskey is making a comeback. Check to see if the rye you are considering is a replication of a three-hundred-year-old product, or simply shares a name. This doesn't mean it isn't great for drinking, but it won't take you way back when.

The natives thought less of George and his intentions. Chief Opechancanough was a leader of the Powhatan Confederacy who spoke the Algonquian language.[3] The chief used deception to gain George's trust. Opechancanough suggested he was open to conversion but secretly was planning attacks against several James River settlements.

"The First Thanksgiving 1621," at Plymouth Plantation painted by Jean Leon Gerome Ferris, circa 1912–1915. A festive occasion.

Thorpe, along with nearly 350 other English men, women, and children were killed in the Indian Massacre of 1622. (Why it is called the "Indian Massacre" is a mystery; it was the pilgrims who were annihilated.) George's body was mutilated and his farm destroyed. His still for making corn whiskey, however, was allegedly unharmed and carted away by the Powhatans.

THE FIRST AMERICAN DISTILLERY

The first commercial distillery in America appeared on Staten Island, NY, in 1640. William Kieft, the Director General of the New Netherland Colony, made the decision to build it and Wilhelm Hendriksen was the master distiller. He is believed to have used corn and rye, making his concoction officially a whiskey. It is

3   Chief Opechancanough was Pocahontas's uncle.

"Indian Massacre of 1622" depicted in cut wood by Matthäus Merian, 1628.
A less festive occasion.

doubtful it was aged for long.

THE IRISH FROM ULSTER ARRIVE

The heritage of whiskey distilling in the new world began in earnest when large numbers of immigrants from Ireland started arriving in the mid-1700s. About half came from Ulster; they were called Scots-Irish (a term of some controversy) because many had already emigrated down to Ireland from Scotland. Since Irish Catholics were prohibited by law from leaving England, most Irish who traveled to the new world were Presbyterian. The Ulster Irish hated British rule because of trade restrictions imposed in the late 1600s. The Irish and Scots hated the English Malt Tax of 1725.

The tax forced many Scottish and Irish distillers underground, as well as into open rebellion. The Scots-Irish felt so oppressed by British rule that many were willing to come to the New World as indentured servants, working without pay for seven to ten years to cover their ship passage. They quickly moved to western Pennsylvania, the Blue Ridge Mountains, and Appalachia. They were well-represented among the first patriots and

THE MASH BILL AND OTHER INGREDIENTS THAT MAKE UP WHISKEY

The Grains

The grains that go into making whiskey are called the "mash bill" or "grain bill." The grains are the same as those that go into making bread:

Rye. Rye is a European grain also easily grown in the middle colonies. It is a crop resistant to disease and extreme weather conditions. It contributes a spicy or peppery flavor to whiskey. If the whiskey contains less than 15% rye it is sometimes called "low rye," more than 15% and it might be called "high rye."

Corn. Corn is a grain that is indigenous to the United States. It was easily grown by the first settlers. The standard corn used in whiskey is called "#2 grade dent," although lots of specialty strains are used.

Wheat. Wheat adds sweetness to whiskey. Most distillers use a red winter wheat.

Barley. Barley is the main ingredient of Scotch whisky and a secondary ingredient of American whiskeys though more distillers are using it as the main grain today. Almost always, barley will be malted; that is, wetted before it is fermented. This step releases enzymes that help the yeast do its job.

Whiskey flavors will vary depending on the type and proportion of each grain in the mash bill and how fine the mash is milled before the process begins.

The Yeast

Yeast is a living, single-celled fungus first observed by Anton van Leeuwenhoek in 1860, long after whisky was already being distilled (yeast is in the air everywhere). It is responsible for fermentation, the process that converts sugars in the grains into ethyl alcohol, carbon dioxide, ATP (a chemical that helps keep the reactions happening), and heat. The most often used yeast in the whiskey industry is *saccharomyces cerevisiae* (which roughly translates to sugar, fungus, beer) but different distillers use different strains that create different flavors. If you intend to make whiskey, be sure not to use the yeasts whose esters create perfume and nitroglycerin; you won't get the taste you're after. The Four Roses Distillery uses five different yeasts and two mash bills to create ten different whiskeys.

The Water

Water for brewing and distilling can come from anywhere, as long as it is uncontaminated. Most often, it comes from local springs or is purchased from elsewhere.

Backset

Backset is the spent mash or "slop" that is left over from the last fermenting run. Typically, it will make up about 25% of the ingredients for the next batch. It contains no alcohol, active yeast, or sugars but it helps keep the acidity, and the taste of whiskey, consistent from batch to batch. Most whiskey today is made with backset and is called "sour mash" whiskey (more on this in Chapter 6). You can find whiskey made with "sweet mash" (no backset) but it is much rarer today.

pioneers, as well as the first to rebel against their new country's government (see Chapter 3, the Whiskey Rebellion) and to turn corn into whiskey, which they were also known to drink in prodigious amounts.

The Scots-Irish brought with them their distilling expertise. Because grapes for wine were hard to come by in Scotland and Ireland, using barley to make beer and then whisky was the way to go. In their new country, corn replaced barley.

THE MOLASSES ACT OF 1733

The first sign that the colonists were fed up with British rule followed the Molasses Act of 1733. It was meant to give English plantation owners in the West Indies a trading advantage over their French, Dutch, and Spanish competitors by placing a levy on non-English molasses and sugar. Problem was, the colonists needed more molasses than the English could provide to make enough rum for export. It led to smuggling and bribery of customs officials. The Stamp Act of 1765 was the more proximal cause for rebellion in the colonies, but the first involved alcohol production.

And it wasn't just taxes that agitated the colonists. The Coercive Acts (called the Intolerable Acts here) were meant to punish colonists for the Boston Tea Party by closing the Boston harbor, providing free housing for British soldiers, and holding the trials of government officials in Britain rather than the colonies, amongst other intolerable actions. Raising taxes was one thing, but doing so without giving the colonists a voice in Parliament was too much. "No taxation without representation" inevitably turned into "live free or die."

Let the revolution begin!

WHAT DOES WHISKEY TASTE LIKE IN THE 18TH CENTURY?

James E. Pepper 1776 Straight Rye Whiskey

Of course, the precise taste of the first whiskey distilled in the 1600s would be extremely hard to reproduce today. George Thorpe left no mash bill, or recipe, from his plantation (and not much of anything else). It also would likely not be appreciated by today's noses and taste buds. That said, some distillers today make an attempt to use original recipes and distilling techniques. Among them is the James E. Pepper Distilling Co. It offers *1776 Straight Rye Whiskey*. The distillery is in Lexington, KY, so this whiskey won't have that east coast terroir of Thorpe's whiskey, but the claim is that the recipe dates back to the Revolutionary War.

The original Pepper distillery was established in 1780 by Elijah Pepper. He remained the master distiller until 1838. Elijah settled in the area near Versailles, KY, and built a distillery at a spring behind the courthouse. During the Whiskey Rebellion in 1794, he was one of only a few distillers who could pay his taxes. He used his earnings to buy up other distillers' land and grain when their businesses went under. Today, the distillery site on Glenn's Creek is a National Historic Landmark. It is the home to the Woodford Reserve Distillery.

Oscar Pepper took over the distillery from his father. Grandson James E. Pepper took over from Oscar in 1867. James E. bred and raced thoroughbreds in the Kentucky Derby and traveled in his own private rail car. He helped introduce the world to the Old-Fashioned cocktail. He used his grandfather's original recipe for whiskey. James remained the distiller until 1906.

The distillery continued through 1958 when the industry hit hard times, at least partly due to the Korean War and changes in Americans' drinking preferences. The brand lay dormant until 2008 when

COL. JAMES E. PEPPER,
A Horseman of International Fame.

James E. Pepper.

it was relaunched by whiskey entrepreneur Amir Peay. A decade-long search for historical records uncovered a letter written by James E. that included the original mash bill. This is used today. The distillery has been rebuilt in Lexington, KY, but the whiskey itself is still sourced from Midwest Grain Products (better known as MGP, see Chapter 16). In 2017, the Pepper distillery began aging its own distillate whiskeys again.

In 2016, *James E. Pepper 1776 Straight Rye Whiskey* won the San Francisco World Spirits Competition Gold Medal.

Just the Facts

Mash Bill	Rye: over 90%
Proof	Proof: 100 ABV: 50%
Age; Barrel Char	"over 3 years"; #3
Chill Filtered?	No

TASTING NOTES

From: James E. Pepper Distilling Company
https://jamesepepper.com

On the bottle: In this bottle lies the oldest and most legendary whiskey legacy in Kentucky history. The same old style and methods have been preserved and restored in this fine whiskey.
Full Flavored; deep . . . notes of mint, cloves, eucalyptus, chocolate & honey.

From: The Scotch Noob (Reviewer: Nathan)
https://scotchnoob.com/2019/06/03/james-e-pepper-1776-100-proof-rye/
Aroma: Spicy and peppery, and slightly vegetal, with clear "young rye" eucalyptus and menthol notes. Fresh mint, orange peel, clove, and root beer (Sassafras). A rest in the glass reveals a few welcome floral notes.
Palate: Thin body. Hardy tongue burn (expected at 100 proof). Green grass and crushed mint, orange zest, and root beer persist on the palate, and the whole is fully flavored but dry (not very sweet).
Finish: Medium-short. The mint carries through, although the finish turns a little bitter. Bitter roots, mild charcoal, and very slight mouth-drying oak tannins. Fades quickly without evolving.
With Water: A few drops of water increase the nose tickle without adding any additional aromas. The palate becomes a bit woody (odd, that) and the finish displays more tannins, plus a rush of black licorice. Water optional.
Overall:. . .a very well put-together rye, if a touch on the young side. Luckily, those youthful notes are all of the grass/mint variety, and not in the "paint thinner" category. A solid rye for the price, and certainly a good choice for whiskey-based cocktails.

From: The Over a Barrel Gang
Looks: Amber, gold.
Aroma: Robust. Dried leaves, butterscotch, vanilla, black pepper, apple, maple, leather.
Flavor: Medium body. Sweet, bitter, salty.
Mouth Feel: Sharp, heavy, round.
Going Down: Strong strength, medium length.
Notes: Very interesting, long finish, wide range of flavors.

Toast

To George Thorpe, a man we owe a debt to yet today, though he might have been a bit too trusting.

DINNER AT BERKELEY HUNDRED, VA, WITH GEORGE THORPE AND CHIEF OPECHANCANOUGH

Cooks in colonial times naturally relied on recipes they brought with them from England or found in imported English cookbooks. There was a problem though; the food stuffs available in North America were not the same as those found in Europe so the cooking techniques of the two continents naturally grew distinct. That's why it was a major event when the first American cookbook appeared in 1796, Amelia Simmons' *American Cookery*. The use of corn in recipes, five of which appeared in Simmons' book, was new to America, as English cooks had little experience with the grain. The book also contained the first recipes for pumpkin and squash pudding. *American Cookery* was such a success a second edition appeared in 1800. The book was reprinted numerous times, sometimes legitimately and sometimes without the author's name or under a different title.

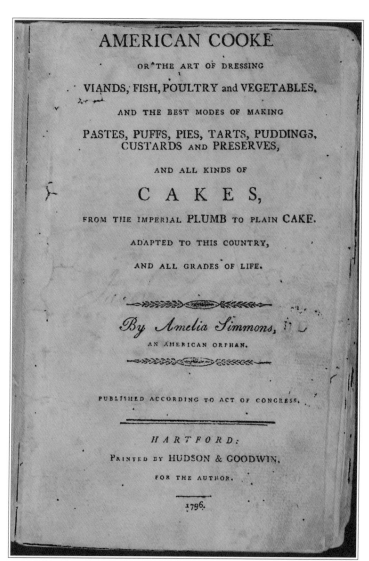

American Cookery.
By Amelia Simmons, 1796.

Recipe: Boiled Lobster

From: Simmons, Amelia (1796). *American Cookery.* Hartford, CT: Hudson & Goodwin. P. 6. [Facsimile published by Dover Publications, New York,1958, with essay by Mary Tolford Wilson. Public domain.]

If you would like to start your meal with a taste of something delicious, try a lobster appetizer. When the European settlers reached North America, lobsters were everywhere on the shore. Because the English soldiers wore red uniforms, it prompted the colonists to refer to them as "Lobster Backs." Being plentiful made lobster a major food source and gave the crustacean a dubious status as the poor man's protein. Native Americans used lobster to fertilize their crops and to bait hooks to catch other fish. Lobster was served in prisons so often that it led to riots by the first American convicts; fear of unrest among inmates led to restrictions on how often it could be served.[4]

The most authentic lobster recipes from colonial times would be the simplest; just boil or throw them on a fire (barbeque grill) and serve small appetizer-sized bites with lemon or butter.

---

4 www.history.com/news/a-taste-of-lobster-history

But Simmons would caution you that saltwater fish should be fresh, and let the buyer beware. Here is her advice (with the original spelling using "ʃ" for "s"):

> Every ʃpecies generally of *ʃalt water Fiʃh*, are beʃt freʃh from the water, tho' the *Hannah Hill, Black Fiʃh, Lobʃter, Oyʃter, Flounder, Baʃs, Cod, Haddock, and Eel*, with many others, may be tranʃported by land many miles, find a good market, and retain a good reliʃh; but as generally, live ones are bought firʃt, deceits are uʃed to give them a freʃhneʃs of appearance, ʃuch as peppering the gills, wetting the fins and tails, and even painting the gills, or wetting with animal blood. Experience and attention will dictate the choice of the beʃt.

Recipe: Garden Stuff

From: Simmons, Amelia. (1796). *American Cookery*. Hartford, CT: Hudson & Goodwin. P. 45. [Facsimile published by Dover Publications, New York, 1958, with essay by Mary Tolford Wilson. Public domain.]

Here are Amelia's directions "To boil all kinds of Garden Stuff." It is also simple by today's cooking standards, but it oddly reflects cooking trends today and makes a good read:

> In dreʃʃing all ʃorts of kitchen garden herbs, take care they are clean waʃhed; that there is no ʃmall ʃnails, or caterpillars between the leaves; and that all the coarʃe outer leaves, and the tops that received any injury by the weather, be taken off; next waʃh them in a good deal of water, and put them in the cullender to drain, care muʃt likewiʃe be taken, that your pot or ʃauce pan be clean, well tinned, and free from ʃand, or greaʃe.

Simmons could have used onions, beets, parsnips, carrots, garlic, asparagus, radishes, cucumbers, and lettuce of various kinds that she grew in her garden. She provided no recipe for a dressing. If she picked proportions of her ingredients to taste, after boiling (or not) it can be assumed she saw little reason to add anything to bring out the flavor. Now you can prepare a warm (or cold) salad, old style.

Simmons was not only a true revolutionary cook but also a modest and open-minded person. She closed the preface to her book by writing for help:

> The candor of the American Ladies is ʃolicitously entreated by the Authoreʃs, as ʃhe is circumscribed in her knowledge, this being an original work in this country. If any future edition appears, ʃhe hopes to render it more valuable.[5]

Indeed, not only original but the first.

---

5   Allow me the same aspiration. Should you find error or suggestions to make this work more valuable, please share.

MUSIC THAT TAKES US BACK TO COLONIAL TIMES

These songs are a mix of tunes that the immigrants from Europe brought with them and some early American originals. Some might have alternate versions of lyrics and different lyrics can share melodies.

Amazing Grace, performed by Judy Collins (1972)

The words to *Amazing Grace* were written by a slave ship captain, John Newton, in 1772 after a particularly violent storm at sea led him to beg for divine mercy. Several years later, he gave up the slave trade and pursued Christian theology. One biographer of Newton suggests the song is performed ten million times a year.

The Escape of Old John Webb, performed by The Kingston Trio (1960)

This is a traditional ballad written about 1730 telling the story of John Webb (or Webber), the mint-master of Salem, MA. He was thrown in prison for using a currency the British government would not accept. The song retells the tale of three brothers, one named Billye, who broke him out of jail. (Oh yes, documents indicate Webb was also a counterfeiter.)

Drink to Me Only with Thine Eyes, performed by Paul Robeson (1958)

John Newton.
Stained glass image, St Peter and Paul Church Olney, Buckinghamshire, South of London.

The lyrics were written by English playwright Ben Johnson, probably in 1616. They were appropriated from *Epistle xxiii*, a love letter in *Epistles of Philostratus*. Robeson was the son of a former slave and a mother of mixed ancestry, including Delaware Indians and English Quakers. He burst on the scene in 1925 when he gave the first African American solo concert devoted to both spiritual and secular songs, including *Go Down Moses*, a spiritual he made famous. In the 1950s Robeson was blacklisted for his political beliefs.

Barbara Allen, performed by Art Garfunkel (1973)

This is a Scottish folk song from the mid-1600s. The earliest reference to it suggests it was a diary entry. There are hundreds of versions.

How Stands the Glass Around, performed by John Towney (1976)

First printed in 1792, according to one story, *How Stands* was sung by British General James Wolfe on the night before he was killed in the Battle of the Plains at Quebec, Canada, in 1759. This version is off Towney's album, *The Top Hits of 1776.*

Drowsy Maggie, performed by Brian Ledbetter & the US Army Old Guard Fife and Drum Corp (2013)

Maggie is an Irish reel from the 1880s. However, there is no certainty about its origin which is likely much earlier. There are more than 160 recordings of this song. But don't get it confused with *Sleepy Maggie*, a completely different collection of tunes.

The Battle of the Kegs, performed by The Committee of Correspondence (1976)

The original Committees of Correspondence were set up by the rebels to maintain communication between the colonies and later between the newly declared states and foreign powers. *Kegs* is a propaganda ballad written in the late eighteenth century by Francis Hopkinson, a signer of the Declaration of Independence. It describes an attempted attack on the British Fleet in Philadelphia on January 6, 1778. The kegs were filled with gunpowder, not whisky.

Chapter 3
A NEW NATION (AND DISTILLERY) IS BORN

There should always be a Sufficient Quantity of Spirits with the Army. . .
it is so essential that it is not to be dispensed with.
—George Washington

GEORGE WASHINGTON

George Washington was a failed politician. Or at least he was in 1755. In his first attempt at being elected to a big-time government office he ran for the Virginia House of Burgesses and lost by a vote count of 271 to 40. But he learned from his defeat and came back to win in 1758.[1] A change in his proposed policies? Not exactly. To secure his victory, Washington gave away about a half-gallon of alcohol per voter; forty-seven gallons of beer, thirty-five of wine, plus cider, brandy and rum, to be exact (Washington kept scrupulous records). Was this buying of votes against the law? Maybe, but it was common practice at the time and even had a name: *swilling the planters with bumbo*. Voters expected free booze. Intoxicating beverages were regularly handed out on the grounds of the polling place, which might have been the local tavern.[2]

Washington would continue to effectively use the dispensation of spirits during the Revolutionary War. He ordered that a gill of alcohol (about a quarter pint) be issued to each soldier every day. There was even an extra nip for someone who had performed an act of bravery. Washington had seen the effects of alcohol during his stint as a lieutenant colonel in the French and Indian War. There, he noticed its positive effects

---

1   He wasn't a terribly successful general at first either, losing five of his first six battles.

2   Allegedly, Paul Revere made his famous ride after drinking enough rum to *make a rabbit bite a bulldog*, though this is disputed. He never made it to Lexington from Concord; he was stopped by the British before he got there. Revere was also the source of most of the rolled copper used to make stills in the colonies. Do you use copper-bottomed Revere cookware?

on soldiers but also its negative ones, and if a soldier was drunk on duty he was punished severely. So thoroughly convinced was the "Father of Our Country" of the salutary effect of spirits that, because imports were restricted, he suggested the government construct public distilleries.

BOTTLING UP THE WHISKEY REBELLION

George Washington.
Penned long after Washington corked the rebellion.

It was the first tax levied by the new government and it went into effect on March 3, 1791. The result was similar to the English's experience with taxing the colonies; many distillers refused to pay it and opposition to the fledgling American government increased.

The tax was harder on small, rural farmers in the western fringes of the colonies than it was for city folk back east.[3] The farmers resented having government agents come to inspect their barns and cellars. Currency was hard to come by in the western states—that is, western Pennsylvania, and what became Kentucky and Tennessee. Instead of cash, settlers on the new frontier used whiskey as a means of exchange when they bartered for other goods. About every sixth farmer took their extra grain to a distillery. Even the trip to Philadelphia—to attend court if they did not pay the tax—created a burden for farmers and other merchants with a still. The trip was hard; it cost time and resources.

THE WHISKEY REBELLION

We know the Revolutionary War came to a successful conclusion, but the Founding Fathers still had issues to contend with in its wake, not the least of which was how to repay the debts incurred by the colonists' uprising. Alexander Hamilton, the first Secretary of the Treasury, insisted that the new federal government and the thirteen states repay all debts rather than leave their creditors *holding the bag*, a sum amounting to about eighty million dollars. There was no income tax, so like many governments before it (the English were exceptionally fond of this strategy), a tax on whiskey was instituted.

Trouble started. Robert Johnson, a tax collector for the counties of Washington and Allegheny, PA, was tarred and feathered and his horse was stolen by a group of men dressed as women. Distillers who paid the tax might find their stills riddled with bullet holes, rendering them useless.

The Whiskey Rebellion peaked when about five thousand tax protesters occupied Pittsburgh, PA.

A Flag of the Whiskey Rebellion.
You can't have a revolution without a flag.
The stripes and stars represented six counties that looked favorably upon the insurrection.
The number of stars changed on different flags.

3   The whiskey tax wasn't the only gripe the westerners had with the government. They felt the government's defenses against Native Americans were lax and they wanted more protection from the French when the new Americans shipped their goods down rivers.

Their dream was to establish a new nation of their own (one suggested name was "Westsylvania"). President Washington grew increasingly apprehensive. He believed the rebellion might be a prelude to a violent uprising, one fashioned after the Reign of Terror that followed the First French Republic when it was established. Indeed, the Whiskey Rebellion was the largest armed resistance in America that occurred between the Revolutionary and Civil Wars.

Washington called up men from militias in Pennsylvania, New Jersey, Virginia, and Maryland. Not lost on him was the fact that this was the first time the new nation tried to raise an army. It was not known how the populous would respond. Would anyone show up to serve the new country? About thirteen thousand men did enlist and Washington led the troops toward the Alleghany Mountains. He then turned matters over to Henry Lee, known as "Light-Horse Harry," and later known as the father of another famous military man, Robert E. Lee. (Harry was also known as a dishonest businessman who fled the country when Robert E. was six).

Washington chose what he thought was the area of rebellion he was most likely to defeat, Pittsburgh. Good choice. By the time George's army reached Pittsburgh in 1794, the rebellion had lost its steam. Perhaps emissaries sent to discuss the situation with the oncoming troops realized they would be far outnumbered (not that the militiamen were any more of a disciplined fighting force than the rebels were). Or, perhaps the currency that the militia men brought with them to purchase goods had filled the coffers of farmers along the way (not that the soldiers didn't *grab* or *lob*; that is, do some looting whether people were or were not at home, respectively). Or, perhaps the fact that the supportive citizens of Pittsburgh had treated the "Whiskey Boys" to such copious amounts of distilled corn that the locals had inadvertently sapped the Boys resolve. Regardless, many rebels decided it was more prudent to lay down their weapons, make peace,

and maybe even head back to the wilderness yet again, to preserve their way of life (and not pay taxes).

Most of the rebel captives were never punished. Two were sentenced to death but were pardoned by Washington. Others were held in jail for a while without a trial (the Bill of Rights, and its Fifth Amendment, ratified on December 15, 1791, was a new idea). Destroyed and confiscated property was the biggest casualty.

The hard feelings subsided as quickly as the soldiers could spend the cash they brought with them. Thomas Jefferson, when he became the third president, abolished the whiskey tax in 1801. It was reinstated again for a few years around the time of the War of 1812, when James Madison was president.

THE DISTILLERY AT MOUNT VERNON

After successfully leading the revolution, acting as first president of the new nation, and putting down the nation's first insurrection, Washington retired to become a gentleman farmer at his most cherished place in the world, his estate at Mount Vernon, VA. George was a good businessman but sometimes his asset columns got a bit *out of whack*. He owned large parcels of land out west. He also either owned or rented over three hundred slaves (half from his wife Martha's dowry, left to her after her first husband died). Yet he struggled for cash most of his life.

An unanticipated turn of events occurred when George hired James Anderson, a Scotsman, to manage his Mount Vernon estate. Anderson realized that what was done with barley in his home country could be done with corn and rye in his adopted land. Anderson proposed that Washington build a grist mill and distillery along Dogue Run, a water source that ambled near the estate. Washington was initially opposed. Martha kept silent. Under great financial pressure, George finally agreed.

Anderson supervised the building of five working copper stills, a malt house, and a grain kiln.

The distillery opened on January 8, 1797. It was staffed by two paid workers and six slaves. Not only was Washington our first president, he was also the only founding father to own and operate a commercial distillery. And it was a successful one at that; it produced 500 gallons of rye whiskey in 1797; 4,500 in 1798; and 10,500 in 1799. In 1799, the distillery brought in about $7,500 in profits (about $120,000 today). By then George was one of the largest whiskey producers in the new country. You could say his liquid assets helped ease his cash problems. George died in 1799. Poor management of the distillery then led to less profit. Washington's original distillery burned down in 1814.

Not to worry, though, whiskey was on the march.

TURNING THE MASH INTO WHISKEY

Mash Preparation
Once the ingredients and proportions of the mash bill are determined, the grains are ground into a meal. Some mills do this using a hammer that crushes the grain. Others use grinder stones. The grain is placed between two circular stones and is crushed between them. The distance between the stones, their speed, their flatness or arc on the grinding side, and whether or not they are carved on the inside can be varied to taste. Making a grain meal for any purpose, not only whiskey, will follow this same process.

Cooking
The ingredients of the ground mash, with water added, are then heated. Different grains are added at different times and at different temperatures. The backset, a part of the leftover from the last whiskey run, is added to create consistency of taste.

Fermentation
The mash is then moved to a large vat and the yeast is added. The ratio of mash-to-yeast is about 25–30 to 1; yeast quickly reproduces itself under the right conditions. You will hear this referred to as "distiller's beer" or "wash."

Distillation
Most American distillers of old used a copper pot still. Alcohol boils before water, about 39° F sooner. The alcohol vapor travels through a copper coil at the top of the still, called a "worm." The worm travels through a water cooling device (no water is added to the vapor) and the condensed alcohol spills into another vat. The resulting distillate will likely be run through the still a second or third time to remove impurities and reach the desired alcohol concentration.

If you visit a modern distillery today, you will likely see a double distillation process, one that uses a column still rather than a pot still, or a hybrid of both configurations. This method is more efficient (the mash can be entered continuously with less frequent cleaning needed) and the distillate can have impurities removed faster. You will hear the separate chambers of the column still referred to as "stripping" sections or "rectifiers." Both remove impurities of different types. Small distillers might yet use copper pot stills (or stills made of other metals, especially stainless steel) because they want a more unique taste.

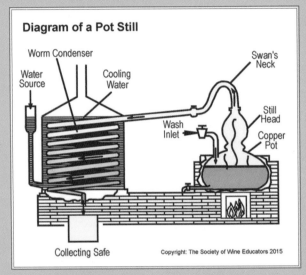

A pot (alembic) still.

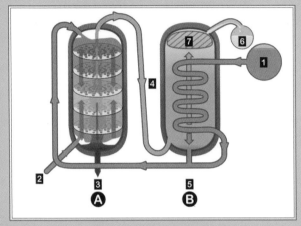

A column still.
Legend: A. Analyzer B. Rectifier 1. Wash 2. Steam 3. Liquid out 4. Alcohol vapor 5. Recycled less volatile components 6. Most volatile components 7. Condenser

WHAT DOES WHISKEY FROM GEORGE WASHINGTON'S DISTILLERY TASTE LIKE?

George Washington Rye Whiskey

The Mount Vernon Ladies Association of the Union, which owns and operates Washington's Mount Vernon estate, began to reconstruct George's distillery in 2004. It went operational in 2007. Washington was a meticulous record keeper so the original detailed plans for the distillery were kept, as were records of how much of each grain was purchased for the original mash bill. The operation was rebuilt nearly exactly as it first existed. (You can visit the distillery, https://www.mountvernon.org/the-estate-gardens/distillery/, and even take online tours, including videos of how the whiskey is made.)

George Washington Rye Whiskey today is made like it was in Washington's time. Mashing is powered by water, the mash is boiled by wood, and there is no modern instrumentation, not even a thermometer. Master distillers from around the country consulted with the new distillery crew to teach them how to recognize good rye whiskey by nose and taste. The rye and corn are sourced from farms in Virginia. Washington's original whiskey was not aged; it went straight into jugs. Some products available today at Mount Vernon have rested in barrels for a while, including a straight rye whiskey aged two years and a premium straight rye whiskey, aged four years and three months, as well as some fruit brandies. Sadly, the Mount Vernon estate is the only place on earth you can purchase Washington's whiskeys. They do not distribute or ship.

In 2017, *George Washington Rye Whiskey* was designated the official spirit of the state of Virginia. In 2019, *George Washington Rye Whiskey* was voted the silver medal by the American Craft Spirits Association for white (unaged) rye, among 500 entrants from thirty-eight states.

Just the Facts

Mash Bill	Corn: 35% Rye: 60% Barley 5%
Proof	Proof: 86 ABV: 43%
Age; Barrel Char	Unaged; no char
Chill Filtered?	Not in the 18th century; distilled twice

TASTING NOTES

From: Courtesy of Mount Vernon Ladies Association

https://www.mountvernon.org/the-estate-gardens/distillery/distilled-spirits-at-mount-vernon/

. . .distilled at least twice before being sent to market. In Washington's time whiskey was not aged and was sold in its original form. The whiskey in this bottle accurately represents that process. . .Mount Vernon staff used Washington's original mash bill and traditional 18th-century methods in the production of this rye whiskey. This included grinding of all the grain in Washington's water-powered gristmill, fermenting in wooden mash tubs, and distilling in copper pot stills heated by wood fires. [The distillery provides no tasting notes.]

From: Whisk(e)y Apostle (Reviewer: Gary Turner)

https://whiskeyapostle.com/2018/03/george-washington-rye-whiskey/

Aroma: Thick, robust cereal, corn bread and freshly baked rye bread; a hint of barley malt and pine.

Palate: Rich, creamy, sweet corn and sweet barley malt with a bite of pepper and a touch of sourdough bread.

Finish: Fairly quick (although more pleasant than the other white dog whiskies evaluated during the same sessions).

Comments: . . .Quite interesting, with a lot more going on in terms of depth of flavor on both the nose and palate, and a thicker mouthfeel. I would absolutely love to try this with some real age on it, based on what I've read about lower proof distillates. Don't get me wrong—this was an expensive taste of history, but it left me with no regrets. . . .Must try.

From: The Over a Barrel Gang

Looks: Clear.

Aroma: Delicate. Apricot, butterscotch, honey, apple, anise, tobacco, grass.

Flavor: Light body. Sweet, bitter.

Mouth Feel: Creamy, sharp, rich.

Going Down: Average strength, short length.

Notes: Deceiving looks, complex and rich.

Old Potrero 18th Century Style Whiskey

If you can't get your hands on a bottle of George's whiskey, *Old Potrero 18th Century Style Whiskey* is an alternative.

Old Potrero is the name that is used by the Hotaling Co. (which used to be Anchor Distilling, located in San Francisco, CA, the same company that makes *Anchor Steam Beer*) for this American whiskey offering. With four and a half years aging, *Old Potrero* has a long rest for colonial times when most whiskey would have been consumed with no aging. The distillers say the mash bill, use of pot stills, and aging process are "an attempt to recreate the original whiskey of America."

Just the Facts

Mash Bill	Corn: 0% Rye: 100% Malt: 0% Wheat: 0% Other: 0%
Proof	Proof: 102.4 ABV: 51.2%
Age; Barrel Char	2 years 6 months; not charred, toasted
Chill Filtered?	Probably not

TASTING NOTES

From: Hotaling & Co., the distiller's website
https://www.hotalingandco.com/brand/hotaling#old-potrero-18th-century

Handmade fine grain new American oak barrels, lightly toasted in the traditional manner, impart a wonderfully subtle flavor. In the 18th century, barrels were made by heating the staves over a fire of oak chips, allowing them to be bent and formed into a barrel shape. During this process, the inside of the barrel would become toasted, but not charred. For aging, several uncharred oak barrels, both new and used, to achieve the balanced complexity that complements this whiskey's traditional heritage.

From: Drinkhacker (Reviewer: Christopher Null)
https://drinkhacker.com/2015/03/03/review-old-potrero-18th-century-style-whiskey-single-malt-straight-rye/

Both new and used barrels are incorporated into the production process. [*Old Potrero is*] extremely unusual from the choice of grain to the exotic barrel program, and it shows in the finished product. At heart this is a young spirit, racy on the nose with raw wood, raw grain, and a bit of hospital character. The body is almost astringent—so much wood character has leeched into this spirit that it's drained of just about everything else. There's a little bit of peppery rye up front, but this fades to a fiery, almost smoky, medicinal character in the finish.

From: The Over a Barrel Gang
Looks: Gold
Aroma: Medium. Maple, peach, vanilla, caramel, hay, butterscotch, brown sugar.
Flavor: Light body. Sweet, salty, bitter.
Mouth Feel: Sharp, bitter.
Going Down: Strong strength, medium length.
Notes: A rye that jumps out of the glass, sharp but surprisingly pleasant, short-lived going down.

Toast

In addition to his obvious bravery, leadership ability, and devotion to his new country, Washington was thought of as a good choice for president because he had sired no heirs; he had two stepdaughters via widow Martha's first marriage. This lessened concerns that a Washington presidency might lead to King George I of the United States of America.

As George Washington led his charges to victory, he remained skeptical of the depth of human character, having said, "Mankind, when left to themselves, are unfit for their own government," and "Few men have virtue to withstand the highest bidder." Still, he also understood the enormity of the role in history he was playing: "I walk on untrodden ground. There is scarcely any part of my conduct which may not hereafter be drawn into precedent."

To George and Martha Washington, the parents of our country.

DINNER AT MOUNT VERNON, VA, WITH GEORGE AND MARTHA WASHINGTON

Martha Washington's cookbook was written and gifted to her by Frances Parke Custis, the mother of her first husband, Daniel Parke Custis. Daniel was a rich planter who likely died of a heart attack. A facsimile, *The Martha Washington Cookbook*, completely modernized (in 1940), was prepared by Marie Kimball. The original resides with the Historical Society of Pennsylvania.

The cookbook was divided into two parts covering "cookery" and "sweetmeats" and had over five hundred recipes. Martha was a renowned hostess, having cooked and supervised meals in at least three different homes: in New York City (the new nation's first capital), Philadelphia, and several stints at Mount Vernon. The Washingtons' residence was always filled with guests, some of great importance and some who showed up out of curiosity.

Both Martha and her husband were most fond of their table at Mount Vernon. George's affinity for cherries is well-known.[4] He also loved a wide variety of fruits, nuts, and fish. He preferred simple meals over fancy ones. The Washingtons' home at Mount Vernon was completely self-sufficient. It had orchards, farm animals, and meat preservation facilities (to cure ham, bacon).[5]

Recipe: Green Peas Soup

From: The Mount Vernon Inn

https://www.mountvernon.org/inn/recipes/

Ingredients:

10 cups fresh or frozen peas or petits pois (small, young green peas), divided

6 cups water, divided

1½ teaspoons salt

¼ teaspoon ground black pepper

½ teaspoon ground mace

2 whole cloves

2 teaspoons dried thyme

1 teaspoon dried marjoram

4 tablespoons unsalted butter

3 to 4 green onions, trimmed and sliced crosswise into 1/2-inch pieces

¼ pound fresh baby spinach, coarsely chopped

2 teaspoons minced fresh mint

3 tablespoons all-purpose flour

Diced toast for garnish (optional)

Shredded fresh calendula blossoms for garnish (optional)

---

4   The story that George cut down a cherry tree and fessed up is only partly apocryphal. He did have two cherry trees removed in an expansion of the main house at Mount Vernon and he never lied about doing it. But he didn't cut them down himself.

5   Thanks to www.foodtimeline.org/presidents.html#washington

Directions:

1. Put 8 cups of the peas and 4 cups of the water in a large saucepan or Dutch oven. Add the salt, pepper, mace, cloves, thyme, and marjoram, cover, and bring to a boil. Reduce the heat and simmer for about 45 minutes, until the peas are very tender.

2. Drain the peas, reserving the cooking liquid in the saucepan. Puree the peas in a food processor or with a food mill. If using a food mill, discard the skins. Press the puree through a sieve into the reserved liquid, stirring to combine thoroughly. Cover and set aside to keep warm.

3. Combine the remaining 2 cups of peas with the remaining 2 cups of water in a medium saucepan. Cover and bring to a boil. Reduce the heat and simmer for 20 to 25 minutes, until the peas are just tender.

4. While the second batch of peas is cooking, melt the butter in a saucepan. Add the green onions, and sauté for about 2 minutes. Add the spinach and mint and stir together, cooking until the spinach has just wilted. Blend in the flour and cook for about 1 minute.

5. Drain the peas, reserving the cooking liquid, and stir the peas into the warm soup along with the spinach mixture. Heat until it begins to simmer, adding the reserved pea-cooking liquid "a little at a time" if the soup is too thick. Season with additional salt and pepper, if necessary.

6. Pour the soup into a tureen, and garnish with diced toast and shredded calendula blossoms, if desired.

This porridge makes an excellent gazpacho. It can be made with frozen sweet peas pureed in a blender. If you serve it in a shot glass, your guests will ask for seconds.

Recipe: Elizabeth's Hors D'oeuvres (Crab Appetizer)

From: The Inn at Mount Vernon

https://www.mountvernon.org/inn/recipes/

Perhaps a more familiar appetizer for the Revolutionary War period would be a crab dish. Crabs from the Chesapeake Bay were a staple at Mount Vernon.

Ingredients:

6 (2½-inch to 3-inch) bread rounds, lightly toasted

1 cup mayonnaise

1 bunch watercress

6 slices tomato

1 egg, hard-boiled

1 pound backfin crabmeat

1 lemon

Directions:

Place toast rounds on platter or individually on plates. Add to each, 1 slice of tomato, portion of crabmeat that has been gone through lightly for shell, and dollop of mayonnaise lightly colored with cocktail sauce. Grate egg and sprinkle on top. Surround with generous amount of crisp watercress. Put a lemon wedge on side.

Recipe: Hoecakes

From: The Mount Vernon Inn

https://www.mountvernon.org/inn/recipes/

George's favorite food was hoecakes and honey with a cup of tea, which he ate most every morning. He understood that his guests might want to start the day with something more substantial, and he and Martha welcomed them with more hearty fare. Today, hoecakes are a rarity, but you can make them, and serve them (silver dollar size) as an appetizer. Why not? This recipe is a modern adaptation of the 18th-century original. It was created by culinary historian Nancy Carter Crump for the book, *Dining with the Washingtons,* (2011, Mount Vernon, VA: Mount Vernon Ladies Association).

Ingredients (serves 15):

½ teaspoon active dry yeast

2½ cups white cornmeal, divided

3 to 4 cups lukewarm water

½ teaspoon salt

1 large egg, lightly beaten

Melted butter for drizzling and serving

Honey or maple syrup for serving

Directions:

1. Mix the yeast and 1¼ cups of the cornmeal in a large bowl. Add 1 cup of the lukewarm water, stirring to combine thoroughly. Mix in ½ cup more of the water, if needed, to give the mixture the consistency of pancake batter. Cover with plastic wrap, and refrigerate for at least 8 hours, or overnight.

2. Preheat the oven to 200°F.

3. When ready to finish the hoecakes, begin by adding ½ to 1 cup of the remaining water to the batter. Stir in the salt and the egg, blending thoroughly.

4. Gradually add the remaining 1¼ cups of cornmeal, alternating with enough additional lukewarm water to make a mixture that is the consistency of waffle batter. Cover with a towel, and set aside at room temperature for 15 to 20 minutes.

5. Heat a griddle on medium-high heat, and lightly grease it with lard or vegetable shortening. Preparing 1 hoecake at a time, drop a scant ¼ cup of the batter onto the griddle and cook on one side for about 5 minutes, or until lightly browned. With a spatula, turn the hoecake over and continue cooking another 4 to 5 minutes, until browned.

6. Place the hoecake on a platter, and set it in the oven to keep warm while making the rest of the batch. Drizzle each batch with melted butter.

7. Serve the hoecakes warm, drizzled with melted butter and honey or maple syrup.

MUSIC THAT TAKES US BACK TO THE REVOLUTIONARY WAR

Yankee Doodle, performed by US Army Chorus (2006)

The opening lines of this ditty may have been written by British soldiers to disparage the American colonists, especially those of Dutch origin. "Yankee" is a corruption of "Janke" (or little Jan, a common Dutch name) used to describe someone as a loser. A "*doodle*," when used as a noun, was a simpleton (we still mindlessly doodle today), and "*dandy*" was someone of lower class who dressed up to try to look more affluent. Despite its origins, the American army adopted the song. When General Charles Cornwallis' men surrendered at Yorktown in 1781, they passed through columns of colonial soldiers singing and playing *Yankee Doodle Dandy*.

The Ballad of the Tea Party, by Arthur F. Schrader (1976)

Tea Party is believed to have been written in 1774, a year after the tax protest by the Sons of Liberty that left chests of British tea floating in Boston harbor. The author of these lyrics is unknown. The tune was borrowed from *Admiral Hosier's Ghost*, itself borrowed from *Come and Listen to My Ditty*.

The Riflemen of Bennington, performed by Bobby Horton (2008)

Riflemen was written just after the Declaration of Independence was signed. Six-hundred-fifty British soldiers tried to raid the colonial supply center at Bennington, VT. They failed.

President's March/Rights of Man/Death of General Wolfe, performed by US Army Old Guard Fife and Drum Corp (2013)

President's March was written to honor George Washington. With new lyrics but the same melody, *Hail Columbia* was the informal national anthem for several decades. The US Fife and Drum Corp, part of the 3rd United States Infantry, performs in Continental Army uniforms. The Corps has been playing Revolutionary War music for over fifty years. It averages about five hundred performances a year, using ensembles of 3 to 33 musicians.

Female Patriots, performed by Dorothy Mesney (1975)

It is hard to find songs written by or about women during colonial times. This song probably was put on vinyl for the first time for Folkway Records in the mid-20th century. An autoharp is sole accompaniment on Mesney's version. The song may have been written around 1768 by Hannah Griffitts, a Quaker poet and songwriter who lived in Philadelphia, PA.

Three Drunken Maidens, performed by Diane Taraz (2010)

Likely originating in the mid-1700s on the Isle of Wight, a refuge for smugglers and hard drinkers, *Drunken Maidens* paints a different picture of women in the colonies than does *Female Patriots.*

Yorktown, performed by Les Parks (2013)

Yorktown commemorates the surrender of the British troops at Yorktown, VA, on October 19, 1781. Lt. General Charles Cornwallis refused to attend the capitulation ceremony. *Yorktown (The World Turned Upside Down),* from the Broadway show *Hamilton,* celebrates the surrender as well (with different lyrics and arrangement).

Fare Thee Well Ye' Sweethearts, performed by The Committee on Correspondence (1976)

First published in 1710, *Sweethearts* is an English folk ballad sung as a duet by separating lovers.

Liberty Song, performed by Arthur F. Shrader (1976)

Liberty Song was written by John Dickinson in 1768. Dickinson also wrote the first draft of the Articles of Confederation.

The World Turned Upside Down, performed by The Colonial Williamsburg Fife and Drums (2014)

While the Continental Army played *Yankee Doodle* the British Soldiers played this song. The final lyrics to the songs are, "Yet let's be content, and the times lament, you see the world turn'd upside down."

Free America(y), performed by Rob Carriker (2002)

Free America(y) was written by Joseph Warren in 1774 to bolster the morale of Colonial troops. Reference is made to Albion, an alternative name for Great Britain. The lyrics point out that Albion had "bow'd to Caesar" and other lords, but "Americans have never fall'n prey." Huzza, huzza, huzza!

Stoney Point, performed by Norman Blake and Tony Rice (1987)

Sir Henry Clinton's British soldiers took control of the Hudson River crossing at Stony Point, NY. He lost it to General Washington and then retook it when it was abandoned by the American troops. It ruined Clinton's reputation. This tune was written to celebrate Washington's victory.

God Save Our States, performed by Dorothy Mesney (1975)

Written in the late 1700s by the prolific songwriter, Anonymous. Does the tune sound familiar? Its *God Save the King* (or Queen, depending on who's in charge in England at the time).

THE STAR-SPANGLED BANNER

It is widely known that Francis Scott Key wrote the *Star-Spangled Banner* after watching the Battle for Fort McHenry outside Baltimore during the War of 1812. But less well-known is that the song was originally called *Defence of Fort M'Henry* and the melody came from an old London drinking club called the Anacreontic Society. Key's version had three verses we do not sing today. The final verse read like this:

O thus be it ever, when free men shall stand
Between their lov'd home and the war's desolation!
Blest with vict'ry and peace, may the Heav'n rescued land
Praise the Power that hath made and preserved us a nation!
Then conquer we must, when our cause it is just,
And this be our motto: "In God is our trust."
And the star-spangled banner in triumph shall wave
O'er the land of the free and the home of the brave!

Star-Spangled Banner original poem. *The Star-Spangled Banner* did not become the national anthem until 1931, when an act of Congress made it so.

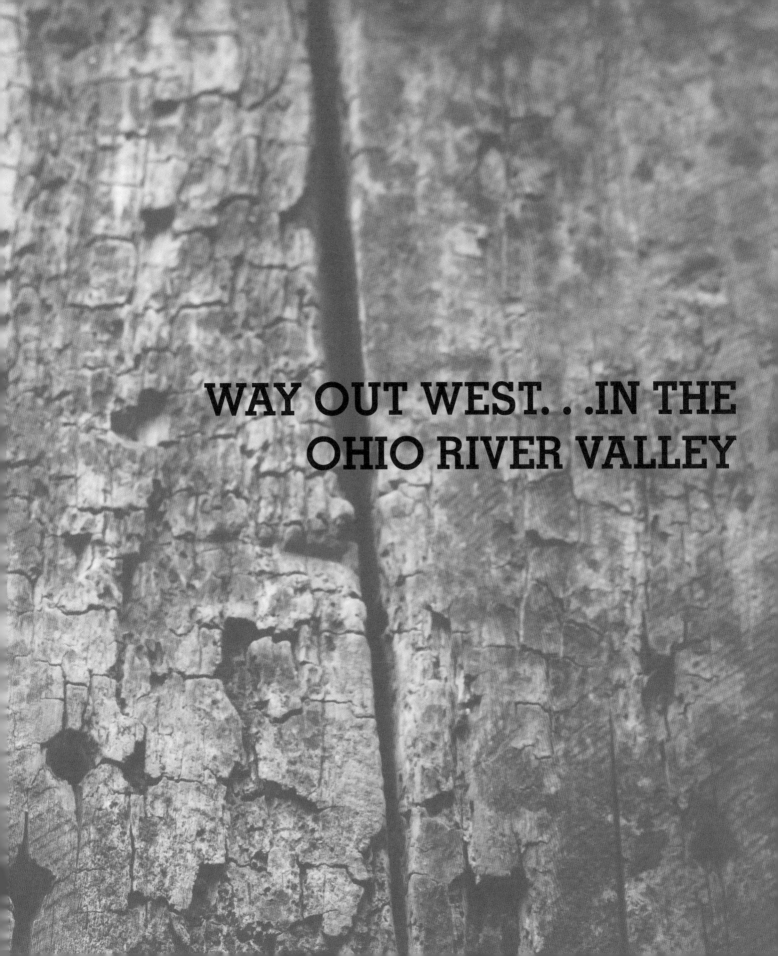

WAY OUT WEST...IN THE
OHIO RIVER VALLEY

Chapter 4
KENTUCKY AND ITS BOURBON FOLLOW SHORTLY

I have never in my life seen a Kentuckian who didn't have a gun, a pack of cards,
and a jug of whiskey.
—Andrew Jackson

THE FIRST PIONEERS

Daniel Boone had been widening the Wilderness Road through the Cumberland Gap and into Kentucky, then part of western Virginia, for a decade before settlers—not trappers, not military men—headed that way. The new United States government had acquired over a quarter-million square miles of land on the western border of Virginia as part of the Treaty of Paris that had ended the Revolutionary War. The Virginia General Assembly allowed settlers to claim up to four hundred acres of Kentucky County land provided they agreed to build a cabin and plant some crops. Couple this legislative action with the disaffection felt by the Whiskey Rebellion rabble-rousers—many of whom were accomplished distillers—who abandoned their homes and took off west when their revolt failed, and the march into Kentucky County was under way.

The first pioneers—those folks who were meaning to settle in the new territory and not use it to hunt then return home (those like Boone)—headed out to cross the Ohio River in early December 1787. Their journey was treacherous not only because of the dense forests and rocky terrain but also because of the cold, harsh winter. To keep them warm on the outside the pioneers built large fires. To keep warm on the inside, whiskey was consumed in copious amounts.

Pittsburgh and Fort Pitt already existed at the confluence of the Monongahela and Allegany Rivers where they form the Ohio River. Pittsburgh was a *rough-and-tumble* settlement filled with a few hundred disorderly people, unlike the more-refined New Englanders who were headed their way to join them on the frontier. It's major "export" at the time was, you guessed it, whiskey.

Not only was whiskey an export, but it was also an integral part of everyday life. It was used to barter. Government-issued money was scarce. The paper money around town could have been issued by any of several different countries with equivalencies hard to reckon, perhaps making transactions seem more like an Abbott & Costello routine than a business deal. Markets for crops were so far distant that perishables would go bad long before they got anywhere near the east coast.

The value of a jug of whiskey, on the other hand, was simple to calculate, and the worth of goods in numbers of jugs was easy to negotiate. An oversupply of good corn and rye was a frequent occurrence, making logical the turning of grain into whiskey; it didn't go bad and everybody wanted it.

Whiskey was so integral to frontier life that church councils formally declared that distilling was permitted by scripture. Spirits were sold at church "revival" meetings. Whiskey was listed as an expense for funerals and medical treatments. You'd be considered *stingy* (cheap) if you didn't offer guests a nip or two when they came visiting.

Some say that "Kentucky" means "meadowlands" in Iroquoian, others say it means "dark and bloody ground." Regardless, the land was thick with trees for log cabins and barrels and the soil was rich for farming, most importantly corn. Daniel Boone was not only an accomplished trail blazer but also a good salesman, writing "I returned home to my family, with a determination to bring them as soon as possible to Kentucky, which I deemed a second paradise. . ." Not so heavenly, Paul Johnson quotes a description of the settlers of Kentucky as "rugged, dirty, brawling, browbeating monsters, six feet high, whose vocation is robbing, drinking, fighting, and terrifying every peaceable man."

William Bard also loved Kentucky. He first visited in 1768 and hatched a plan to travel down the Ohio River from Pittsburgh and mine salt, a commodity much needed in his frontier outpost. His brother, David, received a land grant to start a town and William surveyed and platted the land. In 1780, the Bard brothers held a lottery for one thousand acres of their new land. Lottery winners (there were about thirty-three) simply had to clear and develop their part of paradise. Later, the town's name would become Bardstown, KY; it is now considered the "Bourbon Capital of the World®."

HOW DID BOURBON GET ITS NAME?

Louis XVI of France, never a big fan of the English, was instrumental in bringing about a successful conclusion to the Revolutionary War. French assistance started out in a clandestine manner, but the 1778 Franco-American Treaty (or Treaty of Alliance) moved the military cooperation into the open. It also formally recognized the United States as an independent country.[1] The most famous Frenchman to support the colonies was Marie-Joseph Paul Yves Roch Gilbert du Motier, better known as the Marquis de Lafayette. A French aristocrat (with a name like that he needed a royal coach to carry it around for him), the Marquis took off from France for the colonies against the wishes of his king. He ended up leading troops of the revolution and became an aide and dear friend of George Washington.

Bourbon County. KY, was named after the French House of Bourbon to honor its help during the Revolutionary War. In 1785, it was carved out of Fayette County, VA, (yes, named after the Marquis) and later became part of Kentucky when it was granted statehood in 1792. At one time,

---

1   France wasn't the first country to recognize the new United States. Dubrovik, a small country that doesn't exist today (it is a city in Croatia) was first (and apparently has a document in its museum to prove it). Morocco recognized the United States. in 1777, followed by Holland a year later.

Bourbon County comprised over one-third of all the 120 counties that now make up Kentucky. "Old Bourbon County" now refers to the original geographic area.

Corn whiskey was one of Old Bourbon County's principal exports and its origin was stamped on the barrels used to send it down the river. Prior to the Civil War, most whiskey was sold "white," or unaged, but was sometimes colored with caramel to imitate the amber hue of brandy. The effect of aging on whiskey was discovered when the Kentucky product was ready for shipping down the river in winter but had to rest in the barrels waiting for spring to raise the rivers before it could be loaded onto boats. Then, the ship's jostling and swaying during its long journey produced even more interaction between whiskey and wood. The residents of New Orleans especially took a fancy to the aged corn whiskey with its new color and the taste it acquired on its journey. Predominantly inhabited by French colonists at the time, the good folks of New Orleans also liked the French connection imprinted right on the barrels.

Today, Bourbon County has no whiskey distilleries but one is being built. Most production of Kentucky whiskey is concentrated in the Louisville, Frankfurt, and Bardstown areas. It was not until 1840 that bourbon officially became known as bourbon. Prior to this, it was often labeled "Bourbon County Whiskey" or "Old Bourbon County Whiskey."

WHY KENTUCKY?

So, a lot of spirits drinkers—hunters, trappers, Indian fighters, military men, farmers, the disenfranchised—headed west to make a new life. By 1812, Kentucky had around two thousand licensed distilleries. Twenty years later you could count twenty thousand distilleries on the "western" frontier. And that doesn't include the unlicensed stills. But why did bourbon whiskey take such a firm hold in Kentucky, of all the

possible places? After all, trees and arable land were plentiful throughout the Ohio River valley.

The explanations are numerous. First, Kentucky County's location near a network of rivers certainly was in its favor. The Ohio River, which starts in Pittsburgh, PA, and heads southwest about four hundred miles to Louisville, KY, was generally navigable and fed into the Mississippi River that winds another seven hundred miles to New Orleans and the Gulf of Mexico. New Orleans became a major market for Kentucky goods, especially bourbon whiskey.

Second, ask any thoroughbred racehorse and they will tell you that calcium in the Kentucky water is good for their bones. The water is also great for making whiskey; Kentucky's natural limestone deposits

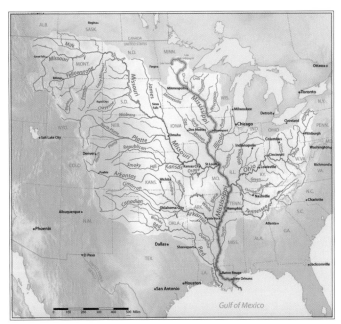

The Missouri and Mississippi River drainage system.
You can join your fellow whiskey pioneers in Pittsburgh, PA, then navigate down the Ohio River to Louisville. Wait on the riverbank for the waters to rise but load your whiskey on the steamboat (overleaf) or flatboat so it gently sways. When spring comes and the river rises, head down the Mississippi to Memphis, TN, Baton Rouge, LA, New Orleans, LA, and on to the world.

A steamboat being loaded with whiskey.
Show Boat it ain't.

filter iron salts from the water that don't taste good in whiskey.[2]

Third, hot summers and cold winters. Maybe that's not a slogan for a chamber of commerce, but it is music to the ears of a modern whiskey producer. Expansion and contraction of wood caused by extreme temperatures move whiskey in and out of the sides of the barrels in which aging whiskey rests. The interaction of the distillate and barrel wood speeds up and strengthens the flavoring that the wood imparts to the whiskey.

Finally, corn was Kentuckians' grain-of-choice. It was hard to grow wheat on the hillsides among all those tree stumps. Necessity is the mother of invention, and in this case, she was a sweet mother indeed.

SOME OF THE EARLIEST KENTUCKY DISTILLING FAMILIES

Today, many bourbon whiskeys have been named for early distillers in Kentucky. Some of the modern-day

distillers have a connection to a founding family, an original distillery, or were instrumental in the early production process. Others, not so much. Some of the honorees were good businessmen who knew how to take advantage of an opportunity when they saw one. Others were respected producers who made a name for themselves by turning out good whiskey. Still others we remember because they had a lot of character.[3]

You learned in the first chapter about Elijah Pepper, who settled in Kentucky the year the Declaration of Independence was signed. He was distilling whiskey in Frankfurt, KY, four years later. But many more followed.

Henry Hudson Wathen settled near Lebanon, KY in 1788 and started distilling in 1790. The second generation of Wathens built a bigger still and the third generation, five grandsons, all joined the business. One grandson moved to Louisville, KY, and built an even larger distillery, called, J. B. Wathen & Brothers. J. B. formed the American Medicinal Spirits Co. just in time; their "medicinal" spirit survived Prohibition. Today, a seventh generation Wathen relative, Charles Medley, and his son, Sam, bottle a brand called *Wathen's Kentucky Straight Bourbon Whiskey Single Barrel*. The whiskey is distilled outside Kentucky but to the company's specification, with lots of corn (77%).

Robert Samuels, who we will learn more about in Chapter 12, arrived in 1780 and probably set up his still shortly thereafter. His family has been distilling whisky (without the "e") on and off (mostly on) since then. His progeny now run Maker's Mark Distillery.

___

2   You can tell a real Kentuckian because they drink their local water and won't touch a drop of that purified, bottled stuff; it's not as good for you.

3   The dates and claims for early Kentucky bourbon distillers are sometimes hard to verify. They also get kinda specific to a particular distilling process, so many claims to being "the first" have to be parsed carefully. Maybe the first still was erected in Kentucky in Harrodsburg in 1774.

George Garvin Brown introduced his first whiskey, *Old Forester*, in 1873. Brown was a pharmaceutical salesman and the founder of the Brown-Forman Corporation, a major owner of several brands, and is still managed today by his descendants. *Old Forester*, named after a Union surgeon in the Civil War, was the first whiskey sold exclusively in sealed bottles, to prevent it from being adulterated.

Evan Williams built what is claimed to be the first commercial distillery in Kentucky in 1783. Williams was an upstanding citizen of Louisville who served his whiskey to his city's first elected Board of Trustees. He was censured for serving it during deliberations and for its poor quality (they called it "*popskull*"). Williams was indicted for serving whiskey without a license.

In the late 1700s, Jacob (Jake) Boehm (Beam) moved his family to central Kentucky and began growing corn. He also distilled whiskey using his father's recipe and sold it to neighbors. It caught on, so much so that the Beam family can lay claim to being the "First Family of Kentucky Bourbon." Jacob's descendants are master distillers spread throughout Kentucky's whiskey industry.

Elijah Craig's "invention" of bourbon whiskey is a claim that is disputed, though he certainly was among the first to age whiskey in a charred oak barrel. The term "bourbon whiskey" can't be found in written records before 1821 and then it was used in a *Western Citizen* newspaper ad. We do know that Elijah was a Baptist minister who was prosecuted for preaching his own brand of scripture. Before moving to Kentucky, he spent much time in Virginia

Elijah Craig.
A stiff upper lip (yes, it is American 19th century slang) helped Elijah get through many a travail.

jails and dungeons. He was "forcibly" removed from the state along with six hundred followers, called the Traveling Church. He continued to preach fire and brimstone as well as start businesses as a paper miller, grist miller, and wool cloth maker, in addition to being a distiller. Craig believed selling alcohol and preaching were not hypocritical because of the many references to wine in the Bible.

While Kentucky had a barrel full of iconic distillers, they had a neighbor in Tennessee that would also make a pretty big name for itself.

BARRELING WHISKEY

The distillate that comes out of the doubler (the second still that removes more impurities) can be aged in barrels to enhance its flavor (or it can be consumed right out of the still as unaged corn whiskey, of course).

To be called bourbon, the spirit must rest in new charred American oak barrels. When it goes into the barrel, bourbon whiskey must be between 110 and 125 proof; distillers can add water if needed.

Charred Oak Barrels

It has been known for ages that putting certain liquid products in barrels can infuse them with interesting flavors. Charring today involves shooting a propane flame into the barrel before it is filled. You won't hear of this being done for wine barrels, so why for whiskey barrels? Charring gives whiskey its straw, gold, or amber color; it also removes impurities that might taste sour. Charring also adds hints of flavors such as caramelized sugars, mild tannins, and vanilla, which are flavors that reside below the barrel's char line.

Once the inside of the barrel has caught fire the fuel source is cut off. Then the flame in the barrel is allowed to continue to produce one of four levels of charring. The lightest char, level #1, means the inside was allowed to burn for about fifteen seconds and the darkest char, level #4, for about 55 seconds. The char level will affect the taste of the whiskey when it is roused from its rest, which might be days or decades.

There are at least four stories concerning how charring whiskey barrels came to be. First, it may have occurred because the oak staves that make up the barrel were overheated in the process of making them more pliable so they would fit together better. Second, a building used by the Elijah Craig Distillery to store barrels might have caught fire but the barrels were used anyway. Third, charring would kill bugs. Fourth, charring might have removed the smell and taste from barrels that previously had been used to store pickles and fish. Nothing romantic here, but all the explanations are certainly utilitarian.

WHAT DOES KENTUCKY WHISKEY TASTE LIKE IN THE 1800s?

Basil Hayden Kentucky Straight Bourbon Whiskey

Basil Hayden brought Catholics to Kentucky from Maryland in the late 18th century, arriving about the same time as Elijah Craig and Jacob Beam. Most distillers at the time used the grains that were at hand. Hayden, having recently arrived from back east, was partial to rye. However, he was a neighbor of Jacob Beam who talked him into using corn. Over two hundred years later, the Noe family (descendants of Beam) paid tribute to Hayden's first recipe with a small batch bourbon, *Basil Hayden Kentucky Straight Bourbon Whiskey*.

Just the Facts

Mash Bill	Corn: 63% Rye: 27% Barley: 10%
Proof	Proof: 80 ABV: 40%
Age; Barrel Char	"Artfully aged to taste"; #4
Chill Filtered?	Yes

TASTING NOTES

The Basil Hayden website describes its straight bourbon whiskey as giving off the aromas of "Spice, tea, [and] a hint of peppermint." The flavor is also described as spicy and with a "gentle bite" but "light-bodied." The finish is characterized as short in length, "Dry, [and] clean."

From: In Search of Elegance (Reviewer: Jason Hambrey)

https://www.insearchofelegance.net/blog/2016/11/14/review-basil-haydens-kentucky-straight-bourbon-whiskey?rq=Basil%20Hayden

Aroma: Light, citrusy and fruity aroma overall—there's a lovely light rye influence in this one, but corn is quite present as well. The rye is quite dominant—it could perhaps fool some to be a light rye whiskey rather than a bourbon. Caramel, vanilla, custard, citrus, green apple skins, without a lot of oak for a bourbon that is close to eight years old. It's hot and peppery in the nose despite the low ABV and light profile. . .

Palate: Light, corn and oak with a bit of a floral nature on top. A taste profile that is simple and quite easy to embrace. . . .Lightly smoky, with fruity notes in the apple and pear camp, with a soft oak integration. Fruit too—apple and pear. Ever so lightly bitter and tannic, and fairly sweet for the light body. There is a decent amount of oiliness, too, in the palate as with many of the other premium Jim Beam products—which some people quite like but isn't quite my favorite.

Finish: A light body on the finish, with some oak, earthy corn—like what you would expect wet corn stalks to smell like after they've been pulled up. Slightly sour, and slightly spicy, as well. The oak wins out in the end.

This is a decent light bourbon, though at the price there are many others I'd recommend before this one at this price point. For someone just getting into bourbons, it's perhaps good because of the very light profile which is fairly easy to embrace.

From: The Over a Barrel Gang
Looks: Gold, amber.
Aroma: Medium. Vanilla, banana, orange, coffee, pepper, honey, maple.
Flavor: Light body. Sweet, salty, bitter.
Mouth Feel: Light, creamy, round, sharp.
Going Down: Soft strength, short length.
Notes: Good starter, people will be surprised a whiskey can be so drinkable; short lived.

Toast
Basil Hayden Kentucky Straight Bourbon Whiskey was not the first bourbon named after Basil Hayden. His grandsons opened a distillery and named their product *Old Grand-Dad*. Some of the bottles today (Basil's mash bill is used) have a drawing of granddad Basil on the label. As Booker Noe so astutely remarked, "I know bourbon gets better with age, because the older I get, the more I like it."

To the wisdom that comes with age and the character that comes with aging.

DINNER AT LEBANON, KY, WITH ELIJAH CRAIG AND THE TRAVELING CHURCH

Besides horses and bourbon, Kentucky is also known for its country ham; bourbon and ham are Kentucky's two top processed agricultural products. Pigs are easy to raise in Kentucky because they don't need fences. You might not be surprised to learn that Kentucky ham is referred to as "hillbilly prosciutto."

If you don't live in Kentucky and don't want to slaughter your own pig, there are a few places you can get Kentucky ham shipped to you. Or, you might be able to purchase it at a specialty store nearby. Here are two preparers of cooked Kentucky Ham.

Recipe: Kentucky Ham

You can order Kentucky spiral-sliced, honey-glazed ham from Browning's Country Ham: https://browningscountryham.com/shop/ham/spiral-sliced-glazed-half-country-ham/
You can also order half-hams from Kentucky Legend: https://kentuckylegend.com/product/half-ham/

It will take no preparation, other than to slice for serving. One or two slices of ham, served on a biscuit along with some fresh berries (blackberries are the state fruit of Kentucky), preserves, or marmalade will do the trick.

Recipe: Baking-Powder Biscuits

From: Gillette, F. L. (1887). *White House Cook Book* Chicago IL: R. S. Peale and Company.
Mrs. Gillette writes in her preface:

In presenting this book of recipes to the public, I do so at the urgent request of friends and relatives. During forty years of practical housekeeping, it has been my custom, after *trying* and *testing* a recipe, and finding it *invariably* a success, and also one of the best of its kind, to copy it into a book, thereby accumulating a considerable amount of reliable and useful information in the culinary line.

But there is more:

. . .this book embodies several original and commendable features, among which may be mentioned its plain print, its simplified method of explanation in preparing an article. . . .Unlike most books, the leaves are broad, and when opened it will not close itself, which obviates the necessity of frequently opening, as is the case with narrow pages.

What could be better?
Ingredients and directions:

Two pints of flour, butter the size of an egg, three heaping teaspoonfuls of baking-powder, and one teaspoonful of salt; make a soft dough of sweet milk or water, knead as little as possible, cut out with the usual biscuit-cutter and bake in rather a quick oven.

Recipe: Kentucky Corn Dodgers

From: Originally, Fox, Minerva Carr. (1904). *The Blue Grass Cookbook.* Reproduced in McLean, Alice (2006), *Cooking in America, 1840–1945.* Newport, CT: Glenwood Press. P. 106.

Probably better known as corn pone.

Sift the best meal made from the white corn, any quantity desired. Salt to taste. Mix with cold water into stiff dough and form into round, long dodgers with the hands. Take the soft dough and form into shape by rolling between the hands, making the dodgers about 4 or 5 inches long and 1½ inches in diameter. Have a griddle hot, grease a little with lard, and put the dodgers on as you roll them. Put in oven and bake thoroughly, when they will be crisp and a rich brown.

This bread does not rise.

MUSIC THAT TAKES US BACK TO DANIEL BOONE'S PARADISE

My Old Kentucky Home, performed by Kate Smith (2005)

Written by Stephen Foster, this was originally an anti-slavery song. It was adopted as the official song of Kentucky in 1928. Words in the original version that we would find offensive today were officially changed by the state of Kentucky in 1986. Kate Smith is best known for her iconic rendition of *God Bless America*.

Camptown Races, performed by The John Halloran Singers (2006)

This is another Steven Foster composition. It was originally a minstrel song titled *Gwine to Run All Night*.

Daniel Boone, performed by Fess Parker (1964)

Okay, they weren't singing this song in the 1800s. It was the theme song to a 1960s TV show of the same name (starring Fess Parker). Born in 1734, Boone, to the dismay of many who grew up watching the show, never wore a coonskin cap; he always wore a beaver felt hat. But he did set out in 1775 to chop a passable trail into the Kentucky wilderness.

Coal Miner's Daughter, performed by Loretta Lynn (1970)

Lynn's signature song. It only made it to #4 on the *Billboard* country music charts when it was first released. But it also was the title of Lynn's autobiography and the movie for which Sissy Spacek won the Academy Award for her portrayal of Loretta. Lynn selected Spacek for the role.

Daniel Boone.

Rawhide, performed by David Grisman (1980)

Composed by Bill Monroe, known as "The Father of Bluegrass Music."

The Road to Kaintuck, performed by June Carter Cash (with Johnny Cash) (1965)

June Carter Cash is credited with composing this song, recorded first by Johnny in 1965 on *Songs of the True West*. This version comes off an album titled *The Appalachians*. If it is an original by Carter, she did an amazing job of writing a traditional tune.

Paradise, performed by the Everly Brothers (1973)

John Prine, a contemporary songwriter, penned this song, titled after the town in Kentucky where his mother grew up. The older Everly brother, Isaac ("Don"), was born in Muhlenberg County, KY, in 1937. Brother Phil was born in Chicago, IL. Their father worked in the Kentucky coal mines from age fourteen. Lucky for us, the family's musical talent drew them away.

Down to the River to Pray, performed by Alison Krauss (2000)

This song might be considered a hymn, spiritual, or Appalachian folk song. It first appeared in the *Slave Songbook of 1867*. Krauss' version appeared in the movie, *Oh Brother, Where Art Thou?*

Eight More Miles to Louisville, performed by Grandpa Jones (2005)

Lewis Marshall Jones was a native Kentuckian, but he spent many years in Kornfield Kounty, as a member of the cast of the TV hit *Hee Haw*. "Outrageous!"

Chapter 5

TENNESSEE WHISKEY: WHO TAUGHT JACK DANIEL TO MAKE WHISKEY?

I heard that little guy is from Tennessee. Probably up here to find out how real good liquor is supposed to be handled.
—Comment overheard by Jack Daniel at the 1904 St. Louis World Fair
before his whiskey won the Gold Medal

DON'T CALL IT BOURBON IF IT'S FROM TENNESSEE

A common belief is that bourbon whiskey must be distilled in Kentucky. Not true. By resolution of Congress on May 4, 1964, bourbon whiskey was designated "a distinct product of the United States" and can be labelled such regardless of which state it comes from. It must be produced in the United States, contain at least 51% corn in the mash bill, and be free of added ingredients. If flavorings are added the label must say so. Straight bourbon whiskey must be distilled at less than 160 proof (so that more flavor from the mash is left in) and aged for a minimum of two years; more on these definitions later.

Tennessee whiskey made its first appearance in 1825 with the "invention" of "The Lincoln County Process" by Tennessean Alfred Eaton. This process involves a filtration system in which the whiskey is dripped through a minimum of ten feet of sugar-maple charcoal before it is put in barrels for aging. This is called leaching. It takes ten days to travel through the filtering. This process is still in use today and distinguishes

SOME CATEGORIES OF AMERICAN WHISKEY

It is time to become familiar with some terms you will see to describe types of whiskey. Many distillers put out multiple expressions of their whiskey and you will have to read carefully to understand what category of whiskey you are drinking.

The United States government definition of the most frequently used terms is the place to start. The definitions below are taken from the Electronic Code of Federal Regulations, e-CFR current as of July 16, 2019, Chapter I, Subchapter A, Part 5, Labeling and Advertising Distilled Spirits.* However, I have tried to translate them a bit from government-ese to English.

Neutral spirits: "Neutral spirits" or "alcohol" are distilled spirits produced from any material at or above 190 proof, and if bottled, must be bottled at not less than 80 proof. "Grain spirits" are neutral spirits distilled from a fermented mash of grain and stored in oak containers.

Whisky: ** "Whisky" is an alcoholic distillate from a fermented mash of grain produced at less than 190 proof in such manner that "the distillate possesses the taste, aroma, and characteristics generally attributed to whisky" [that clears things up]. It is stored in oak containers (except that corn whisky need not be so stored), and bottled at not less than 80 proof. It also includes mixtures of such distillates for which no specific standards of identity are prescribed.

Bourbon and other whiskies: "Bourbon whisky," "rye whisky," "wheat whisky," "malt whisky," and "rye malt whisky" are produced at 160 proof or less from a fermented mash of not less than 51% corn, rye, wheat, malted barley, or malted rye grain, respectively, and stored at not more than 125 proof in charred new oak containers. This includes mixtures of whiskies of the same type.

Corn whisky: "Corn whisky" is produced not exceeding 160 proof from a fermented mash of not less than 80% corn grain. If it is stored in oak containers, it should not be stored at more than 125 proof in used or uncharred new oak containers and not subjected in any manner to treatment with charred wood.

Straight whisky: "Straight whisky" conforms to the standards prescribed above and is stored in the type of oak container prescribed for a period of two years or more. Straight whisky includes mixtures of straight whiskies of the same type produced in the same state.

---

*   https://www.ecfr.gov/cgi-bin/retrieveECFR?gp=&SID=9b2a0a59ad7bdd15023465091823490c&n=27y1.0.1.1.3&r=PART&ty=HTML#27:1.0.1.1.3.3.25.1

**   Note that for some reason the regulators chose to drop the "e" from "whisky" in the regulations, even though the "e" was included in the declaration that pronounced bourbon whiskey a distinct product of the United States.

Tennessee whiskey from bourbon and all other American whiskeys.[1] While Tennessee whiskey could be called bourbon, don't call it that when talking to a Tennessean.

---

1   A document in the Filson Historical Society, in Louisville, KY, written prior to 1820, describes local distillers filtering whiskey through white flannel, clean white sand, and pulverized charcoal.

JASPER NEWTON "JACK" DANIEL

The exact date of Jasper Newton Daniel's birth is a matter of some dispute. He was probably born in 1849 just prior to his mother Lucinda's death, though his birth record was lost in a fire. We do know for sure that Jack was the youngest of ten children fathered by Callaway Daniel. Jack was the runt of the litter; he grew to be only five feet four inches tall and was known for running everywhere, perhaps a strategy he learned to keep up with other people. Jack didn't like his stepmother; she scared him and he felt neglected. At age six, he trotted out of the house and took up with his neighbor "Uncle" Felix Waggoner on Waggoner's farm next door.

Jasper Newton "Jack" Daniel.

Another neighbor, Daniel Call, a lay preacher, inherited his father's store. It had a whiskey still in back. Jack was fascinated by the still so when Call asked if Jack would like to come to work for him, Jack agreed. Call's wife, Mary Jane, frowned on the whiskey business but liked Jack. She taught Jack math by showing him the store's books. In his late teens, Jack decided to peddle the whiskey in the surrounding area.

To all our benefit, a prohibitionist preacher came to town and gave a sermon at Call's church. This ignited anti-alcohol sentiment; the parishioners, especially Mary Jane, began to wonder why their preacher owned a still and sold whiskey. Understanding what he was up against, Call sold the whiskey still to Jack on credit. (Something good came of the temperance movement). After the Civil War, Jack moved the still to a site closer to transportation.

In 1904, Jack, the cool *dude,*[2] secretly entered *Jack Daniel's Old No. 7 Tennessee Whiskey* in competition at the St. Louis World's Fair. He took the train there by himself and told few of his mission. At the Fair, he was ridiculed for his dress (a top hat, swallow-tailed jacket), small stature, and for coming from Tennessee. When *No. 7* won the competition, the big whiskey distillers discouraged newspapers from circulating the news.

In 1911, Jack *flew off the handle* one morning when he couldn't open the distillery's safe. He kicked it, contracted gangrene in the toe he injured, and later *kicked the bucket*[3] from blood poisoning. The safe is still at the distillery. The distillery is now on the National Register of Historic Places and produces over a dozen different varieties of whiskeys. Over twelve million cases were sold in 2016.

HOW DID *JACK DANIEL'S OLD NO. 7* GET ITS NAME?

Is *No. 7* aged for 7 years? It's aged between five and six years. Is *No. 7* its license number? Nope. Lucky number 7 from dice rolling? Probably not. One biographer of Jack says a merchant friend in Tullahoma, TN, had a chain of seven stores. Another biographer says the distillery lost some barrels of whiskey. As they were found numbers were put on them to keep track. Orders started to come in asking for more whiskey from the 7th barrel.

---

2   Though we associate the slang term *dude* with surfers in the 1970s, it dates back to the late 19th century and was short for "doodle." Originally, a dude was an overly fastidious man, or popinjay.

3   This slang term is of no known origin but first appeared in the Dictionary of Vulgar Tongue in 1785. It may have originated from hangings where the hangee stood on a bucket or pail that was kick out from under him. It is now used simply as "to die."

George Green seated next to Jack Daniel in a photograph taken in the mid-1800s.

NATHAN "UNCLE NEAREST" GREEN

The origin of Jack Daniel's distilling expertise is even more history-filled than his unique life story. For a century, Dan Call was credited with teaching Jack how to make whiskey. Then, in the 1990s, Jack Daniel's Distillery uncovered a photograph that changed everything. In the photo of the distillery workers, Jack is sitting next to an African American man whose position is front and center, unusual for an image taken in the south at that time. The story goes that Jack met a boy about his age who was the son of a slave who worked for Dan Call. The boy's name was George Green. He and Jack became close friends. George showed Jack the still house and when Jack asked Dan Call if he could work there, Dan said "yes." Jack met the distiller, George's father, Nathan Green, known to most as Uncle Nearest Green. No one knows how Uncle Nearest got the nickname, but his descendants suggest it comes from "nearest and dearest." It was Uncle Nearest who taught Jack how to make Tennessee whiskey.

The photo gave new credibility to a 1967 biography written about Jack by Ben Green (no relation), *Jack Daniel's Legacy.* The book was reissued in 2017 and it makes fifty mentions of a slave family named Green. The distillery has embraced this history and has a display in its tour waiting room dedicated to the Green family. Uncle Nearest is now recognized as the first African American master distiller in America. Clay Risen, in an article written in the *New York Times*, remarked that "Enslaved men not only made up the bulk of the distilling labor force, but often played crucial skilled roles in the whiskey-making process." After emancipation, Green earned a respectable living practicing his trade.

But the story doesn't end there. Fawn Weaver, an entrepreneur, investor, best-selling author (*Happy Wives Club*), historian, daughter of a Motown Records executive, and spouse of a Sony Pictures Entertainment vice president, read an article about Jack Daniel on an airplane ride to Singapore. While on the trip, her niece was killed in a motorcycle accident and Weaver decided to turn her grief into a new mission in life: resurrecting the legacy of Nathan Green. Weaver bought Dan Call's old farm and hired archivists, archeologists, and genealogists to resurrect the role Nathan Green played in the birth of Tennessee whiskey. Weaver began the *Uncle Nearest* whiskey label and is writing a history of him. She is restoring the Call farmhouse and renovated the African American Highview Cemetery where Uncle Nearest is buried, across the road from where Jack Daniel rests. There is now a ten-foot-high memorial to Green. She is building a distillery and concert venue on Sand Creek

BARREL AGING AND STORING WHISKEY

The aging process for whiskey can be short or long, but if it's called "bourbon" it must pass through a new charred oak barrel. The effects of aging will be determined by how much time the whiskey spends in the barrel, the size of the barrel, and the temperature (and temperature changes) outside the barrel. The most frequently used barrels contain fifty-three gallons (two-hundred liters) of whiskey, or about 267 bottles. Smaller barrels holding thirteen gallons are also used, often with the intent of speeding up the aging process.

You may often hear talk of what rickhouse (or warehouse) a whiskey rested in, how high up in the rickhouses it was stored, and whether it was on the end of a rack or in the middle. All these factors can modify a whiskey's taste by affecting the interaction of the wood and the whiskey inside the barrel. Distillers use a team of tasters to determine when a barrel of whiskey is ready and which barrels to mix together to get the taste they are after.

An age statement on a bottle of whiskey is only required if the whiskey is less than four years old but distillers often prominently display older ages on labels as marketing devices. If whiskeys of different ages are mixed together, the label must display the age of the spirit taken from the youngest barrel. Government requirements about reporting age on labels are always under discussion. Some distillers are removing age statements, to the consternation of their loyalists.

Farm in Shelbyville, TN, the original site of the Call farm.

Weaver has set up the Nearest Green Foundation which pays for all his descendants to attend colleges and graduate schools throughout the United States, as long as they keep their grades up. There has always been a descendent of Nathan Green working at the Jack Daniel's Distillery.

A friendship like that of Jack and George was unusual, perhaps punishable, prior to the nation's most tumultuous time.

WHAT DOES WHISKEY TASTE LIKE IN JACK DANIEL'S DAY?

Jack Daniel's Old No. 7 Tennessee Whiskey

The original *Old No. 7* is Jack Daniel's leading product. All the distillery's products use the same mash bill but different types of barrels (see *Sinatra Select* in Chapter 13 later on) or different numbers of charcoal filterings (*Gentleman Jack* undergoes a second filtering), barrel chars, or blending.

Just the Facts

Mash Bill	Corn: 80% Rye: 8% Barley: 12%
Proof	Proof: 80 ABV: 40%
Age; Barrel Char	No Age Statement; #3
Chill Filtered?	Filtered through sugar maple charcoal

TASTING NOTES

From: Jack Daniel Distillery website

https://www.jackdaniels.com/en-us/

Mellowed drop by drop through 10-feet of sugar maple charcoal, then matured in handcrafted barrels of our own making. And our Tennessee Whiskey doesn't follow a calendar. It's only ready when our tasters say it is. We judge it by the way it looks. By its aroma. And of course, by the way it tastes. It's how Jack Daniel himself did it over a century ago. And how we still do it today.

A balance of sweet and oaky flavor.

From: The Whiskey Sidekick (Reviewer: "The Sidekicks in America")

https://www.whiskeysidekick.com/whiskeyreviews/reviews/jack-daniels-old-no-7

Color & Consistency: Light honey with thin, quick legs.

Nose: Light alcohol, pretty mellow actually with a hint of confectioner's sugar.

Taste: Nutty, buttery & bitey. Salty peanut butter.

Finish: Lingers a while, oak with some brown sugar. Like a smoldering campfire in your mouth.

Conclusion: The only way to get more American than Jack Daniel's is if you bottled the amount of freedom in 50 Bald Eagles, drank it while flying the Flag standing on the roof of a Walmart® on the 4th of July eating a Big Mac®.

From: The Over a Barrel Gang
Looks: Gold, amber.
Aroma: Delicate. Butterscotch, honey, vanilla, cinnamon, banana.
Flavor: Medium body. Sweet, salty.
Mouth Feel: Round, creamy.
Going Down: Medium strength, medium length.
Notes: Round and interesting.

Uncle Nearest 1856 Premium Whiskey

Uncle Nearest 1856 Premium Whiskey now sells in more than four thousand locations around the world and is the fastest selling label in the British Airways Concorde Lounge at Heathrow Airport. The whiskey is still sourced from two Tennessee distilleries, most likely the Cascade Hollow Distillery (owned by the George Dickel Distillery[4]) and Prichard Distillery, but a unique product from the Nearest Green Distillery is on the way.

TASTING NOTES:

From: Uncle Nearest Website

The Uncle Nearest website describes its color as "light caramel" and "straw/hay." The aroma is also called "hay" with "peach and apricot" and "caramel corn and sweet maple." On the palate, it tastes of caramel with "hints of maple. . .dried fruit and floral notes," some sweets and spices "reminiscent of freshly baked oatmeal raisin cookies." The finish is portrayed as long and rich with hints of vanilla.

From: Whiskey Consensus (Reviewer: Eric Stumbo)

https://whiskeyconsensus.com/uncle-nearest-1856-review/

Color: Medium Gold
Aroma: Brazil nuts, cherry cough syrup, toffee, and nutmeg
Palate: Chocolate covered almonds, cold medicine, and the familiar but faint Flintstone's Vitamin.
Finish: Charcoal joins the chocolate and almond with a lingering coffee bean.
In closing:. . . if you're interested in giving the Uncle Nearest brand a try, I would personally suggest you start with the 1856 before moving onto the higher priced 1820 release. Although I'd say you could find more appropriately priced alternatives for both labels, these are still unique options and worth a try.

Just the Facts	
Mash Bill	Corn: 84% Rye: 8% Barley: 8%
Proof	Proof: 100 ABV: 50%
Age; Barrel Char	No Age Statement; #4
Chill Filtered?	No

---

4   George Dickel bought, sold, and distilled whiskey in Tennessee for over three decades during the mid-1800s. He and his business partners also bought numerous distilleries in the area. Today, there are over a half dozen brands coming from the Cascades Hollow Distillery.

From: The Over a Barrel Gang

Looks: Amber, gold.

Aroma: Delicate. Chocolate, butterscotch, apple, licorice, caramel, pepper, orange, wood.

Flavor: Medium body. Sweet, salty, umami.

Mouth Feel: Round, rich, sharp.

Going Down: Soft strength, medium length.

Notes: Decent whiskey, rounded and easy going; nothing crazy.

Toast

A whiskey lover's old saying: "To times you'll never remember with people you'll never forget." Thanks to Fawn Weaver, Uncle Nearest Green is a person we will never forget.

To Jack Daniel, Nearest and George Green, and their immortalized friendship.

DINNER AT LYNCHBURG, TN, WITH JACK DANIEL AND NATHAN AND GEORGE GREEN

Tennessee's cooking heritage is much like that of Kentucky and western North Carolina. (I'm sure there are Tennessee chefs who will disagree.) But pickled watermelon rinds and barbequed ribs didn't make the Kentucky selections, so you will find them here. Pickling recipes have nearly disappeared from cookbooks. However, pickled watermelon rind remains popular in the South. You can buy prepared pickled watermelon rinds in a jar. Memphis-Style ribs are served "dry" without a sauce and get their flavoring from a dry rub instead. The rib rub is made from a variety of spices, often reflecting the chef's secret recipe.

Recipe: Pickled Watermelon Rind

From: Virant, Paul. (2012). *The Preservation Kitchen*. Berkeley, CA: Ten Speed. Page 49-50.

My family has always embraced Southern cooking, from my mom's skillet-fried chicken to my brother's Carolina barbecue. This pickle is a tribute to that rich culinary culture.

Made from an ingredient that typically goes straight into the compost bin, watermelon rind makes for a humble pickle. Actually, it's a pickle only in the sense that a splash of vinegar curbs some of the preserve's sticky sweetness. The not-insignificant amount of sugar in this recipe is added in three stages, which allows the sugar and spices to gradually permeate the rind. The layering process also changes the texture of the rind, turning it translucent, similar to what happens when you candy citrus peel. In the end, the layers contribute to a pickle destined for cured meat. Adding these layers takes patience—plan on making this pickle over the course of several days—but the result is a perfect condiment for salty cured meat. I also like to serve it alongside grilled bread, sliced prosciutto, and arugula dressed with lemon juice and olive oil.

Makes 3 pints

Ingredients

Ingredients	Volume	Ounces	Grams	Percent
Peeled watermelon rind, finely diced	6 cups (from about 1 medium or two small melons)	2 pounds	907 grams	25.50%
Water	6 cups	48 ounces	1360 grams	39%
Kosher salt	¼ cup plus two tablespoons	3¼ ounces	92 grams	2.50%
Sugar	3 cups	1 pound, 7 ounces	652 grams	18.50%
Champagne Vinegar	1½ cups	12 ounces	340 grams	9.50%

Ingredients	Volume	Ounces	Grams	Percent
Lemon, sliced thinly	1½ lemons	6 ounces	170 grams	5%
Cinnamon sticks	3 cups	X	X	X
Allspice berries	1½ teaspoons	X	X	X
Cloves	1½ teaspoons	X	X	X

Directions:

1. Place the rind in a large bowl. In a separate bowl, mix together the water and salt. Pour the salted water over the watermelon rind and let stand for 4 hours, then drain and rinse. Transfer the rind to a pot and cover with about 1 inch of fresh water. Bring to a boil, decrease to a simmer, and cook until tender, about 20 minutes. The rinds will start to look translucent, like slices of onions. Drain and chill.

2. In a pot over medium-high heat, simmer together 1 cup of the sugar, the vinegar, and the lemon slices. In a dry sauté pan over medium heat, toast the cinnamon, allspice berries, and cloves until fragrant. Mix the spices into the vinegar and pour over the rind. Cover and refrigerate for at least 24 hours or up to 2 days.

3. Strain the brine into a pot, reserving the rind and spices. Place the pot over medium-high heat, mix in 1 cup of the sugar, and bring to boil. Pour over the rind, cover, and refrigerate for another 24 hours or up to 2 days.

4. Strain the brine into a pot, reserving the rind and spices. Place the pot over medium-high heat, mix in the remaining 1 cup sugar, and bring to boil. Meanwhile, scald 3 pint jars in a large pot of simmering water fitted with a rack—you will use this pot to process the jars. Right before filling, put the jars on the counter. Divide the rind among the jars. Place 1 cinnamon stick in each jar. Soak the lids in a pan of hot water to soften the rubber seal.

5. Transfer the brine to a heat-proof pitcher and pour over the rind, leaving a ½-inch space from the rim of the jar. Check the jars for air pockets, adding more liquid if necessary to fill in gaps. Wipe the rims with a clean towel, seal with the lids, then screw on the bands until snug but not tight.
   Place the jars in the pot with the rack and add enough water to cover the jars by about 1 inch. Bring the water to a boil and process the jars for 15 minutes (start the timer when the water reaches a boil). Turn off the heat and leave the jars in the water for a few minutes. Remove the jars from the water and let cool completely.

Recipe: Memphis-Style BBQ Ribs

From: https://en.wikibooks.org/wiki/Cookbook:Memphis-Style_BBQ_Ribs

Ingredients (serves 6):

    1 slab pork spareribs

    6 tbsp rib rub

    1 cup tomato paste

    ½ cup molasses

    ¼ cup apple cider vinegar

    2 tbsp Worcestershire sauce

    2 tbsp soy sauce

    Hickory chunks

Directions:

1. Season spareribs with rib rub.
2. Refrigerate for at least 1 hour.
3. Place chunks in smoker or charcoal grill set for indirect heat at 250°F (120C).
4. Combine liquid ingredients and bring to a boil over high heat.
5. Reduce liquid by ⅓.
6. Place spareribs into smoker or grill for 4–5 hours, basting occasionally with sauce.
7. Brush remaining sauce on top of ribs and place on a medium high grill until browned.
8. The internal temperature of the ribs before removing from the grill needs to be at least 145°F (63°C).
9. Let rest for 10 minutes, covered, and carve.

Rib Rub:

    2 cups smoked paprika

    ¼ cup salt

    1 cup brown sugar

    3 tbsp cayenne pepper (you can change this at will)

    ¼ cup dry mustard

    ¼ cup garlic powder

    ¼ cup dried rosemary

    1 tbsp cinnamon

Directions

1. Combine all ingredients in a container with a shaker lid.

MUSIC THAT TAKES US BACK TO GOOD OLD ROCKY TOP

Cherokee Dancer, performed by Jay Red Eagle (2009)

The early 1800s were a tragic time for the Cherokee tribe. Native Americans from Tennessee, Georgia, Alabama, and North Carolina (sixteen thousand Cherokees) were forcibly removed from their homes and made to march twelve hundred miles to "Indian Territory," the infamous "Trail of Tears." One quarter of the natives died on the way. Jay Red Eagle, an enrolled member of the Cherokee tribe, is an award-winning flutist.

Electricity, performed by Paul Burch (2005)

The shocking implications of technological innovation.

Preacher Got Drunk and Laid His Bible Down, performed by Tennessee Ramblers (2007)

The Ramblers were popular in east Tennessee from the 1920s to the 1940s. Founder William "Fiddlin' Bill" Sievers was a barber before starting the Ramblers with his children.

Moonshiner and His Money, performed by Charlie Bowman and His Brothers (2007)

Bowman, a country fiddle pioneer, toured the United States with string bands and vaudeville shows throughout the 1920s. Luckily, he lived to experience the folk revival of the early 1960s.

A. P., Maybelle (June Carter Cash's Mother), and Sara Carter.

Can the Circle Be Unbroken, performed by The Carter Family (1927)

The Carter Family is the first family of American country music. The first generation of musicians—A. P., Maybelle, and Sara—hailed from Maces Springs, VA, in Poor County, just across the border from Black Mountain, KY. A. P. traveled the rural roadways collecting folk songs. This well-known song has lyrics by Ada Habershon and music by Charles Gabriel, rearranged by A. P.

Memphis Blues, by W. C. Handy (1909)

William Christopher Handy, the "Father of the Blues," was born in Alabama but his strongest musical influences came from the Mississippi Delta and Memphis, TN, where for many years he played on Beale Street. *Memphis Blues* was written as a campaign song for a mayoral candidate.

Crying Won't Help You, performed by B. B. King (1956)

If Handy was the father of the Blues, B. B. was the King. King also haunted Beale Street for many years and played live on the local radio stations. King wrote this song (or at least wrote it down), shortly before it was recorded.

Rocky Top, performed by The Obsorne Brothers (1967)

Rocky Top is one of Tennessee's ten state songs. The song became so popular that the Red Clay Ramblers, who played it in many a bar, wrote a satire called *Play Rocky Top (or I'll Punch Your Lights Out)*.

Wildwood Flower, performed by Reese Witherspoon (2005)

You can hear this traditional number with lyrics recorded by many artists. Witherspoon sings it in the movie *Walk the Line* (the Johnny Cash story) for which she won the Academy Award for Best Actress.

Statue of W. C. Handy in Handy Park, Memphis, TN.

Cumberland Gap, performed by Earl Scruggs (1980)

This is an Appalachian folk song first recorded in 1924. The Cumberland Gap transported citizens of the thirteen colonies to the western frontier, Tennessee and Kentucky at the time. Earl Scruggs three-fingered banjo picking helped define bluegrass music as we know it today. Can you sing the theme song to *The Beverly Hillbillies (The Ballad of Jed Clampett)*? It was written by Les Flatt & Earl Scruggs.

Tennessee Waltz, performed by Patti Page (1950)

This song is also one of the state songs of Tennessee. It was #4 of the ten state songs. Millions of copies of this version were sold in the 1950s. In the many cover versions, the gender of the singer is varied depending on who is getting jilted.

Jack Daniel's, If You Please, performed by David Allen Coe (1985)

When David Allen Coe drinks too much Jack Daniel's he tells his boss to *Take This Job and Shove It*, probably Coe's best-known song (Johnny Paycheck made it popular, but Coe wrote it).

THE MOST UNCIVIL WAR

Chapter 6
A HOUSE DIVIDED AND REUNITED

When the commanding officer gave out whiskey, I yielded to his better judgement.
—Abstentious Union Soldier

WHISKEY IN THE EXECUTIVE MANSION BEFORE THE CIVIL WAR[1]

Presidents with an opinion about the advisability of drinking whiskey are not hard to find. Often, their love, hate, and personal experience with our native spirit played an important role in the events of their day. Here are a few pre-Civil War anecdotes about drinking among our nation's leading men.[2]

Andrew Jackson, (7th president, 1829–1837). Andrew Jackson grew up in Salisbury NC, where one resident said that he was "the most roaring, rollicking, game-cocking, horse-racing, card playing, mischievous fellow that ever lived in Salisbury." He made his name killing Native Americans in Florida during Creek War.

Jackson was a populist and a controversial choice to hold the highest office in the land. He was also the first frontier president. His presidency got off to a memorable start when the Executive Mansion was vandalized by his overzealous supporters at the reception following his inauguration. Being on less than amiable terms with his predecessor, John Quincy Adams (whom he lost to in the presidential election of 1824), the residence was left with no security. The reception was overrun by a mob and the furniture was destroyed. Jon Meacham, in his biography of Jackson, *American Lion*, quotes a congressman as saying that, "the glasses [were] broken, the

---

1   A special shout-out to Mark Will-Weber for his wonderful book, *Mint Julips with Teddy Roosevelt: The complete history of presidential drinking* (2014), upon which much of the recounting of whiskey in the Executive Mansion, later named the White House, is based. Will-Webber's book is both factual and a *hoot* to read.

2   Not every president gets a shout-out because not every president had an interesting relationship with alcohol.

pails of liquor upset, and the most painful confusion prevailed."

Whatever location Jackson found himself in, his heart remained at the Hermitage in Nashville, TN, where over three hundred slaves were said to have worked. He had his own distillery at the Hermitage from which he sold whiskey to merchants in the area.[3]

William Henry Harrison (9th president, 1841). Harrison's father was a signer of the Declaration of Independence. Harrison ran his "Log Cabin" campaign for president, positioning himself as the candidate of the common man.[4] He was a hero for his service in the War of 1812, during which he used *bust head* (strong whiskey) to help subdue the Native Americans. In Fort Wayne, IN, he would not let the tribal chiefs have whiskey until they had marked a treaty that turned over three million acres of farmland. Harrison was president for thirty-two days then died of pneumonia. Harrison may have been the third president to own at least a portion of a distillery.

James K. Polk (11th president, 1845–1849). Polk was not a whiskey drinker and his wife, Sarah, banned

A painting of the White House reception after Jackson's inauguration.
He is surrounded by aides to keep him safe.

whiskey and dancing from the White House. But his political foe Sam Houston, the President of Texas at the time, alleged to have consumed a barrel of whiskey a day, was known to the Native Americans as "The Big Drunk." Houston said of Polk, "He drank too much water."

Millard Fillmore (13th president, 1850–53). Fillmore took the temperance pledge but deserves some mention because, well, nobody else seems to mention him. At the first meeting of the Society to Promote Respect and Recognition of Millard Fillmore at a Baltimore waterfront pub in 1985, our thirteenth president was eulogized with a quote that is probably better remembered than he: "What he lacked in charisma he made up for in mediocrity." There were about thirty people at the gathering.

Franklin Pierce (14th president, 1853–57). Pierce's drinking ruined both his health and public image. A longtime imbiber—a fact conveniently omitted from his biography written by Nathaniel Hawthorne—he signed the temperance pledge in the 1830s but died of cirrhosis of the liver. Hmm. Jefferson Davis, the President of the Confederacy, served as the secretary of war under Pierce.

James Buchanan (15th president, 1857–1861). A 2018 survey of 157 presidential scholars by Sienna College rated Buchanan next-to-last among all presidents (only Andrew Johnson ranked worse). His *weak-kneed* response in the face of the impending Civil

---

3   Today's whiskey *Old Hickory* carries Jackson's image on the label but it is not based on his process. Jackson gained the nickname "Old Hickory" because it, and he, were considered "the hardest wood in creation."

4   A log cabin shaped whiskey bottle fashioned by the E.C. Booz Distillery was part of the campaign's swag. Hence, the term "booze."

War certainly didn't help. He also was known for his ability to drink large amounts of wine and whiskey without getting *tight* (showing any effects). He died of gout, worsened by a diet of rich food and too much alcohol.

ABRAHAM LINCOLN (16TH PRESIDENT, 1861–1865) AND HIS CIVIL WAR COHORT

Abraham Lincoln was a native-born Kentuckian and the son of a part-time distiller. When his father moved Abe and the family to Indiana (before their move to Illinois) he traded his Kentucky farm for twenty dollars in cash and whiskey. Abe was not a noted whiskey drinker himself but Jefferson Davis, also a native of Kentucky, was a lover of his home state's signature product. Indeed, Davis was court-marshalled as a student at West Point for spiking the refreshment at a Christmas party. Robert E. Lee favored bourbon whiskey as well but abstained as much as he could, allegedly confessing, "I like whiskey, I always did, and that is why I never drink it."[5] General William Tecumseh Sherman, the scourge of the South, carried his maps in his saddlebags, along with a flask of whiskey and a stash of cigars.

THE CIVIL WAR WHISKEY STRATEGY

In 1861, as the Civil War began, the Union reinstituted the excise tax on alcoholic beverages. That tax is still levied today.

As the war raged, Lincoln was quoted as saying, "I hope to have God on my side, but I must have Kentucky." It is not clear whether Lincoln was referring to the state's strategic location, its natural resources, or both. Pennsylvania, a big distilling state, was firmly on the Union side, as was

Maryland (although it did permit slavery) but not so Kentucky. Slavery was not outlawed in Kentucky, and at first, the state remained neutral. It was a "brother-against-brother" border state whose citizens relied for their economic well-being on whiskey drinkers (among other consumer goods, of course) down the Ohio River and out on the frontier. But Kentucky politicians were of divided loyalty. When the Confederacy tried to take Kentucky, its legislature asked the Union for help. By 1862, the territory was under Union control (Lincoln's wish granted).

The Union army had control of the important whiskey-producing border states between the North and South. Most of the war was fought on Southern soil, so in addition to a distillery advantage the Northern soldiers had access to the whiskey stored in the homes and barns they occupied. The Union also had a firm hold on trade channels (rivers, seaports) and the industrial infrastructure needed to supply alcohol. Whiskey was plentiful enough that it was frequently used as an anesthetic for injured soldiers.

The situation was different in the South. Its railroads were crippled by the fighting, and blockades limited access to the ocean and major inland waterways. The Confederacy also had limited manpower and limited grains needed for making whiskey. Many Southern states even prohibited whiskey production so grain could be used for food. In 1860, whiskey cost twenty-five cents a gallon; in 1863, it cost thirty-five *blue backs* (Confederate dollars) a gallon.

ULYSSES S. GRANT

By far the most famous whiskey drinker at the time of the Civil War and the era of Reconstruction that followed was Ulysses S. Grant. Born Hiram Ulysses Grant, his given names were reversed when he enrolled at the United States Military Academy and he did not change it. He removed "Hiram" and added the "S"

---

5   Lee was offered the command of the Union army by Lincoln but turned him down because of his devotion to his home state of Virginia.

for his mother's maiden name, Simpson.[6]

Upon graduating from West Point, Grant served bravely in the Mexican-American War. After about ten years of service, amid allegations he was a heavy drinker, he resigned his military post in California to return to his wife, Julia, and two sons (one he had never seen before). His time as a civilian didn't work out. Grant was unsuccessful as a farmer and in real estate in Missouri. He was reduced to selling firewood before humbling himself by going to work as a clerk in his father's store.

When Fort Sumter in South Carolina was fired on by Confederate soldiers, Grant rejoined the military. Even then, his career got off to a rocky start. He was denied appointments until finally landing the command of a rag-tag regiment of Illinois volunteers. He imposed discipline on his troops and things started to look up for him.

At least this was so until the Battle of Shiloh (or Pittsburgh Landing) in western Tennessee, about a year into the Civil War. The Confederacy had won most skirmishes but the Union "won" the

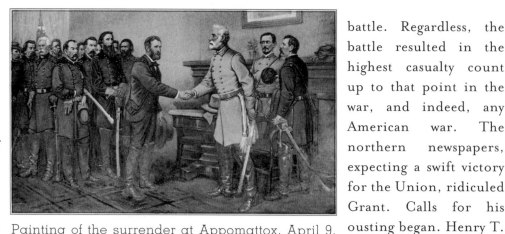
Painting of the surrender at Appomattox, April 9, 1885.

battle. Regardless, the battle resulted in the highest casualty count up to that point in the war, and indeed, any American war. The northern newspapers, expecting a swift victory for the Union, ridiculed Grant. Calls for his ousting began. Henry T. Blow, a Representative from Missouri, went to President Lincoln with charges that Grant was a drunkard. Abe kept his faith in Grant, famously responding, "I wish I knew what brand of whiskey he drinks. I would send a barrel to all of my other generals."

That Grant had a drinking problem is indisputable. It is also the case that alcoholism was a family trait, passed on to Ulysses from his father and from Ulysses to his own children. His loyal personal secretary during the war, Horace Porter, was charged with keeping Grant sober. He was largely successful with aid from Julia. Together they kept Ulysses on the straight and narrow when they were around, but bouts of heavy drinking still persisted.

If heavy drinking was Grant's major fault, naiveté and blind loyalty ran a close second and third. As president, Grant had to knit the nation back together. But while trying to carry out Reconstruction his administration was plagued by scandal and corruption, largely because Grant could not believe

---

6   Another story, likely apocryphal, suggests Grant did not want the initials on his equipment to read HUG. In his lifetime, the U.S. in his name came to stand for "unconditional surrender."

Grant stumbles to re-election.

his friends would engage in duplicity. The most famous episode is known in history as The Whiskey Ring.

THE WHISKEY RING

After the war, Grant served as General of the Army and then was elected president in 1868. Also, when the war was over, dishonest distillers from Milwaukee, WI, to New Orleans, LA, began turning out cheap imitations of "barrel-aged Kentucky"

Whiskey Ring cartoon, 1875 by Granger.

bourbon. They made and sold a lot more of a fake product doctored to look like aged whiskey than the government knew about. One of their deceptions was to remove tax stamps from barrels and use them again. Federal officials *in cahoots* with the ring took bribes to keep this secret and tip off the distillers when government raids were imminent. However, a subsequent investigation resulted in the arrest of three hundred distillers and government employees.[7]

The trail of payoffs led straight to the Executive Mansion. Investigators found that a close friend of Grant's and his chief of staff at the time, Orville Babcock, was alerting the crooked businessmen about upcoming raids of their distilleries. It was alleged that Grant knew about the Whiskey Ring but was being threatened with the disclosure of an

affair, was being bribed with money from the Ring to help him win reelection, and was silenced by members of his family who were involved. None of these accusations proved true.

That's the naive part of Grant's character. The loyalty part finds its denouement when Grant provided written testimony on Babcock's behalf to a grand jury. Babcock won acquittal.[8]

For all his failings, Grant was at the helm of the United States through its most divisive and treacherous time. Grant died of throat cancer in the summer of 1885. He was close to a pauper at his death (though he was revered by Union veterans of the Civil War) and he feared for the well-being of his wife and family. He was writing his memoirs and finished them days before he passed on.

DR. JAMES C. CROW

We know *Old Crow* bourbon was Ulysses' favorite whiskey because it was mentioned in a letter by a dinner guest who wrote that it was the brand reached for by Grant.[9]

Dr. James C. Crow was a Scottish physician and chemist who arrived in Kentucky in 1823. Crow was the first to introduce the saccharometer (an instrument for measuring the sugar content in

---

7   In New York City after the Civil War, distillers who were evading the whiskey tax were subjected to raids by United States soldiers sent by Grant, sometimes numbering over a thousand men. They smashed stills and barrels but the intrepid distillers quickly did their repairs and were back in business. The raids, which lasted two years, came to be known as "The Whiskey War."

8   Grant dismissed Babcock from his position at his side but appointed him a district lighthouse director. About a decade later, Babcock drowned off the coast of Florida while on duty.

9   Other famous drinkers of *Old Crow* include Mark Twain and Hunter S. Thompson.

SOUR AND SWEET MASH

The sour mash process uses the mash left in the still from a previous run to start the next run. The stillage has a slightly acid taste, hence the term sour mash. Sweet mash is made with fresh yeast for each batch. Sour mash creates uniformity in taste from batch to batch, because the yeast is as similar as possible and it kills unwelcomed bacteria. It is also said to improve the taste of the distillate. Most distillers today use the sour mash process, but sweet mash is making a comeback, especially with craft distillers.

a solution) and thermometer into the process of distilling and (arguably[10]) was the first to use the sour mash process.

Old Crow also has a place in American history because of the role it played in establishing trademark law at the turn of the 20th century. Whiskeys with the name *Old Crow* were manufactured in at least three distilleries. The W. A. Gaines Company held several trademarks on *Old Crow* and sued other distillers for using the same or similar names. Gaines sued a company using the name *White Crow*. He won. Then he lost cases against *Raven Valley* and *Old Jay*.[11] These cases were used to set standards on what was fair competition in the marketplace. The courts determined it was okay to compete over quality, price, packaging, and advertising. However, the criteria set for trademark infringement was whether a brand name would cause confusion among the public. So, while *White Crow* was verboten, *Wild Turkey* was okay.

But, would it cause confusion among the public if one of America's premier personalities was known by two names?

---

10   There are recipes for sweet and sour mash written by a woman, Catherine Carpenter from Casey County, KY. Date: 1818.

---

11   The "Old" in whiskey names is not an allusion to the spirit's age but to a dear friend . . . old buddy, old pal.

WHAT DOES U. S. GRANT'S FAVORITE WHISKEY TASTE LIKE?

Old Crow Kentucky Straight Bourbon Whiskey

If you look for *Old Crow* on your liquor store shelf today, don't look up. While it was *top shelf* (among the best) when Grant drank it, and it is aged at least three years, it has moved down the shelves since then. *Old Crow* is inexpensive. A slightly more expensive expression, *Old Crow Reserve*, is aged for a minimum of four years and bottled at 86 proof (43% ABV).

Talk about old school—*Old Crow* does not have a website. The web addresses listed on the bottle take you to pages for "The Olds" (*Old Overholt*, and *Old Grand-Dad*), and for making smart choices when you drink. Josh Peters (see below) suggests *Old Crow* is *Jim Beam* (White Label) that has been aged only half as long.

Just the Facts

Mash Bill	Corn: 75% Rye: 13% Barley:12 %
Proof	Proof: 80 ABV: 40
Age; Barrel Char	Minimum of three years; #4
Chill Filtered?	Yes, if it is *Jim Beam* (White Label)

TASTING NOTES

From: The Whiskey Jug (Reviewer: Josh Peters)

https://thewhiskeyjug.com/bourbon-whiskey/old-crow-review/

Color: Pale caramel

Aroma: A bit medicinal at first but that wash gives way to a sugary bourbon and a very pronounced corn. There's a bit of honey and waxy sugary smell to it that, combined with the corn, reminds me of a bag of candy corn. . .some underripe citrus and a raw almost pancake batter–like quality to the overall nose. A splash of water will help kick up some of the vanilla.

Palate: Caramel and corn battle it out on the palate with a buttered corn on the cob flavor. . . There is a touch of citrus, but not much of the vanilla that is very often found in bourbon. With only a touch of oak and a slightly medicinal quality hanging out in the glass it has a very young flavor profile and feels a bit wild. A splash of water or ice brings out more of the vanilla, but even then, it feels a bit unbalanced. Relatively smooth and easily drinkable with only a bit of burn.

Finish: Buttery popcorn that fades to a buttery caramel corn and then back to buttery popcorn before fading out a grainy flavor.

U. S. Grant painting from *Vanity Fair* magazine, June 1, 1872.

From: The Over a Barrel Gang
Looks: Gold, pale straw.
Aroma: Medium. Butterscotch, chocolate, vanilla, caramel, honey.
Flavor: Medium body. Sweet, salty.
Mouth Feel: Creamy, delicate, light, round.
Going Down: Medium strength, short length.
Notes: Light on the nose, nice and easygoing but short lived; not bad for the bottom shelf.

Toast
In addition to his penchant to drink too much, Grant constantly had a pipe or cigar in his hand, with an ashtray at his bedside and a new smoke for when he arose in the morning. This was reflected in one of his most revealing quotes: "Cheap cigars come in handy; they stifle the odor of cheap politicians."

To U. S. Grant and to resolution and reconciliation.

DINNER AT THE EXECUTIVE MANSION, WASHINGTON, DC, WITH ULYSSES S. AND JULIA GRANT

According to Executive Mansion records,[12] Julia Grant fired the army cook her husband brought with him whose skills resembled those of, well, an army cook. She hired to take his place an Italian kitchen steward and chef who planned opulent multi-course meals when the Grants entertained guests. However, for family meals Ulysses preferred simpler dishes such as rice pudding, turkey, and roast beef for dinner (his favorite meal was breakfast).[13]

When the newly married Grants were entertaining for the first time—having four or five of Ulysses's fellow officers to dinner—Julia was terrified. She had come from a slave-holding Missouri family and had been brought up with no knowledge at all of cooking. Her husband reassured her, telling her that he could "run up a savory mess himself, if need be." He had roasted apples at West Point and had even been known to cook a fowl. Julia survived that first company dinner and went on to become a respectable cook.

Recipe: Veal Olives

From: First Presbyterian Church. (1892). *Our own cook book*. Galena IL: Gazette Printing House. p.18. (Public domain.)

This recipe was one of Julia's favorites. Why it was called "Veal Olives" is a mystery; there are no olives in the recipe.

Ingredients:
  Leg of Veal
  Grated bread
  Butter
  Onion
  Salt and pepper
  Eggs
  Cloves

Directions [in Julia Grant's own words]:
Slice as large pieces as you can get from a leg of veal; make stuffing of grated bread, butter, a little onion, minced, salt, pepper, and spread over the slices. Beat an egg and put over the stuffing; roll each slice tightly and tie with a thread; stick a few cloves in them, grate bread thickly over them after they are put in the skillet, with butter and onions chopped fine; then done lay them in a dish. Make your gravy and pour over them. Take the threads off and garnish with eggs, boiled hard, and serve. To be cut in slices.

---

12 www.foodtimeline.org/presidents.html#grant

13 It is said that Grant had come to abhor the sight of blood. He asked that his meat always be prepared well-done.

Something a Little Different: Jennie June's *American Cookery*

Jennie June's *American Cookery*, written by J.C. Croly, first appeared in 1866. Croly dedicated the book "To the young housekeepers of America" (housekeepers at the time meant homeowners). In addition to receipts (that is, recipes) it contained advice on all phases of housekeeping, including kitchen furnishings, household management ("the most perfect system of management is, undoubtedly, that which outwardly betrays itself least"), hints on frugality, rules for eating ("eat slowly"), use of fuel ("There is no department of housekeeping in which our national spirit of waste and extravagance is more clearly identified than in our use of fuel."). In addition to the chapters you typically see in cookbooks that group by foodstuff (soups, salads, eggs, vegetables, meats, etc.), Croly included a chapter on "Food for Invalids,"—that is, people who are sick. She gives nursing advice ("Neatness, cleanliness, and promptitude are the great requisites in a sick chamber.") and provides twenty-three recipes that seem chosen for ease of digestion. There are also chapters on food for infants, children, New Year's parties, and Jewish cooking (contributed by "a superior Jewish housekeeper in New York"), to name but a few. There is even a chapter on "Washing Day" (". . .the dreaded event of every household, large, and small").

Recipe: Filet of Beef with Anchovy

From: Croly, J. C. (1878). *American Cookery Book.* New York: The American News Company. P. 38. (Public domain.)

This recipe sounds awful but somehow makes the mouth water.

> Soak five or six anchovies in water for about two hours, split them and put the fillet with them, mixed with some bacon; boil it on a slow fire with a small quantity of broth, a glass of white wine, a garlic clove, two cloves, and a bunch of herbs. When sufficiently done, strain the sauce, add to it a piece of butter rolled in flour, two teaspoons of cream, and a few capers; mix in a little yoke of egg, and pour it over the fillet.

Recipe: Minced Veal with Macaroni

From: Croly, J. C. (1878). *American Cookery Book.* New York: The American News Company. P. 48. (Public domain.)

Here's a recipe from June that's a bit less intimidating.

> Mince up cold veal with a slice of ham, a little grated rind of lemon, a little salt, and a few spoonsful of broth or gravy. Simmer gently, taking care that it does not boil. Serve it upon small squares of buttered toast, and surround it with a border of macaroni, cooked without cheese.

MUSIC THAT TAKES US BACK TO THE CIVIL WAR

Throughout the 19ᵗʰ and early 20ᵗʰ century, minstrel, medicine, and vaudeville shows had a profound influence on American music. However, in the four chapters that follow, the musical focus is on people, places, and events with more focused ties to the way Americans were living and what they were experiencing.

Home, Sweet Home, performed by University of Saint Mary's Choir (2006)

Home, Sweet Home was written for an opera by American lyricist John Howard Payne and English composer Sir Henry Bishop. The song was a favorite of both Northern and Southern soldiers during the Civil War. The soldiers would play their instruments at night to lift their spirits and, because their campsites were often close, to frighten the other side. On at least two documented occasions, one side began playing *Home Sweet Home* and the other side joined in. Learning of this, the only people frightened were the Union Army brass. They feared it might encourage desertions. They banned playing it.

John Brown's Body, performed by Paul Robeson (2007, remastered)

John Brown was an abolitionist who led the famous raid on Harper's Ferry, VA. The raid was meant to start a slave rebellion. If the melody sounds like *Battle Hymn of the Republic* (see below) it should; *Battle Hymn* is set to the same tune.

Harper's Weekly illustration of attack on John Brown's Fort.

Battle Cry of Freedom, performed by the 2ⁿᵈ South Carolina String Band (2000)

This song was so popular after the Civil War that printing presses couldn't keep up with the demand. It was suggested it be adopted as the national anthem.

When Johnny Comes Marching Home, performed by the Mitch Miller Orchestra (remastered 2013)

Johnny is most closely associated with the South but was written to appeal to both sides in the Civil War; Johnny was the most popular given name at the time. The writer, Patrick Gilmore, admitted to "appropriating" the melody for *Johnny* from a tune he heard someone humming. Folk music belongs to everyone; and as Pete Seeger said, "Plagiarism is basic to all culture."

No More Auction Block for Me, performed by Odetta (1973)

A Black spiritual that was performed by free Black soldiers during the Civil War as a marching song. Bob Dylan also covered this song; it is claimed to provide the structure for *Blowin' in the Wind*. Odetta Holms was an inspirational voice of the civil rights movement of the 1960s.

American Trilogy, performed by Mickey Newbury (2011)

Dixie Land was likely written by Ohioans but was adopted as the de facto national anthem of the Confederate States. *Battle Hymn of the Republic* was written by Julia Ward Howe and first published in 1862. *Hush Little Baby*, a lullaby of unknown origin, is thought to have originated in the South. (Elvis Presley also recorded *Trilogy*.)

Wayfaring Stranger, performed by Emmylou Harris (1980)

The origin of this song is lost in time. It could have been written as a spiritual or even by Portuguese settlers in the southern Appalachia mountains. The arrangements are numerous.

Vacant Chair, performed by Kathy Matea (1991)

George F. Root wrote the music for this poem written by Henry S. Washburn. Matea is a country/folk/bluegrass singer. The song expresses the grief of the family of a soldier who does not return from the war.

Like a Songbird That Has Fallen, performed by The Reel Time Travelers (2003)

This song by Henry and T-Bone Burnett is from the movie, *Cold Mountain*.

Chapter 7
THE FIRST VOICE OF THE AMERICAN COMMON MAN

Too much of anything is bad, but too much good whiskey is barely enough.
—Mark Twain

SAMUEL CLEMENS (A.K.A. MARK TWAIN)

Samuel Langhorne Clemens was born November 30, 1835, two weeks after Haley's Comet reached its closest point to the Earth (its perihelion). In his 1909 autobiography, he wrote:

> I came in with Halley's comet in 1835. It is coming again next year, and I expect to go out with it. It will be the greatest disappointment of my life if I don't go out with Halley's comet. The Almighty has said, no doubt: 'Now here are these two unaccountable freaks; they came in together, they must go out together.'

They did. Clemens died the day after Halley's Comet again reached perihelion on its subsequent visit to our solar system. In the intervening seventy-five years, while the comet traveled the heavens, Clemens traveled the United States and the world. He wrote, and wrote, and wrote, and left a chronicle—almost always humorous, often profound, often controversial—of what it meant to be an American in the 19th century. He also left a trail of empty whiskey bottles.

A visage as distinct as his writing.

Boyhood

Samuel's father, John, was of Scots-Irish descent. John was a lawyer, owned a general store, and held three government positions, as county clerk, county commissioner, and attorney general in Missouri.

Samuel seemed less ambitious. He held many odd jobs in and around Hannibal. He worked as:

- a clerk in a grocery store (he was fired for eating the sugar);
- a clerk in a bookstore (a job he didn't like because "the customers bothered me so much I could not read with any comfort");
- a clerk in an apothecary shop ("my prescriptions were unlucky, and we appeared to sell more stomach pumps than soda water");
- a newspaper deliverer; and
- an assistant in a blacksmith's shop.

Then he turned thirteen.

At age fifteen, Clemens left school and became a printer's apprentice at his brother's newspaper, the *Hannibal Courier*, finally finding work that vaguely suited him. It would provide enough compensation over the next decade or so that he could eat and buy clothes. It also led to his career as a writer. Samuel became incredibly proficient at typesetting and would write newspaper pieces directly into the printing machine. Most were written under pseudonyms; he sometimes kept up squabbles with himself in the letters section of the newspaper. After a whiskey tax was passed, he wrote a letter saying it was now patriotic to get drunk. His brother noticed that people around town were buying his paper to read Samuel's pieces.

But Clemens had wanderlust and soon took off. Before leaving, his mother had him put his hand on a bible and solemnly swear that he would not play

Mark Twain portrait, 1867.

cards or drink a drop of alcohol. He worked as a typesetter in New York City, Philadelphia, St. Louis, and Cincinnati. While in New York City, he was disparaged in the printer's office because he did not drink. The printers proudly claimed "to be able to drink more red whisky than men in any other trade. . ." Clemens must have been thought of as a disgrace to the profession. His pledge to his mother lasted about nine years. If he had kept the pledge, this chapter might have ended here.[1]

Steamboats

In Clemens's time, working on a steamboat was the true romantic adventure. Upon returning to Missouri, he trained to be a riverboat pilot. Throughout his life, he would proclaim that piloting a steamboat was the time he cherished most.[2] It was on the steamboat that Clemens' discovered the pen name he would be known by internationally. The leadsman on the riverboat would yell "mark twain" when the river was about twelve feet deep and safe to navigate.

---

1   Many years later, Twain made a similar pledge to Oliva Langdon, the woman he would marry, in order to win the approval of her father. Cigars were substituted for card playing in the pledge, but whiskey remained. Again, Twain broke his promise.

2   There is one sad caveat to this story. After Samuel helped his younger brother, Henry, get a job tending a steamboat boiler, the boiler exploded and took his sibling's life. Clemens wrote about his brother's death for the rest of his days. Some believe this episode contributed greatly to his acerbic view of mankind. He also came to believe in the paranormal, especially telepathy and precognition, believing he foresaw his brother's death.

The Civil War

While Samuel was in St. Louis in his twenties, the Civil War broke out. It is not clear that he had any sympathy for the Confederate cause, but he did join two friends and enlisted to be an irregular of the Missouri State Guard. The trio left the big city to help protect Hannibal from attack by Union forces. They joined a unit of about a dozen Guards (no two of whom dressed alike) and carried knives, shotguns, and squirrel rifles, whatever weapons were available. Samuel arrived for duty on the back of a mule named Paint Brush, carrying a valise and umbrella.

None of the irregulars had before slept under the stars for more than a night or two. A rumor circulated that Union troops were marching toward Hannibal. The irregulars took up positions and after shooting some rustling wildflowers, they ran away. One drunken Guard heard footsteps and called for the password. Hearing no reply, he shot—his own horse lay dead.[3]

At this point, Clemens was done with the war and headed west. He didn't stop until he reached Nevada. He would later write that war was ". . . the killing of strangers against whom you feel no personal animosity; strangers whom, in other circumstances, you would help if you found them in trouble, and who would help you if you needed it . . ."

Nevada

As Clemens moved west, he tried his hand at buying mine claims and even did some mining himself. He had no luck and went to work in a quartz mine. Arduous manual labor did not suit him. The $10 a week he was paid appalled him. He asked for a rise to $400,000 a month. He was fired.

In Virginia City, NV, Clemens found work as an editor of the *Territorial Enterprise*. Here, he first used his

---

3   Twain tells an enhanced version of this story in a memoir titled, *The Private History of a Campaign that Failed.*

pseudonym, Mark Twain. People loved his stories and his destiny was found. But again, his acid tongue got him in trouble. Twain wrote something nasty about the publisher of a competing newspaper and the man challenged Twain to a duel. Realizing that dueling was illegal and the publisher was a better shot than he, he could see no good end to this episode, win or lose. He *skedaddled* to San Francisco in 1864.

San Francisco in the Mid-1860s

Twain *tramped* about the San Francisco saloons, both fancy and rough, and the bohemian neighborhoods, writing all the time, and once was jailed for public drunkenness. Most significantly, while visiting Angel's Camp at the lower elevations of the Sierra Mountains, he heard a tale told by a miner. Twain turned the tale into a short story, titled *Jim Smiley and His Jumping Frog*, that would make him renowned nationally when it was published in the *New York Saturday Post* (1865) and then reprinted far and wide as *The Celebrated Jumping Frog of Calaveras County*.

Life on the Mississippi

Later in life, in his book recounting his days on the steamboats, *Life on the Mississippi* (1883), Twain turned his sociological eye toward the American west and the role whiskey played in its settlement:

> How solemn and beautiful is the thought that the earliest pioneer of civilization, the van-leader of civilization, is never the steamboat, never the railroad, never the newspaper, never the Sabbath-school, never the missionary—but always whiskey! Such is the case. Look history over; you will see. The missionary comes after the whiskey—I mean he arrives after the whiskey has arrived; next comes the poor immigrant, with ax and hoe and rifle; next, the trader; next, the miscellaneous rush; next, the gambler, the desperado, the highwayman,

THE FIRST ARRIVAL.

The First Arrival (from *Life on the Mississippi*).

and all their kindred in sin of both sexes; and next, the smart chap who has bought up an old grant that covers all the land; this brings the lawyer tribe; the vigilance committee brings the undertaker. All these interests bring the newspaper; the newspaper starts up politics and a railroad; all hands turn to and build a church and a jail—and behold! civilization is established forever in the land. But whiskey, you see, was the van-leader in this beneficent work. It always is . . . Westward the Jug of Empire takes its way.

Thoughts on Politicians and Twain's "Run" for President

In *Mark Twain's Notebooks*, published in 1898, Twain wrote about his short stint in Washington D.C. as secretary to Senator William M. Stewart in 1867. Twain wrote his famous take on politicians, remarking about Congress, "Whisky [was] taken into Committee rooms in demijohns [jugs] & carried out in demagogues."[4]

---

4   But Stewart was no more impressed by Clemens than Clemens was by Congress, writing in his remembrance of their first meeting:

I was seated at my window one morning when a very disreputable-looking person slouched into the room. He was arrayed in a seedy suit, which hung upon his lean frame in bunches with no style worth mentioning. A sheaf of scraggy black hair leaked out of a battered old slouch hat, like stuffing from an ancient Colonial sofa, and an evil-smelling cigar butt, very much frazzled, protruded from the corner of his mouth. He had a very sinister appearance. He was a

THE GREATEST FRIENDSHIP IN WHISKEY HISTORY

From his boyhood, Samuel Clemens was an admirer of Ulysses Grant, finding great pleasure when he distributed newspapers describing Grant's exploits in the Mexican War.

Two or three days prevented their first meeting in that wildflower field that Clemens and his buddies were "protecting" outside Hannibal, MO; Grant was in charge of the approaching Union troops. Had his friend's horse not given his life in the line of duty, there is no telling how history might have changed.

Twain and Grant's friendship was cemented in 1879 in an unusual way, but maybe not so unusual for Twain. He was asked to give a toast to Grant at a dinner in Chicago. Grant sat impassively while others delivered testimonials to him. Twain took it as a challenge to make Grant lose his composure. He remarked before the crowd that in Grant's infancy he tried "to find some way to get his big toe in his mouth." Stunned silence. Twain continued, "And if the child is but the father of the man there are mighty few who will doubt that he succeeded." Grant broke up and the celebrity roast was born. Thereafter, Twain sought out Grant's company whenever possible and they became dear friends.

About five years later, Grant agreed to write articles for the magazine *Century* recounting several battles in the Civil War. Knowing he was dying of throat cancer and fearing that his wife, Julia, faced penury after his death, Ulysses also agreed to publish his memoirs with the same publisher. True to his modesty and naiveté as a businessman, he consented to an agreement that would give him a mere 10% royalty.

A start-up publisher was aghast at the pittance the Grants would receive. This publishing house made Ulysses a much better offer, giving him a 20% royalty, a $10,000 advance, and assigning the rights to Julia upon Ulysses' death. All told, the royalties paid to Julia amounted to nearly half a million dollars, and the publisher made about $200,000. The publisher was Mark Twain. After one visit, Twain wrote in his notebook, "One marked feature of General Grant's character is his exceeding gentleness, goodness, and sweetness. I wonder it has not been more spoken of."

In the age of the muckrakers (1879), Twain announced his bid for the presidency. He launched his campaign with a preemptive admission of past transgressions:

I am going to own up to all the wickedness I have done. . . I admit that I treed a rheumatic grandfather of mine on the winter of 1850. . . I ran him out of the front door in his nightshirt at the point of a shotgun & caused him to bowl up a maple tree, where he remained all night, while I emptied shot into his legs. I did this because he snored. I will do it again if I ever have another grandfather.

Thus began and ended Twain's presidential campaign.

Twain was clearly an admirer of the *golden elixir*, but he was not the only one drinking whiskey west of the Mississippi River.

man I had known around the Nevada mining camps several years before, and his name was Samuel L. Clemens.

SOME CELEBRATED (AND BANNED) BOOKS OF MARK TWAIN

Innocents Abroad (1867)

Considered the first travelogue, it is a narrative in first person about a boat trip with stops in Europe and the Middle East. Twain got in trouble for its unflattering portraits of some travelers and cities.

Roughing It (1872)

Tom Sawyer (1876)

The Prince and the Pauper (1882)

Life on the Mississippi (1883)

Adventures of Huckleberry Finn (1884)

H. L. Menken called *Finn* "perhaps the greatest novel ever written in English" and Twain the "true father of our national literature." T. S. Eliot called it "a masterpiece." The Concord Library called it "trash." Almost from the day of its publication, the book was immersed in controversy for Twain's use (more than two hundred times) of a racial epithet from the era's vernacular and its ambiguous portrayal of the slave, Jim. But, it was also vilified for its portrayal of the friendship that grew between Jim, Tom Sawyer, and Huck. It is one of the most frequently banned books of all time.

A Connecticut Yankee in King Arthur's Court (1889)

Pudd'nhead Wilson (1894)

An adult mystery novel. Twain, living in Italy at the time and strapped for cash, serialized the novel before putting it in book form. It contains a scathing critique of racism and slavery. In the shadow of the *Plessy v. Ferguson* case, the story hinges on two infants who are switched at birth, a white child who becomes a slave, and a child of a fraction African American ancestry who becomes a privileged white man.

WHAT DOES WHISKEY TASTE LIKE IN THE LATE 1800s?

E. H. Taylor, Jr. Small Batch Straight Kentucky Bourbon Whiskey

Like his friend, U. S. Grant, Twain was a fan of *Old Crow* whiskey. His likeness was used in a 1950s campaign for the brand. So, let's try something different.

Edmund Hayes Taylor, Jr. was a descendent of two United States presidents, James Madison and Zachery Taylor. He also was the founder of many distilleries around Kentucky, first in partnership with George T. Stagg, then as Stagg's business and legal adversary. He founded or was associated with venerated distilleries such as O.F.C. (Old Fashioned Copper), Carlisle, J. S. Taylor, and Old Taylor. *E. H. Taylor, Jr. Small Batch Straight Kentucky Bourbon Whiskey* is now made at the enormously successful Buffalo Trace Distillery. The J. S. Taylor distillery is now being restored as Castle and Key Distillery.

But we are most indebted to E. H. for his campaign to ensure the quality of whiskey. His efforts led to the Bottled in Bond Act (1897), a reaction to the frequent adulteration of whiskey. The Act was the first law to protect consumers. To be recognized as Bottled in Bond (B-in-B) a whiskey must be produced at one distillery during one distillation season (January–June or July–December). It must be aged in a federally bonded warehouse for at least four years under United States government supervision and bottled at 100 proof (50% ABV). The label must identify the distillery, and if different, where the whiskey was bottled. Only whiskey produced in the United States may be designated as B-in-B. The Pure Food and Drug Act

Twain and Rudyard Kipling in a 1950s *Old Crow* advertisement.

(enacted in 1907) followed shortly after the B-in-B Act.

E. H. Taylor, Jr. Small Batch Straight Kentucky Bourbon has won over three dozen awards in competition.

Just the Facts

Mash Bill	Not made public, but believed to be Buffalo Trace mash bill #1 (less than 10% rye)
Proof	Proof: 100 ABV: 50%
Age; Barrel Char	No Age Statement; #4
Chill Filtered?	Yes

TASTING NOTES

From: The Buffalo Trace Distillery website
https://www.buffalotracedistillery.com/brands/eh-taylor

Made by hand, this Small Batch Bourbon Whiskey has been aged inside century old warehouses constructed by E.H. Taylor, Jr. Barrels are evaluated and selected to create a perfect blend of distinctive character that is like no other. This bourbon is a true sipping bourbon that honors the uncompromising legacy of E.H. Taylor, Jr.

Tastes of caramel corn sweetness, mingled with butterscotch and licorice. The aftertaste is a soft mouth-feel that turns into subtle spices of pepper and tobacco.

From: Bourbon & Banter (Reviewer: Lee Stang)
https://www.bourbonbanter.com/drink/drink-reviews/bourbon-reviews/colonel-e-h-taylor-jr-small-batch-bottled-bond-kentucky-straight-bourbon-whiskey/#.XVqSolB7nusIn

Aroma: Brown Sugar, Vanilla, Cherries, Nuts, Some Alcohol
Palate: Vanilla, Wood, Spice
Finish: A creamy start on the front of the tongue that turns into a burst of lingering spice on the back of the mouth and tongue. Nice warming of the chest.
Overall: . . .I think the EHT Small Batch is the best bourbon for the money on the market. A great sipping bourbon that is also great on the rocks as well. Sometimes it is a little hard to find. . . The EHT Small Batch is a great bourbon to have around.

From: The Over a Barrel Gang
Looks: Amber, gold.
Aroma: Delicate. Corn, chocolate, allspice, orange, brown sugar, leather, wood.
Flavor: Medium body. Sweet, salty, umami, bitter.
Mouth Feel: Sharp, round, rich.
Going Down: Medium strength, medium length.
Notes: Great intro bourbon; complex but refined and round.

Toast

Mark Twain began smoking when he was nine years old. He practiced moderation in smoking cigars, though, asserting that he had a rule to "never smoke more than one at a time." His love of bourbon and cigars led him to another pledge, one much different from the one he made to his mother and his father-in-law: "If I cannot drink bourbon and smoke cigars in Heaven, then I shall not go."

To Mark Twain, the first voice of the American common man.

DINNER AT NOOK FARM, HARTFORD, CT, WITH SAMUEL AND OLIVIA CLEMENS

A Tramp Abroad

Twain published *A Tramp Abroad* in 1880. It is a travelogue but also contains autobiographical sections, short stories, and essays. It is one of five books he wrote on his travels. On his excursions overseas, Twain longed for the foods of his home. In *Tramp*, he provided a list of the foods he wanted at "a modest, private affair, all to myself" upon his return to the United States. He then listed about sixty to eighty dishes, depending on how you count. One of his requests was for bacon and greens, originally published as *Wicked Good Collard Greens* in Southern Favorites.

Recipe: Bacon Collard Greens

From: Taste of Home website https://www.tasteofhome.com/recipes/bacon-collard-greens/

Ingredients (serves 9):

- 2 pounds collard greens
- 4 thick-sliced bacon strips, chopped
- 1 cup chopped sweet onion
- 5 cups reduced-sodium chicken broth
- 1 cup sun-dried tomatoes (not packed in oil), chopped
- ½ teaspoon garlic powder
- ¼ teaspoon salt
- ¼ teaspoon crushed red pepper flakes

Directions:

1. Trim thick stems from collard greens; coarsely chop leaves. In a Dutch oven, sauté bacon for 3 minutes. Add onion; cook 8–9 minutes longer or until onion is tender and bacon is crisp. Add greens; cook just until wilted.
2. Stir in remaining ingredients. Bring to a boil. Reduce heat; cover and simmer for 45–50 minutes or until greens are tender.

Twain also had a roast turkey on his wish list, Thanksgiving-style. So why no cranberry sauce?

Godey's Lady's Book

Godey's Lady's Book was the most popular magazine for women for most of the 19th century. It had a national readership that topped out at about 150,000 during the 1860s. Sarah Josepha Hale was the editor for forty years. Hale was also an early feminist who fought for causes such as property rights for women and allowing women to serve as teachers in public schools. Her recipes (in what may have been the first cooking section in a popular magazine) were not meant for the wealthy but for middle class households. The magazine assiduously avoided any political commentary while the Civil War was fought. That said, *Godey's* was published in Philadelphia and

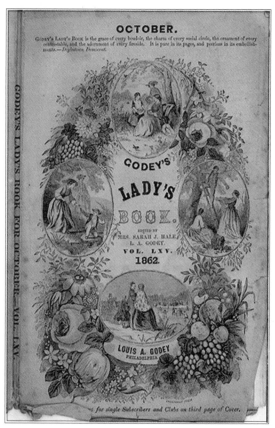

Godey's Lady's book cover, October 1862.

most of the recipes, though not all, were contributed by readers from the northern states. Meat was scarce in the South due to the blockades.[5]

Recipe: Sauce for Roast Beef or Mutton

From: Spaulding, Lily May & Spaulding, John. (1999). *Civil War Recipes: Recipes from the Pages of Godey's Lady's Book*. Lexington, KY: University of Kentucky. P. 179. (Public domain.)

Grate horseradish on a bread grater into a basin; then add two tablespoons of cream, with a little mustard and salt; mix them well together; then add four tablespoons of the best vinegar, and mix the whole thoroughly. The vinegar and cream are both cold; add a little powder white sugar. This is a very fine sauce; it may be served in a small tureen.

This is a very hot sauce!

---

5   Twain, in *Life on the Mississippi*, wrote that an issue of *Godey's* was to be found in every fine dwelling along the river. In the parlor you would find a "current number of the chaste and innocuous *Godey's 'Lady's Book'*, with painted fashion-plate of wax figure women with mouths all alike—lips and eyelids the same size—each five-foot woman with a two-inch wedge sticking from under her dress and letting-on to be half of her foot." Little escaped Twain's jaundiced eye.

MUSIC THAT TAKES US BACK TO MARK TWAIN'S TIME

Lift Every Voice and Sing, performed by Street Corner Renaissance (2011)

Lift Every Voice was penned and put to music by the Johnson brothers, James and John, ten years before Mark Twain died. Over a century later, Beyonce sang it at the Coachella Music Festival. It is considered by many to be Black National Anthem. Street Corner Renaissance is an a cappella group of men who gave up their first careers to pursue their dream.

Stephen Foster.

Oh Susannah, performed by James Taylor (1970)

This is the third selection written by Stephen Foster to make a playlist. Foster, an alcoholic, lived to be a mere thirty-seven years old (1826–1864). But that was long enough for him to write some three hundred songs, many for minstrel shows. It was also long enough for him to become known as "The Father of American Music." In addition to the three songs on the playlists, Foster is also the composer of *The Swanee River (Old Folks at Home)* and *Jeanie With the Light Brown Hair*.

When the Saints Go Marching In, performed by Louis Armstrong and His Orchestra (1950)

An African American spiritual turned into a jazz standard by Louis "Satchmo" Armstrong, a New Orleans native, in 1938. Armstrong's version of *What a Wonderful World* is still the standard. Armstrong was accepted by both black and white music lovers but was criticized by other Black musicians because he played before segregated audiences.

Chopsticks, performed by Liberace (1952)

The Chop Waltz was written by female British composer Euphoria Allen under a male pseudonym. Although not strictly American in origin, innumerable American children learned this tune at their first piano lesson (and it may be the only piano tune they can still play). Can you play it as well as Wladziu Valentino Liberace (born in Wisconsin)?

She'll Be Comin' 'Round the Mountain, performed by Jewel (2011)

This song has its origin as a Christian spiritual. Who is "she"? She is the chariot that Christ is said to be driving upon his return. Jewel recorded this version for an album of children's songs, *The Merry Goes Round*.

Maple Leaf Rag, performed by Scott Joplin (1987)

Joplin, "The King of Ragtime" never recorded this song. It was preserved on music sheets and piano rolls for player pianos. Joplin was intent on making ragtime music acceptable; in all, he wrote forty-four rags, one ballet, and two operas.

I've Been Working on The Railroad, performed by John Denver (1997)

Railroad is based on an African American spiritual about working on the levee on the Mississippi River. It might have been derived from an Irish hymn. Like several songs on this playlist, this traditional folk song is now considered a children's song.

Cover of sheet music of *Maple Leaf Rag*, 3rd Edition.

There'll Be a Hot Time in the Old Town Tonight, performed by LaVern Baker (1958)

More ragtime. Allegedly written after its writers saw from a train window a group of children starting a fire. The train was at a station in a place called Old Town. If you like Baker's sound, try *Tweedle Dee* and *Go Jim Dandy*.

Swing Low, Sweet Chariot, performed by the Fisk Jubilee Singers (1909)

This song was written by a Choctaw Indian freedman. The Fisk Jubilee Singers sang *Swing Low* when they toured the US raising money for Fisk University. This version is the earliest known recording. A version by Joan Baez was performed at the Woodstock Music Festival.

OH, GIVE ME A HOME. . .

Chapter 8
OPENING THE WEST: COWBOYS AND OUTLAWS

[Wyatt Earp], having tried and failed to invent a better future for himself,
in the end he invented a better past.
—Andrew C. Isenberg

THE LOUISIANA PURCHASE AND THE LEWIS AND CLARK EXPEDITION

In 1804, the Corps of Discovery, led by Merriweather Lewis and William Clark, headed out of St. Charles, MO, to explore the vast Louisiana territory that Thomas Jefferson had purchased from the French. Their

mission was to map the waterways between the Mississippi River and the Pacific Ocean for purposes of promoting commerce and to catalog the natural resources. Lewis, twenty-nine years old at the time, brought with him six barrels of whiskey. The whiskey was needed to trade with Indians and trappers, for medicine, and for rewarding the good behavior of the thirty-one men on the expedition. The whiskey didn't last long.

Prior to becoming an explorer, Lewis was a military man who had helped suppress the 1791 Whiskey Rebellion in Pittsburgh. After the expedition, Lewis

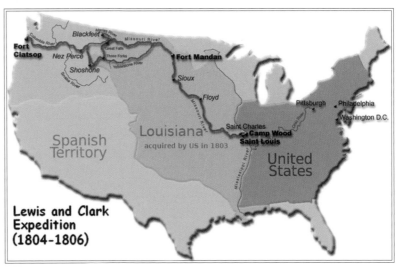

The route of the Lewis and Clark Expedition.

had trouble adjusting to a quiet life in politics as governor of the Louisiana territory. In 1809, he succumbed to drinking and depression, and while staying at an inn called Grinder's Stand in Tennessee, he is believed to have shot himself in the head with his pistol.

THE RENDEZVOUS

Over the decades following the Corps of Discovery, the first white men to venture west were fur traders; they were explorers only by necessity. The trappers were motivated not by a belief in the importance of westward expansion but out of a desire to make money. They slept on the ground and lived off the land by hunting and trapping for food.

The Rendezvous—the first was held in the Rocky Mountains in the early 1800s—was the precursor to our modern-day trade show. Men who lived and hunted by themselves for the better part of a year could get mighty lonesome. So, they came together annually to trade furs for money, whiskey, and tobacco. Regrettably, these get-togethers also played a major role in the decline of Native American nations and culture. The traders brought with them new diseases. They decimated the natives' sources of food. The indigenous people also had their first brush with the white man's *firewater*. This low-quality whiskey would be diluted and adulterated even further to make ample quantities of what became known as *Indian liquor*.

The Indian Trade and Intercourse Act (actually six acts) was passed by Congress between 1790 and 1834. One of its supposed intended effects, beyond asserting the federal government's supremacy over the states for making treaties, was to protect Natives Americans from land speculators and unscrupulous traders by putting the federal government in charge of trade and land deals with the Indian tribes, rather than the individual states and private traders. The Act was hardly effective in suppressing private trade. They were even less effective in protecting the Natives Americans from the government itself. But then again, the Act was only meant to protect the natives against exploitation by private interests.

The hunters, traders, and native tribes were about to have a lot of company.

AFTER THE CIVIL WAR, WHAT WAS THERE TO DO?

Imagine you are returning home to Georgia or the Carolinas after fighting for the Confederacy in the Civil War. You find many of your friends and relatives have perished, your family property is in shambles, and there is hardly a functioning economy. Or, imagine you are a freed slave. The work available looks no different than before emancipation, if you can find any work at all.

What to do? You hear that herds and herds of cattle are roaming free in Northern Texas, abandoned in the anarchy following Mexico's separation from Spain (1821), the War of Texas Independence (1832–1836), and the Mexican War (1846–1848). Maybe it's time to head west and start afresh, where *flush times were at the flood*.

The Cowboy

Unlike our romantic image, the first cowboys were mostly young southern whites displaced by the war and freed slaves, joined by Mexican vaqueros (the origin of the noun *buckaroos*). The cowboys were transient workers who often toiled six days a week, sixteen hours a day for pay of about thirty dollars a month.[1] In 1871, a Kansas newspaper described the typical cowboy as "unlearned and illiterate, with few wants and meager ambition," who had a "diet of Navy plug and whisky."

---

1   Cowboys were not averse to withholding their services. The Cowboy Strike of 1883 was but one of many that riled cattle owners. The strikes were, however, largely unsuccessful.

Tent saloon, Laramie, WY, 1868.

Cowboy entertainment was simple and rough. On the range, they sang and swapped stories around the campfire. The songs were soft and slow, rarely up tempo, lest the *doggies* get spooked—even one calf—and a stampede ensue.

On payday, the *cowpokes*[2] hustled into town where they could have *brunch* and find many people—legit and not so legit—ready to relieve them of their hard-earned dollars. There were saloons, dance halls with *soiled doves*, and more saloons. And whiskey. Whiskey cost two to four dollars a gallon. Part of that cost went to a large permanent Federal Excise Tax on distilled spirits. It was the only sure-fire way the government had to get cowboys to pay taxes.

---

2   The noun *cowpoke* or *cowpuncher* is derived from a long stick that cowboys used to prod cattle onto railroad cars by poking them.

The Saloon

As the west was settled, cowboys could find saloons along the trail, in makeshift tents with dirt floors and lanterns, or in elegant brick and wood establishments near railroad stops. Here the cowboys would enter through those familiar swinging doors—a never-completely successful attempt to let air flow through while keeping dust out. The saloons were presided over by the saloonkeeper, a man of local renown.

Mark Twain picked up quickly on the emerging social hierarchy of the new western communities, which he recounted in his book, *Roughing It* (1872):

In Nevada, for a time, the lawyer, the editor, the banker, the chief desperado, the chief gambler, and the saloonkeeper, occupied the same level in society, and it was the highest. The cheapest and easiest way to become an

Judge Roy Bean's Saloon and "Hall of Justice", Langtry, TX, c. 1900.
Bean is holding court, seated on a barrel with a law book open.

influential man and be looked up to by the community at large, was to stand behind a bar, wear a cluster-diamond pin, and sell whisky. I am not sure but that the saloonkeeper held a shade higher rank than any other member of society. His opinion had weight. It was his privilege to say how the elections should go. No great movement could succeed without the countenance and direction of the saloonkeepers. It was a high favor when the chief saloonkeeper consented to serve in the legislature or the board of aldermen.

The saloons in town were not only the place where men drank, read newspapers, and conducted business, but they were also the setting for cultural activities and moral advancement. They often served as a courthouse (Judge Roy Bean presided over legal matters in saloons) and a place to preach. Many saloonkeepers were former clergy who had exchanged their cloth for a rag.[3]

The saloon was also a pharmacy; that is, the place to get the medicine that all strata of society thought could cure your ills—whiskey. Whiskey was believed to strengthen your heart, improve your respiration (no small problem given the time you spent breathing dust and dirt), cure your chills and fevers (as well as malaria), and help your kidneys.

Many saloons had a metal barricade that the "pharmacists" could pull down and secure if they needed to leave their station unattended. Hence the *bar* you still *mosey on up to* to get your, um, prescription. Because so many cowboys had little coin or script (the new westerners had a deep distrust of paper money) they would often pay for a glass of whiskey with a bullet, a *shot* if you will.

_____

3   Horace Greeley lectured against drinking in the bar of the Denver House. He was attended to with good humor.

The Whiskey

The big producers of whiskey for the western towns were located in Kentucky, Tennessee, and Illinois. Favorite brands included *Old Crow*, *Old Tub*, *Old Pepper*, *Old Gideon*, *Old Anderson's Little Brown Jug*, and *Old Hermitage*. But many whiskeys that started out as bourbon, or straight ethyl alcohol, often had something bad happen to them along their way out west. "Extenders" were added by the people shipping and distributing the whiskey and by those upstanding citizens, the saloon keepers. It would be mixed with prune juice, pepper, iodine, tobacco juice, and gunpowder.[4] A frontier traveler, Irwin S. Cobb, would write, "It smells like gangrene starting in a mildewed silo, it tastes like the wrath to come, and when you absorb a deep swig of it you have all the sensations of having swallowed a lighted kerosene lamp."

The lawman stands alone.
Notice the spittoons?

---

4   In *Roughing It*, Twain wrote that there were tales of a bottle of whiskey, "that killed nine men in three hours, and that an unoffending stranger that smelled the cork was disabled for life." In 1904, Michael J. Owens patented the automated bottling machine. This went a long way toward improving the quality of whiskey shipped long distances.

The Lawman

Wyatt Berry Stapp Earp, came to personify the Wild West lawman. Before he became a deputy sheriff, he tried his hand at lots of different professions, including saloon owner, gambler, burglar, horse thief, and proprietor of a house of ill repute (run by his common-law wife). He did many of these things while also carrying a badge. Despite his surroundings, Earp was an abstainer for most of his life. Not so his father; when the town of Monmouth, IL, passed a law prohibiting the sale of alcohol in the 1850s, Nicholas Earp managed to act as both the town's constable charged with enforcing the ordinance and as a bootlegger.

Earp and his brothers often traveled from boomtown to boomtown. One brother would check out a new town and then summon the siblings. Their brother-from-another-mother was John Henry "Doc" Holiday, a dentist who suffered from and eventually succumbed to tuberculosis. He was also a gambler (preferring the card game Faro) and heavy drinker who was accused of robbing a stagecoach. He was a good shot; you can find accounts that claim Holiday killed between two and thirty men, but the fact that he was good with a gun is undisputed.

The most famous shootout of the old west was the "Gunfight at the O.K. Corral." The Earps along with Holiday represented the law (what there was of it) in Tombstone, AZ, and their adversaries were part of a loose group of outlaws known as "The Cowboys" who had a well-deserved reputation for stealing cattle. How the feud started has many versions, including one version in which the Cowboys had stolen six Army mules. The Earps went to retrieve the Army's property but were unsuccessful. Another claims the Cowboys refused to leave their guns at the sheriff's office (an early version of gun control in the west) before entering a saloon and gambling establishment. Yet another claims the feud started earlier when Wyatt made eyes at Josephine Marcus, the girlfriend of a Tombstone saloon owner and a friend of the Cowboys.[5] All these stories may be true, somewhat. The renowned gunfight didn't take place in a corral but in an alleyway and lasted about thirty seconds. The shootout resulted in losses for both sides.

After the gunfight, Earp had many more sordid adventures throughout the West. Wyatt and Josephine were together for nearly fifty years, on and off, for good and not-so-good. Josephine tried to sanitize Wyatt's life, arguing to biographers that he never owned a saloon, never promoted prostitution, and never drank. Her efforts proved fruitless.

While in Los Angeles, CA, in the early 1900s, Earp became a consultant for silent cowboy movies. He made friends and acquaintances of the movie director John Ford, the writer Jack London, and even the actor Charlie Chaplin. The cowboy movie actors Thomas S. Hart and Tom Mix were pallbearers at Earp's funeral when he died in 1929, at age eighty.

As colorful as the individuals were who made up the Wild West, the places they inhabited took on an identity equally as distinct.

---

5   Josephine would become Wyatt's common-law wife. He had two others. His one clearly legal wife died of typhoid fever early in his life. Josephine was the last.

WHAT DOES WHISKEY TASTE LIKE 'ROUND THE CAMPFIRE?

Bulleit 95 Rye Frontier Whiskey

You won't be asked to sip some pure grain alcohol "flavored" with iodine and tobacco juice in order to get an authentic taste of what the cowboys drank. Instead, try the much more appealing *Bulleit 95 Rye Frontier Whiskey*. Rye whiskey was a staple in the Wild West but fell out of favor after Prohibition. It made a triumphant return around 2008.

In the early 1990s, Seagram Distilling Company started to work on a "frontier whiskey" concept. The company hoped to make a whiskey that tasted like something Wyatt Earp might drink. It wanted to use the name "Bullet" but thought the federal regulators would frown on that choice. Seagram discovered an attorney in Kentucky, Tom Bulleit, whose family had been making whiskey for five generations. Seagram bought the brand. With Tom's involvement, it created a new bourbon based on Augustus Bulleit's recipe, Tom's great-great-grandfather. They refashioned a "high rye" bourbon (28% rye) as well as a *Bulleit 95 Rye Frontier Whiskey*, which has a mash bill that is ninety-five rye.

The *Bulleit* labels on store shelves and in drinking establishments today are sourced from other distilleries but the mash bill and distilling process are fashioned to remain true to the family's heritage. A new Bulleit distillery opened in Shelbyville, KY, in 2017, which means its product is still being aged. The new distillery is buying ingredients from local farmers and is using sustainable energy sources. Even the bottle, with the name embossed on the glass, is meant to evoke visions of the old west.

Bulleit 95 Rye Frontier Whiskey has won many awards, including gold medals at the San Francisco World Spirits Competition. It is a favorite among bartenders as a cocktail mixer.

Just the Facts

Mash Bill	Corn: 0% Rye: 95% Barley: 5%
Proof	Proof: 90 ABV: 45%
Age; Barrel Char	No age statement but straight (at least 2 years); #4
Chill Filtered?	?

TASTING NOTES

From: Bulleit 95 brand website (Diageo North America, Inc.)
https://www.bulleit.com/whiskeys/bulleit-rye/

Russet in color, with rich oaky aromas. The taste is exceptionally smooth, with hints of vanilla, honey, and spice. Finish is crisp and clean, with long, lingering flavors.

From: The Rum Howler (Reviewer: Chip Dykstra)

https://therumhowlerblog.com/whisky-reviews/american-whiskey/bulleit-bourbon-frontier-whiskey/

In the Glass: . . .a richly coloured whiskey with a hue that reminded me of a shiny new copper penny. The whiskey imparts a light sheen on the sides of the glass when swirled and moderately thick legs form on the inside of the glass. The initial nose which featured honeycomb, rich new oak and a light toffee with accents of tobacco was quite pleasing. As I let the glass breathe, the woody aroma of new oak remained strong, but it did not overpower the honeycomb and toffee scents which remained firm. The breezes above the glass also contain some nice rye accents, and some soft vanilla. There is a bit of rough and tumble in the air as well, but considering that the Bulleit Bourbon is bottled at 45 % alcohol by volume, I am impressed that the astringency does not really climb to a level that would concern me in any way.

In the Mouth: I really like the first sip of the bourbon. There is a bit of a spicy swat that tickles the tonsils, but there is also a nice maple and caramel sweetness which accompanies that spicy swat and makes you want to take another sip. I can taste oak planks which are seeping just a little fresh sap from the wood pores, some delightful rye spices, and a nice impression of maple and caramel. I also detect a nice smattering of cloves, cinnamon and vanilla. When I add an ice-cube to the glass, the sweetness of the whisky is diminished and some lightly bitter notes of oak tannin seem to take hold of the whiskey. (I decided rather quickly that adding ice was not an experience to be repeated.) Like it was on the nose, the whisky has a bit of rough and tumble character in the glass. Again, I am not put off by the sensation, as in fact, I rather enjoy the full flavoured character the whiskey displays in the mouth.

In the Throat: The sweet honeycomb and maple flavours of the Bulleit Bourbon really give the whiskey length in the finish. Rich baking spices build upon the palate as you sip, and your throat feels a nice spicy warmth well after the glass is consumed. Those flavours of maple, cinnamon and cloves seem to be the last to fade away.

The Afterburn: Bulleit Bourbon Frontier Whiskey really surprised me as I sipped and sampled it. I like how the typical bourbon flavours of freshly cut oak planks with its sap seeping from the wood is held in check such that I can really appreciate those lovely caramel and maple flavours. Even though this is a 45% alcohol by volume whiskey, the overall flavour is much more approachable than many other whiskeys bottled at a lower proof.

From: The Over a Barrel Gang

Looks: Gold, pale straw.

Aroma: Light. Black pepper, vanilla, butterscotch, clove, orange, apple, berry, peach, wood.

Flavor: Medium body. Sweet, bitter.

Mouth Feel: Sharp, creamy, delicate.

Going Down: Medium strength, medium length.

Notes: Nose is bigger than the body and bouquet.

Toast

William Claude Dukenfield, better known as W. C. Fields, was an actor born in 1880. Though he is best remembered for his films in the first half of the 20th century, he was an avowed whiskey drinker. One of his many quotable quotations can be hoisted to the men and women who risked everything, if they had anything, to open the American West. It could almost serve as their motto:

"When life hands you lemons, make whiskey sours."

DINNER AT GRAND HOTEL (BIG NOSE KATE'S SALOON), TOMBSTONE, AZ, WITH WYATT EARP & JOSEPHINE MARCUS

Cowboys congregated around the chuck wagon at mealtime is an image reproduced in many accounts of life on the Wild West trail. Their *grub slinger* had most likely honed his skills while a cook during the Civil War. His chuck wagon was stocked with staples such as salt, coffee, canned vegetables, and beans. Not surprisingly, he served plenty of beef since he had an unending supply walking alongside the wagon. Cowboys referred to beans as *whistle berries* for obvious reasons; think of that hysterical dinner scene in the movie *Blazing Saddles*.

To add to authenticity, you might want to consider celebrating the Wild West by biting into a sourdough roll or two. Sourdough bread was a staple in cowboy and gold mining country because it stayed fresh longer than other breads.

Chuck wagon dinner, c. 1908.
Reservation for twenty, please.

Recipe: Broiled (Grilled) Beef Ribs

From: Monahan, S. (2015). *The Cowboy Cookbook: Recipes and Tales from Campfires, Cookouts, and Chuck Wagons.* Guilford, CT: TwoDot. P. 36

Ingredients (serves 6–8):

    2 pounds beef short ribs
    Salt and pepper to taste

Directions:

1. Heat your coals or grill to medium-high heat.
2. Season ribs with salt and pepper, then sear the ribs on one side for about 10 minutes and then on the other side for another 10 minutes.
3. Allow to rest for about 5 minutes, and then slice thinly.

Recipe: Pork and Navy Beans.

From: Monahan, S. (2015). *The Cowboy Cookbook: Recipes and Tales from Campfires, Cookouts, and Chuck Wagons.* Guilford, CT: TwoDot. P. 36

Ingredients (serves 8–10):

2 cups navy beans

1 teaspoon salt

Pepper to taste

½ pound salt pork, quartered

2 tablespoons molasses

Directions:

1. Soak beans overnight in water. The next day drain and rinse. Place into a large Dutch oven or stockpot and cover with water. Bring to a boil over high heat.
2. Drain and place in baking dish. Salt and pepper the beans, and stir. Place the pork in the center of the bans then top with the molasses. Cover and bake at 325°F for 5 hours until tender.

Note: You can also make these in a slow cooker. After soaking the beans all night, place all ingredients in slow cooker and cook for at least 8 hours on low.

MUSIC THAT TAKES US BACK TO THE COWBOYS' CAMPFIRE

Home on the Range, sung by Riders in the Sky (1982)

Range was originally published as a poem. The singing group Riders in the Sky has been playing cowboy music since 1977. They were inducted into the Grand Ole Opry in 1982. You can hear them on the soundtrack of several Pixar movies, including *Toy Story 2*.

Cattle Call, performed by Eddie Arnold (1970)

Cattle Call was written and recorded in 1934 by American songwriter and musician Tex Owen. From 1945 through 1983, Eddie Arnold had 145 charted songs, including twenty-eight #1 hits. According to *Billboard* Magazine, he holds the record for the most Top 10 hits on the Country Charts. He usually performed wearing a tuxedo, not the typical cowboy outfit.

I Want to Be a Cowboy's Sweetheart, performed by Patsy Montana and the Prairie Ramblers (1935)

Yodeling is a European singing tradition made popular in American music halls of the 1830s.

The Ballad of High Noon (Do Not Forsake Me, O My Darling), performed by Tex Ritter (1952)

High Noon won the 1952 Academy Award for Best Original Song in a movie. When most people think of traditional western values, they think of rugged individualism. Not completely true; many western movies contained a subtext of gun control, respect for the environment, and the importance of community cohesiveness. *High Noon* was one of them.

Legend of Wyatt Earp, performed by Hugh O'Brien with Ken Darby's Orchestra (1957)

This is the theme song to the television show with the same name. O'Brien played Earp in the series. Earp claimed to be a teetotaler but became the incarnation of the Wild West. How'd he do that? He read the 1901 novel *The Virginian* and he moved to Hollywood.

Rawhide, performed by Frankie Lane (1958)

Rawhide is another TV show theme song. One drover on the show was played by Clint Eastwood (as Rowdy Yates). Eastwood wouldn't get really famous until he played "The Man with No Name" in Sergio Leone's spaghetti westerns (*A Fistful of Dollars*). To film "No Name," Eastwood had to bring his own gear to Italy. It wasn't clear what would happen if Eastwood lost his hat. You heard this song in *The Blues Brothers* movie.

Riders in the Sky, performed by Sons of the Pioneers (1990)

Not written until long after the cattle drives were over (1948), *Riders* is still considered one of the greatest Western songs of all time. The Pioneers, singing since the 1930s, are one of the groups that defined Western music. In 1931, a young truck driver and fruit picker named Leonard Slye, later known as Roy Rogers, joined a group called the Rocky Mountaineers, later to become the Pioneers. And yes, you heard this song, sung by Riders in the Sky, in *The Blues Brothers 2000* movie.

Cool Water, performed by Lazy B Wranglers (date unknown)

About a man, his mule, and an oasis in the dessert. `Nuff said.

He's a Lone Ranger, performed by Dom Flemons (2018)

This song, written by Flemons for his album *Black Cowboy,* appears on this collection of traditional and new songs. It is not about the Lone Ranger you know from radio, television, and movies. It is based on the legend of Bass Reeves, a slave who beat his owner and fled to the Indian Country during the Civil War. He was the first black deputy United States marshal west of the Mississippi River. After the 13th Amendment passed, he returned to Arkansas and became a farmer. During his career as a marshal, he is said to have arrested more than three thousand wanted lawbreakers and to have killed fourteen outlaws, all in self-defense, of course.

Poncho and Lefty, performed by Willie Nelson and Merle Haggard (1983)

Poncho and Lefty was written by (John) Townes Van Zandt, a legendary writer of country songs, born in Fort Worth, TX. This version is the best known, having reached #1 on the Hot Country Billboard chart in 1983. Like too many other great country songwriters, Van Zandt succumbed to drug and alcohol addiction, though the cause of his death, at fifty-two, was listed as cardiac arrhythmia.

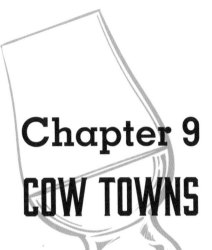

Chapter 9
COW TOWNS

The Worst Liquors, The Poorest Cigars, and a Miserable Billiard Table.
—Sign outside a Junction City, KS, saloon.

WHERE CAN YOU GET A DRINK AROUND HERE?

Hell on Wheels

Leland Stanford Sr. and Thomas C. Durant both missed when they took their swings at the Golden Spike that completed the Transcontinental Railroad at Promontory Summit, UT in 1869. Nevertheless, the meeting of the tracks was a true accomplishment of human engineering.[1] It was also a testament to the superhuman endurance displayed by the railroad laborers. However, contrary to legend, the spike wasn't golden but ordinary iron. From the east, the Union Pacific Railroad employed many men who were Civil War veterans, Irish immigrants, Swedes, Danes, and Finns, as well as freed slaves. The Central Pacific Railroad coming from the west didn't have the *passel* of unemployed men ready to work for a pittance. It sent for workers from China, who numbered eleven thousand by 1868.

As the tracks of the Union Pacific were laid, a small community of surveyors, merchants, craftsmen, gamblers, and dance hall and saloon keepers led the way.[2] These temporary towns would pull up stakes and move

---

1   The Erie Canal predated this engineering feat by over half a century. Its laborers were paid room and board, $.50, and 32 oz. of whiskey a day. That's a lot of whiskey. In Baltimore, Johns Hopkins, a wholesale grocery owner and liquor distributor, financed the first railroad from Maryland to Ohio. That must have involved a lot of whiskey as well.

2   The Central Pacific didn't have the same type of temporary communities. The Chinese rarely drank, preferring opium instead, and gambled mostly among themselves, not in gambling halls.

The completion of the Transcontinental Railroad, Promontory, UT, May 10, 1869.
Do you see any African American or Chinese faces? Do you see the bottles?

ahead of the laborers. The towns were called "Hell on Wheels."[3] This name may have been descriptive but it sure wasn't invented by a Chamber of Commerce. The whiskey was dispensed from tents, sometimes before the roofs were up, and sometimes from prefabricated buildings that were moved on flatcars. If a town would take root in a particular place, the saloon was likely the first permanent building. Some of the names that were bestowed on whiskey to capture its taste were *skull varnish* or *coffin varnish*, *tarantula juice*, *snake water*, and *bug juice*.

Benton, WY, in 1868 was the prototypical Hell on Wheels. Wrote Samuel Bowles, a "tourist":

One to two thousand men, and a dozen or two women where encamped on the alkali plain in tents and board shanties; not a tree, not a shrub, not a blade of grass was visible; the dust ankle deep as we walked through it, and so fine and volatile that the slightest breeze loaded the air with it, irritating every sense and poisoning half of them; a village of a few variety stores and shops, and many restaurants and grog shops; by day disgusting, by night dangerous; almost everybody dirty, many filthy, and with the marks of the lowest vice; averaging a murder a day; gambling and drinking, hurdy-gurdy dancing. . .it fairly festered in

---

3   John Ford's movie in 1924, *The Iron Horse*, presented a romantic vision of these towns. The AMC television miniseries, *Hell on Wheels*, did so as well, but perhaps not as romanticized.

Benton, Wyoming Territory, 1868.

corruption, disorder and death, and would have rotted, even in this dry air, had it outlasted a brief sixty-day life.

Mr. Bowles needed a new travel agent.

The railroads would bring settlers by the thousands as well as prospectors seeking their fortune in the gold mines of the West (an employee found flakes of gold by Sutter's Mill along the American River and set off the California Gold Rush of 1849). The railroad also transported whiskey, rye, and corn to Colorado, Nebraska, Arizona, and California.

Kansas

Dodge City, KS, sitting near the Santa Fe Trail and the Arkansas River, became a crossroads for cattle drives headed north from Texas, especially when the railroad arrived—the Atchison, Topeka, and

The Long Branch Saloon, Dodge City, KS, in 1874. Front Street, Dodge City, KS, 1874, with Robert Wright and Charles Rath's General Store, Chalk Beeson's Long Branch, George M. Hoover's liquor and cigar store, and Frederick Zimmermann's gun and hardware store.

Santa Fe. It also became the quintessential town of the Wild West, hosting not only cowboys but many gunfighters as well. The first commercial structure in Dodge City was a tent saloon for buffalo hunters. By 1876, Dodge City had a population of about 1,200 inhabitants. It also had nineteen licensed

Chester (Dennis Weaver), Miss Kitty (Amanda Blake), and Marshall Matt Dillion (James Arness). Outside the Long Branch Saloon in the television series, *Gunsmoke*.

whiskey-selling establishments, the most famous of which was the Long Branch, an establishment that would become the centerpiece of the radio and television series *Gunsmoke*. In a typical year, Dodge City's residents and guests consumed three hundred barrels of whiskey. If there were three thousand drinkers, residents, and transients, that is about five and a half gallons each.

In 1880, the state of Kansas passed a law prohibiting the manufacture and sale of intoxicating liquors. The saloon keepers were not happy; they put up a reward of $1,200 to be paid "to the widow of the s.o.b. who informs on the saloon men. Here is an opportunity for some enterprising woman who possesses a husband [she] wishes to get rid of."

Colorado

Alcohol consumption in Dodge City might have been staggering (get it?), but the city was not without competition. One visitor estimated that in Leadville, CO, there was one tavern for every eight inhabitants. In 1879, Leadville had ten dry-goods stores, four banks, thirty-one restaurants, four churches, 120 saloons, nineteen beer halls, and 228 gambling houses. Oscar Wilde was among Leadville's famous visitors. He was impressed: "I have also lectured in

THE WHISKEY TRUST

In 1881, the cowboys were drinking whiskey of all manner of quality. And the producers in Peoria, IL, were busy figuring out how to profit most from the national thirst. By 1887, there were over six dozen distilleries in Peoria, and they banded together to form the Distillers' and Cattle Feeders' Trust, known to most as the Whiskey Trust. The Trust's aim was to control production and prices. The principle means of doing so was to buy up small distilleries (whether they wished to be purchased or not) then either close them down or cut production. Small distillers who resisted the Trust's overtures were put out of business, sometimes violently. For example, the H. H. Shufeldt distillery in Chicago, IL, owned by prominent businessman Thomas Lynch, was the target of a dynamiting and several arson attempts, but it was never proved these were the work of the Ring. Demand for whiskey would remain robust but by limiting the supply, prices would rise.

The Trust began to lose its grip on the market in 1891 and 1892, when distillers in St. Louis and Philadelphia stood in opposition. Some of the owners of distilleries controlled by the Trust also rebelled against the price fixing. By the mid-1890s, the Trust had lost its control of the industry. When Theodore Roosevelt became president, breaking up all sorts of trusts became one of his priorities, earning him the title of "The Trust Buster."

Leadville, the greatest mining-city in the Rocky Mountains. . . They asked me to supper. . .the first course was whiskey, the second whiskey and the third whiskey. Over the piano was printed a notice: Please do not shoot the piano player. He is doing his best."

Salt Lake City, UT

Brigham Young was not only the second president of the Church of Jesus Christ of Latter-day Saints and the first governor of the Utah Territory, but also the sole distiller of "whiskey" in his western kingdom. He not only supervised the making of whiskey from wheat but also supervised its distribution and sale by the church's elders. That said, public drunkenness was not a major problem in Salt Lake City, UT.[4] In his book *Roughing It*, Mark Twain (what would whiskey lovers do without him?) gave a vivid description of his encounter with Mormon whiskey while he traveled through Utah:

> It was the exclusive Mormon refresher, "valley tan." Valley tan (or, at least, one form of valley tan) is a kind of whiskey, or first cousin to it; is of Mormon invention and manufactured only in Utah. Tradition says it is made of (imported) fire and brimstone. If I remember rightly no public drinking saloons were allowed in the kingdom of Brigham Young, and no private drinking permitted among the faithful, except they confined themselves to valley tan.

---

4   You probably knew that Young had many wives, estimates varying from fifty-five into the eighties. You probably didn't know that the Utah Territory (parts of Utah, Nevada, Wyoming, and Colorado today) was the first territory to give women the right to vote. Louisa Swain cast the first lawful ballot by a woman on September 6, 1870.

Joseph Smith and Brigham Young.

HAVE YOU EVER DRUNK "HOOCH"?

Hooch was an oft-used synonym for whiskey during the Alaskan Gold Rush, named after the Hoochino Indians who made strong, illegal whiskey to serve the miners. According to La-Belle Brooks-Vincent, it could "transform a poor miner into a millionaire for a time and also make a millionaire miner a poor man."

THE WILD WEST GETS TAMED

By the early twentieth century the era of the Wild West had passed. The railroads helped bring the long cattle drives to an end. The wild herds of bison vanished, often being shot for sport from passing railroad cars. The Homestead Act of 1862 brought farmers and barbwire fences. The Act gave 160 acres to a settler if he lived on the land for five years, built a modest home, and grew crops. In the thirty years following 1870 the number of farms grew from 2.6 million to 5.7 million. Westward ho civilization.

Western Movies

While the hardships of real cowboys and life in boom towns would recede from popular memory, the

COWBOY POETRY

Before we leave the cowboys, let's check in with Baxter Black, the preeminent expositor of cowboy poetry. Black was a large animal veterinarian who took to writing poetry and stories of the West when he was about forty years old, in the mid-1980s. This excerpt is from his poem, *The Hell Creek Bar*. Note that the calm cadence of the poem is reminiscent of western music, or maybe the soft clippety-clop of a horse's hooves:

In the Hell Creek Bar by the light of a star you'll find yourself where the cowboys are all talkin' 'bout horses they rode. The buckers they've known, the times they were thrown and the stories they tell might cut to the bone. . .long as the whiskey flowed.

And amongst this crew who'd forked a few, they could rally on and ballyhoo and make ya buy a round or two just to hear one more. They'd crack a smile like a crocodile then try to put the truth on trial and all the while their lies would pile like beernut bags on the barroom floor.

romantic notion of the Wild West would maintain a special place for whiskey during the golden age of the western movies, or the *Oaters*:

- In *Stagecoach* (1939), the movie that made John Wayne a star, a meek character (played by an actor named Donald Meek) is a whiskey drummer, a traveling whiskey salesman;
- In *High Noon* (1952), when the characters walk up to the bar, the bartender sets down the shot glass and bottle without a word being exchanged;
- In *Shane* (1953), about half of the movie (and nearly all of the action) takes place in Grafton's General Mercantile Co. Sundries and Saloon;
- In *The Magnificent Seven* (1960), Yul Brenner (as Chris Adams) and Steve McQueen (as Vin Tanner) meet by driving a funeral coach through a town to overcome the good citizens' resistance to burying a Native American on Boot Hill. How do they cement their new-found friendship? You guessed it, by sharing a bottle of whiskey.[5]

WHISKEY IN THE EXECUTIVE MANSION AFTER THE CIVIL WAR

Andrew Johnson (17th president, 1865–1869). Andrew Johnson was Lincoln's second vice president. He was a known drinker who consumed so much whiskey at Lincoln's inauguration that he gave a long-winded and offensive speech after being sworn in. Lincoln was appalled and gave the order that Johnson not speak when the proceeding moved outside.

Rutherford B. Hayes (19th president, 1877–1881). Hayes's election was steeped in controversy, and only resolved as part of a deal to remove federal troops from the South after the Civil War ended. His father owned a whiskey distillery in Columbus, OH, but he belonged to the Sons of Temperance. To appease his wife, Hayes banned alcohol from the Executive Mansion.

---

5   In his book, *Dream West: Politics and Religion in Cowboy Movies* (2013), Douglas Brode makes the argument that "cowboy politics" were far more of nuisance than personified

in both the fictional and real-life John Wayne and Clint Eastwood. The "go it alone" attitude we think of as central to the Wild West ethic is rejected in at least three movies listed above. Sergio Leone, the brains behind Eastwood's spaghetti westerns, clearly had leftist leanings, which can be found in his movies, if you can see past the gunfire.

Chester A. Arthur (21ˢᵗ president, 1881–1885). Arthur never won an election; he became president after James Garfield was assassinated. Arthur was a socialite who ate and drank too much. Upon seeing a man who Ben Franklin would have said was *in his cups,* Arthur set out some drinking etiquette: "No gentleman ever sees another man drunk . . ."

Benjamin Harrison (23ʳᵈ president, 1889–1893). Harrison was the grandson of the ninth president, William Henry Harrison (who died after serving only thirty-one days in office). He was president when the temperance movement was gathering steam. A religious man, he was a moderate drinker in private, but he abstained in public. During the Civil War, he told his wife that he traveled four miles to bring his troops a ration of whiskey while they stood in the rain. Andrew Carnegie, the industrial tycoon and philanthropist, sent him a barrel of *Dewar's* Scotch. Harrison thanked him by writing, "It was very nice of you to think of me as needing a 'brace' this winter in dealing with Congress."

William McKinley (25ᵗʰ president, 1897–1901). McKinley often had a whiskey as a nightcap (but his real passion was cigars, supposedly smoking several dozen in a week). Carnegie also sent him a barrel of *Dewar's* scotch whisky. McKinley was assassinated by a man who was brought up in a saloon and had imbibed before the assassination. The temperance movement used this as part of the argument to ban booze. But McKinley, on his death bed, asked that his assassin not be harmed. Not heeded, the assassin was electrocuted.

In the Wild West, people seemed to tolerate a broad variety of lifestyles—except for the occasional bloody feud, of course. As the century closed, would the American polity *writ large* accept itself as such a polymorphous society, or would it push back against diversity?

WHAT DOES WHISKEY TASTE LIKE IN MORMON COUNTRY?

High West American Prairie Bourbon

The High West Distillery in Park City is the first legal distillery in Utah after the 1870s. In 2016, owners Jane and David Perkins sold it to Constellation Brands, Victor, NY, for $160 million. That suggests something special is going on here.

High West American Prairie Bourbon is not so much a replica of the type of bourbon cowboys in the 1880s might have drunk but a celebration of it (we know there was a lot of variation in the quality of whiskey in the Wild West, to say the least). It is a top-secret blend of whiskeys purchased elsewhere while the barrels of the home distillery mature.

Ten percent of the after-tax revenue from each bottle is donated by the distillery to the American Prairie Reserve in Montana. The Reserve is a five thousand–square mile tract of land (that's about the size of Connecticut) being restored to look like what Lewis and Clark would have seen when they traveled through Montana.

Just the Facts

Mash Bill	Blend of mash bills. Corn: 75–84% Rye: 8–21 % Barley: 4–8 %
Proof	Proof: 92 ABV: 46%
Age; Barrel Char	Blend of ages. At least two years, up to 13 years; #4 on the staves, #2 on the heads
Chill Filtered?	No

TASTING NOTES

From: High West Distillery

https://www.highwest.com/products/american-prairie-bourbon.php

   Aroma: Light caramel and sweet vanilla

   Palate: Rich and earthy on the palate with well-balanced flavors of candy corn, honey nougat and sweet corn bread biscuits

   Finish: Vanilla with a hint of caramel apple

From: Spokane Whiskey Club (Reviewer: J. Briggs)

https://spokanewhiskeyclub.com/2017/11/10/high-west-american-prairie-bourbon-review/

Aroma: Rye. Rye everywhere with floral notes, dry eraser, rubber, clove, minty grass and pine. No obvious sweetness to speak of. Slight clove with fresh cedar. Applesauce.

Palate: Grapefruit rind, rye and black pepper. Some butterscotch.

Finish: Pith, citrus peel. Spices with a metallic twinge. Bitter tannins and drying. Short.

Comment: Bourbon lovers won't be outlandishly enthused but rye lovers will rejoice in the streets. Definitely some nice rye aromas, which is always a fine thing. I wonder what kind of whiskey American Prairie is trying to be, though. . .

From: The Over a Barrel Gang

Looks: Amber, gold,

Aroma: Light. Maple, caramel, honey, banana, vanilla, clove, orange, tobacco.

Flavor: Medium body. Sweet, bitter, salty.

Mouth Feel: Creamy, round, sharp.

Going Down: Medium strength, medium length.

Notes: Complex, excellent blend.

Toast

One more from W. C. Fields:

"Always carry a flagon of whiskey in case of a snake bite. Furthermore, always carry a small snake."

DINNER AT SALT LAKE CITY, UT, WITH BRIGHAM YOUNG AND HIS MANY WIVES

Generally speaking, Utah food culture is Mormon food culture. Mormons love socializing around a good helping of food (who doesn't). According to the author of *The Essential Mormon Cookbook*, "no matter what event you're at in Utah, there are a few staple 'Mormon' foods you'll likely find." You may be familiar with Utah's Famous Green Jell-O. Utah has historically consumed more Jell-O per capita than any other state in the nation and state officials bestowed on Jell-O the title of official state snack. Funeral Potatoes and Frog's Eye Salad may be new to you.

Recipe: Utah's Famous Green Jell-O

From: Jensen, J. B. (2018). *The Essential Mormon Cookbook*. Salt Lake City, UT: Deseret Book. P. 35.

Ingredients (serves 12):

    I cup water

    I (6-ounce) package lime Jell-O

    ½ cup sugar

    2 tablespoons fresh lemon juice (optional)

    I cup crushed pineapple, undrained

    2 cups whipped cream

Directions:

    Bring water to a boil. Put Jell-O and sugar in medium-sized bowl; add boiling water, stirring until gelatin is dissolved. Add lemon juice, if desired. Stir in crushed pineapple. Refrigerate until syrupy. Whip cream until stiff. Fold into Jell-O mixture. Place in 9 x 13-inch pan. Refrigerate for several hours until firm.

Recipe: Frog's Eye Salad

From: Jensen, J. B. (2018). *The Essential Mormon Cookbook*. Salt Lake City, UT: Deseret Book. P. 165.

No frogs are harmed in the making of this salad.

Ingredients (serves 12):

    I cup acini de pepe pasta

    I (20-ounce) can pineapple tidbits, juice reserved

    I (20-ounce) can crushed pineapple

    2 (15-ounce) cans mandarin oranges

    I (12-ounce) tub frozen whipped topping, thawed

    2 cups miniature marshmallows

    I cup flaked coconut (optional)

    ½ cup chopped maraschino cherries (optional)

    Green food coloring

Directions (serves 12):

Cook pasta according to package directions: drain well and set aside to cool. Pour reserved pineapple juice over pasta. Add pineapple tidbits, crushed pineapple, mandarin oranges, whipped topping, and marshmallows. Stir in coconut and cherries, if desired. Stir in green food coloring, one drop at a time, to desired color. Place in refrigerator overnight.

Recipe: Funeral Potatoes

From: Jensen, J. B. (2018). *The Essential Mormon Cookbook*. Salt Lake City, UT: Deseret Book. P. 126.

No one needs to die to make this salad.

Ingredients (serves 12):

12 large potatoes or 1 (32-ounce) bag frozen shredded hash browns

2 (10¾-ounce) cans cream of chicken soup

2 cups sour cream

1 cup grated cheddar cheese

½ cup butter, melted

½ cup chopped onion

2 cups crushed corn flakes

2 tablespoons melted butter

Directions:

Peel potatoes and boil for 30 minutes, until just tender. Cool and grate into a greased 9x13-inch baking dish (or put hash browns into the baking dish). Combine soup concentrate, sour cream, cheese, the ½ cup melted butter, and onions. Gently blend into potatoes. Combine crushed corn flakes and the 2 tablespoons melted butter. Sprinkle on top. Bake at 350°F for 30 minutes.

MUSIC THAT TAKES US BACK TO DODGE CITY

Songs that sing the praises of cities and states are scattered throughout popular music. Mobility is endemic to the American way of life. But no genre captured wanderlust and a sense of place better than did the cowboys and early western music.

Don't Fence Me In, performed by Roy Rogers (1948)[6]

This is a song about Wild Cat Kelley, who wants to hit the road. It is an ode to life on the prairie.

Tumbling Tumble Weeds, performed by Gene Autry (1980)

On the Western Writers Top 100 list, Autry recorded this song in 1935 for the soundtrack of a movie by the same name. It also appears in the film *The Big Lebowski* but, regrettably, was left off the soundtrack album.

The Wayward Wind, performed by Gogi Grant (1956)

This is a medley of Gogi Grant's (née Myrtle Audrey Arinsberg) hit. But a big one it was. It also made the Western Writers of America Top 100 songs of all time. The Beatles covered this song on their tours in 1960 and 1961.

The Yellow Rose of Texas, performed by Ernest Tubbs (1961)

Another Top 100 western song of all time. *Yellow Rose* has been covered by at least twenty artists, including The Countdown Kids (on *150 Fun Songs for Kids*).

El Paso, performed by Marty Robbins (1957)

El Paso was a huge hit for Marty Robbins in 1960, reaching #1 on two different Billboard charts. On this version, Bob Weir sings lead and Jerry Garcia, both of Grateful Dead fame, sing harmony.

Streets of Laredo, performed by Marty Robbins (1960)

Yet another Top 100 western songs of all time.

---

6   Speaking of singing cowboys, Herb Jeffries was a Black baritone who, in the 1930s, starred in what were called "race" Western movies, aimed at Black audiences, including *Harlem on the Prairie, Two-Gun Man from Harlem,* and *Harlem Rides Again.*

San Antonio Rose, performed by Bob Wills and His Texas Cowboys (1940)

Wills wrote this song as an instrumental but then his band members wrote the lyrics. Cover versions are numerous, probably most famously by Bing Crosby. Wills is considered the "Father of Western Swing" music. Waylon Jennings pays homage to Wills in his song, *Bob Wills is Still the King.*

'Neath the Blue Montana Skies, performed by Gene Autry (1939)

From a movie by the same name, starring "The Singing Cowboy" himself.

Amarillo by Morning, performed by George Strait (1985)

Strait's signature song, *Amarillo* was conceived by its songwriter, Terry Strafford, while driving home to Amarillo after a gig in San Antonio, TX. The song is on the Western Writers of America's Top 100 list.

Happy Trails, performed by Roy Rogers and Dale Evans (1952)

This was the theme song to *The Roy Rogers Show.* Roy, Dale, Trigger (Roy's horse), and Bullet (their German shepherd) had four different sidekicks, most recognizably George "Gabby" Hayes. Upon Trigger's death, Rogers had him stuffed. You can visit Trigger in Branson, MO.

Dale Evans and Roy Rogers c. 1950.

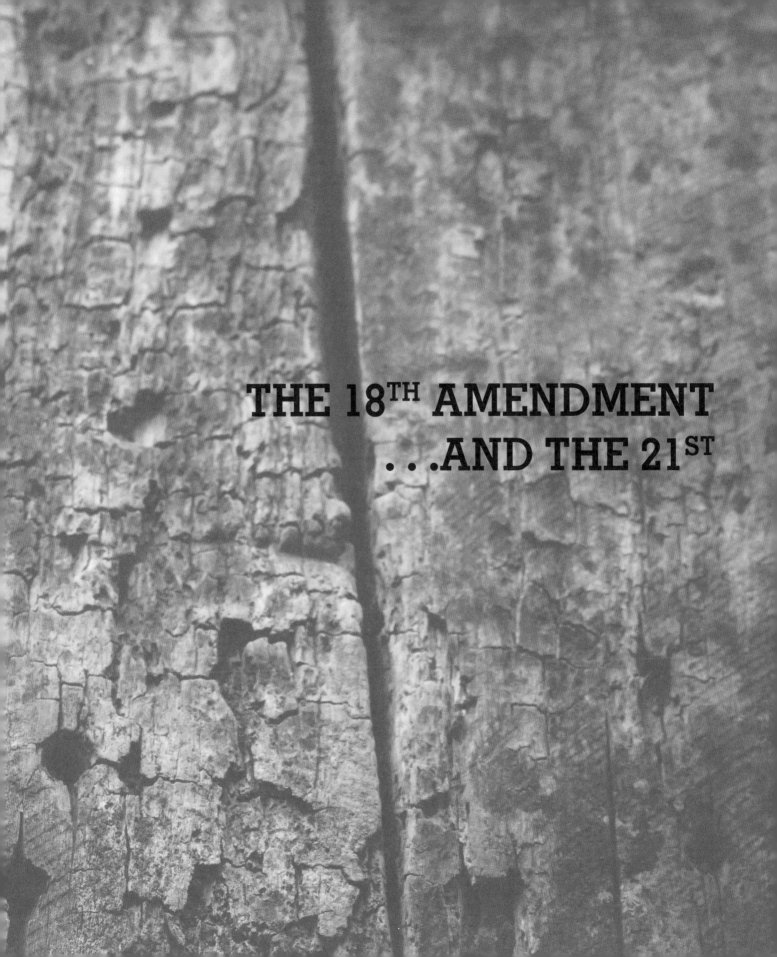

THE 18TH AMENDMENT
...AND THE 21ST

Chapter 10
BANNING BOOZE AND SHUNNING STRANGERS

Prohibition is better than no liquor at all.
—Will Rogers

EXTRA! EXTRA! PROHIBITION HAS WHISKEY OVER A BARREL!

The 18th Amendment to the United States Constitution was ratified by three-fourths of the states in January 1919. The Volstead Act that followed made it unlawful for any person to "manufacture, sell, barter, give away, transport, import, export, deliver, furnish, receive or possess any intoxicating liquors except as allowed under the act." That pretty much covered all the bases. However, wine for sacramental purposes was allowed. Consumption of other intoxicants for other purposes was also allowed as long as the beverage was in stock before the law went into effect, in January 1920. And, alcohol could still be used as medicine.

But the roots of Prohibition go much farther back in American history. It was not until the United States was turning into a modern and multicultural society that the temperance movement won the battle (but not the war).

The Roots of the Temperance Movement

Prohibition might have happened decades earlier had it not been for the nation's divide over slavery. Long before the Civil War, in 1826, the American Temperance Society was established in Boston. Within a decade, the society had thousands of local chapters and tens of thousands of members.[1] But the strongest supporters in the North also supported the abolition of slavery. The coupling of these two issues kept the movement divided from Southerners who might otherwise have joined the anti-alcohol crusade.

After the Civil War, temperance gained steam in the South, not least because it was a way to keep alcohol away

---

1   Walt Whitman, the author of one of the greatest American poems, "Leaves of Grass," wrote only one novel. *Evan Williams, or the Inebriate,* published in 1842, described in first person how the evils of drinking could ruin a life.

The Drunkards Progress, a lithograph by Nathaniel Currier in 1846.
Currier and Ives produced "cheap and popular" prints for over seventy years.

Carrie Nation.

from freed slaves.[2] It also gained momentum in the West where women settlers wanted to keep their men out of saloons. The Women's Christian Temperance Union was founded in 1874 in Cleveland, OH (remember, Ohio was still the West then). Anne Wittenmyer, a relief worker who established homes for children orphaned by the Civil War, became the first WTCU president.[3] The most influential temperance organization was the Anti-Saloon League, established in 1893 and led by Reverend Howard Hyde Russell. The League's motto was "the church in action against the saloon."

---

2   John Stith Pemberton was a druggist in the late 19th century who abhorred the drinking of alcohol. As an alternative, he concocted a new drink you might have tasted, Coca-Cola. Using Coke as a prophylactic to drinking alcohol lasted decades, though the original formula is thought to have contained cocaine. During World War II, Dwight Eisenhower did all he could to keep the troops supplied with Coke, to keep them away from the harder stuff.

3   It should be mentioned that the temperance movement was notable as one of the first forays of women into public debates about social policy.

But the image of the temperance movement that struck fear into the hearts of drinkers everywhere was undoubtedly that of Carrie Amelia Moore, known to all as Carrie Nation.

Carrie was born in 1846 in Kentucky and was raised there as well as in Missouri and Texas. In 1867, she married a physician, Dr. Charles Gloyd. Gloyd was not only a doctor but also an alcoholic. Carrie was widowed when Charles succumbed to demon alcohol and was buried in a drunkard's grave. Less than ten years later, Carrie married David Nation, a lawyer and church minister. But Carrie was not only speaking with her husband in those days; she believed she spoke directly with Jesus as well. And Jesus told her to destroy saloons.[4] David eventually divorced Carrie because he felt her sanity was slipping away. He was also concerned about her unusual way of combating (and "combatting" is the word) the consumption of alcohol.

In 1873, Eliza Jane Thompson led seventy women down the streets of her hometown of Hillsboro, OH, to drugstores and bars. The women stood outside, sang

---

4   Carrie Nation also hated sex, tobacco, and Teddy Roosevelt.

hymns, and prayed. After the newspapers covered the story, over fifty thousand promoters of temperance followed suit. But that didn't go far enough for Carrie Nation. In 1900, she gathered her supporters, went into a drugstore in Kansas, rolled out a cask of brandy, smashed it with a sledgehammer, and set fire to the contents. Carrie wasn't nearly done. Later that year she used her ax to destroy an entire saloon in Kiowa, OK. Carrie was jailed over thirty times in many of the places she visited, including Wichita, KS. She died of a stroke in 1911. She didn't live to see Prohibition.

PROHIBITION BECOMES LAW: A NEW CLASS OF CRIMINALS IS CREATED

The success of the temperance movement in the early 1900s certainly had as much to do with native-born Americans' abhorrence of freed slaves and new immigrants—and the changes their unfamiliar ways were bringing to society—as it did with a distaste for alcohol.[5] "Immigrants" here includes Irish Catholics, Italians, and Eastern Europeans. In addition to their alien ways, many were believed to be political radicals. And then there was the increasing anti-German feelings arising out of World War I.[6]

Prohibitionists perceived the saloon as draining the immigrants of their wages and keeping them from their families. It didn't matter that immigrants had lower rates of alcoholism than native-born citizens and that drinking in America was less per capita than it had been before the immigrants arrived. And, urban drinking establishments were much more than home wreckers.

---

5   The Prohibition movement was joined by the second iteration of the Ku Klux Klan, started in Georgia around 1915.

6   The Great War may have given impetus for Prohibition in another way as well. Many returning soldiers were suffering from "shell shock," what today we call post-traumatic stress disorder. There was no treatment for this as yet unrecognized malady. Drinking became a way for these soldiers to self-medicate.

As had been true in the settlement of the West, local saloons in urban areas were the places to find many of the social services needed by the new poor immigrants. It was the gathering place, at least for men, after work.

"Fake news" is not an invention of the twenty-first century. A propaganda pamphlet espousing Prohibition claimed that alcohol could lead to spontaneous self-combustion, that 10% of the population died each year because people drank too much, and that 80% of America's criminals came out of saloons. Supporters of Prohibition also believed it would be good for the economy.

THE WETS

Where were the drinkers, the *Wets*, while all this was going on? Mostly, they paid the *Drys* little notice except, of course, if it was their establishment that was targeted for a street prayer meeting or for getting smashed to smithereens by a black-clad woman with a Bible in one hand and an axe in the other.

But one man, George Garvin Brown, took it upon himself to combat the temperance movement by appealing to that same higher authority. Brown was a deeply religious man whose association with his church was endangered by his involvement in the whiskey business. In 1910, Brown countered the Drys by using the "word of the Lord;" he published a pamphlet titled *The Holy Bible Repudiates Prohibition*. In it, he quoted passages from the Bible that showed "divine" approval of the consumption of alcoholic beverages. To wit:

> Deut. 14: "And thou shalt bestow that money for whatever thy soul lusteth after, for oxen, or for sheep, or for wine, or for strong drink, or for whatsoever thy soul desireth; and thou shalt eat there before the Lord thy God, and thou shalt rejoice, thou and thine household."

When passage of the 18th Amendment became inevitable, the Wets made plans to circumvent Prohibition

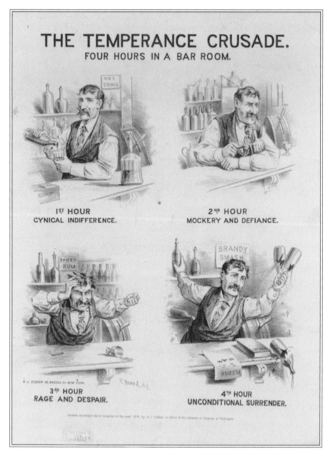

Four Hours in a Bar Room by Frank Beard, 1874.

and the new law that would enforce it. In 1918, the Sears, Roebuck & Co. catalog (the Amazon of its day) ran an advertisement for home distilling equipment, a new hobby adopted by many Americans. The Los Angeles Library had every book on how to distill alcohol at home checked out, and most never returned. And, given the laws permit of medicinal alcohol, lots of people started to get sick.

WHISKEY WILL CURE WHAT AILS YOU, ONE WAY OR ANOTHER

Whiskey as Medicine

The Volstead Act made the exception that alcohol could be used for medicinal purposes. It could even be manufactured and transported across state lines if the intent was to relieve physical suffering. Two years into Prohibition, the American Medical Association endorsed alcohol as medication. Whiskey was approved for the treatment of twenty-seven "ailments" and physicians, dentists, and veterinarians were licensed to dispense it. Of course, you needed a doctor's note to purchase whiskey from a pharmacist. One famous prescription—perhaps taking things a bit too far—read "take three ounces every hour for stimulant until stimulated." So many people became "ill" that the number of bottles of whiskey a person could legally obtain was eventually restricted to one bottle every ten days.

In true American fashion, several savvy entrepreneurs realized there was a fortune to be made in the medicinal whiskey business. Six companies were given licenses to continue selling bonded spirits. The Brown-Forman Company marketed its *Old Forester* brand of whiskey to pharmacies. And the pharmacies did not suffer either. The Walgreens drugstore chain grew from twenty stores in 1920 to 525 by end of the decade.

Whiskey as Poison

People had to watch what they drank. Wets certainly wanted to avoid drinking industrial alcohol, regardless of what it had been mixed with or how golden brown it looked. The federal government required that toxins be added to the alcohol used by industry. If people got *spifflicated* (drunk) on this concoction it could cause blindness, nerve damage, or cost them their lives; in New York City, unless drinkers were careful—meaning they were "receiving medical treatment" or had a trustworthy source—a huge percentage of the alcohol contained poison.[7]

---

7   And don't believe that the debate over the health implication of consuming alcohol faded away with the end of prohibition. We all know the health risks associated with overconsumption, both long and short term. Potential health benefits of moderate consumption also have been cataloged (https://www.wideopencountry.com/10-health-benefits-drinking-whiskey/).

When Prohibition first took effect, it had some successes. The death rate due to alcoholism dropped noticeably. Productivity on the job improved, partly due to a decrease in absenteeism. Prohibition also had some interesting unintended consequences.

THE SPEAKEASY

The disappearance of the saloon marked the appearance of illegal drinking establishments, known as speakeasies.[8]

Gone with the saloon was the association between working-class male drinking and social drinking. The patrons of speakeasies didn't cross many barriers of social class, being composed mostly by *bluenoses* (upper-class) and middle-class whites, who suddenly found themselves to be a new form of "criminal." Speakeasy patrons might enter through a secret passageway. They might be asked for a password or use a secret knock. Once inside, swingers and *flappers* (women who dressed in a particular fashionable way) could request their favorite bourbon and gin by the name of the manufacturer (if they could afford it). They could drink a *jorum of skee* (gangster slang for hard liquor), smoke *gaspers* (cigarettes), listen to the best music in town, and liaise with that special someone.

Women Leave the Home

Before and during World War I, women in large numbers, mostly unmarried or the spouses of soldiers with no children, took jobs outside their homes. Their new independent status as wage earners led women to one realization: things weren't going back to the way they used to be. Women began drinking and smoking in public. They fully participated in the speakeasy culture. Less affluent women would be present in speakeasies as employees.

8 No one talked about these illegal watering holes except in hushed tones. They had to "speak easy."

A Crack in the Racial Boundaries

A breach also occurred in racial boundaries. While most speakeasies were owned by whites, the most lavish ones were predominantly located in African American neighborhoods, such as the South Side in Chicago and Harlem in New York City. African Americans worked and entertained, most notably as jazz performers. White musicians would go to a speakeasy and steal jazz riffs to play in their gigs downtown. But the increasing popularity of jazz did bring recording deals for African American artists, a first. The Cotton Club in Harlem was a whites-only establishment except, of course, if you could sing or play swing music. Some African American talent would transcend the racial barrier to perform in legitimate establishments for Whites, including renowned musicians such as Duke Ellington, Louis Armstrong ("Satchmo"), and William "Count" Basie, and singers such as Ethel Waters, Bessie Smith, Billie Holiday, and Lena Horne.

THE END OF PROHIBITION

One reason for the end of Prohibition was simple . . . it did not work. In 1922, New York City had about

Billie Holiday.

THE COCKTAIL

A cocktail is a drink that mixes alcoholic beverages, sometimes multiple different alcoholic beverages, with other beverages, most often fruit juice or soda. Bitters are also often added. A person who is a creative cocktail mixer can become a cherished member of a bar staff, or make many friends.

There are at least seven proposed derivations of the word "cocktail," some not suited for genteel company. Regardless of where the term originally came from, I like the visual explanation.

An old-fashioned whiskey cocktail and a real old-fashioned cock's tail.

Prohibition was a boon to the cocktail. It was a way to make poor-tasting whiskey palatable. Also, because whiskey needs to be aged, drinking gin came into fashion.

five thousand speakeasies. By 1927, that number had jumped to at least thirty thousand, twice the number of establishments serving alcohol when drinking was legal. Similar growth in the number of places you could get a drink have been documented for Washington, DC, Boston, and even Kansas, the first state to shut its legitimate saloons. Prohibition led to more drinking of distilled spirits in place of beer or wine. It also caused a general erosion of respect for the law; smoking marijuana increased because it was still legal.

Another reason why prohibition failed was the tepid government attempt at implementing the law. Public officials simply did not provide the funding needed for effective enforcement.

But perhaps the greatest impetus for the repeal of the 18th Amendment was the Great Depression. Remember the excise tax on alcoholic beverages? The alcohol industry helped fill the Treasury's coffers. Alcohol was a great source of revenue for the government, but the excise tax became less necessary when the tax on income was first collected in 1913. The income tax worked great as long as people had income to tax.[9]

There is another interesting fact about the

---

9   You might argue that whiskey caused the Great Depression. When Benjamin Strong (the Governor of the New York Federal Reserve Bank) instituted the credit policy that led to wild stock speculation, he is quoted as saying, "I will give a little shot of whiskey to the Stock Market." Okay, maybe it was just a metaphor.

THE EXCISE TAX (AGAIN)

The end of Prohibition brought with it the system we still use today for collecting federal excise taxes on beer, wine, and distilled spirits. Excise taxes are not sales taxes, so they are not displayed on a cash register receipt. They are typically paid by the producer and are part of the cost of the alcoholic beverage. That also means the state and local sales tax is calculated with the excise tax as part of the cost of the product. In 2019, the excise tax on whiskey was $13.50 a gallon. Based on alcohol equivalence, the distilled beverage tax is about three times that on beer and wine. Some states and local governments add their own excise tax in addition to their sales tax. These taxes vary from locality to locality. By the time the taxes are all added up, they can account for half the price of a bottle of whiskey.

Prohibition also left behind a three-tiered system of alcohol distribution. Alcoholic beverage producers can only sell to distributors. Distributors, who are either state-employees or licensed by the state, are entrusted with ensuring the excise taxes are paid. The distributor then sells the beverage to the retailer, who can then sell it to the consumer. *

*I once stood in a distillery gift shop and asked to purchase some of my favorite whiskey. The salesperson told me it was sold out, but if I waited an hour or so "some might be back from the distributor." Sure enough, the whiskey returned. The producer had to send it to the distributor who then taxed it and sold it back to the producer, who was now a retailer. Alexander Hamilton would be proud; so would Rube Goldberg.

18th Amendment. It is the only amendment to the Constitution that restricted the freedoms of American citizens instead of protecting or expanding them. The 18th Amendment was repealed on December 5, 1933 with the passage of the 21st Amendment.[10, 11]

Besides opening doors for white women and some African Americans, Prohibition had another positive effect. To enforce prohibition, police and federal agents looking for illegal alcohol would conduct raids of private homes. Public outcry regarding this practice helped spur laws restricting search and seizure. The restrictions meant enforcers of the law would be required to have a search warrant, describing what contraband they were looking for and why they thought they would find it, in order to enter someone's home. If they didn't have a warrant, any evidence of wrongdoing the agents found could not be used in court.

Prohibition certainly changed lifestyles in American cities. But in rural areas, that whiskey still producing illegal *white lightning* was always a part of life and, Prohibition or not, it was business as usual.

---

10   Today, there are still over thirty United States counties and cities that prohibit the sale or manufacture of alcoholic beverages within their jurisdiction.

11   Alcoholics Anonymous was founded in 1935, by two alcoholics, a stockbroker and a proctologist. Today, it is estimated to have around two million members.

WHAT DOES SPEAKEASY WHISKEY TASTE LIKE?

Old Forester 1920 Prohibition Style Kentucky Straight Bourbon Whisky

The Old Forester Distillery in Louisville, KY, was one of the six producers of whiskey granted a license to continue distilling during Prohibition. Though it is now owned by the Brown-Forman company, the brand is the longest continuously available bourbon whiskey, closing in on its 150th birthday. *Old Forester 1920 Prohibition Style Kentucky Straight Bourbon Whisky* is meant to bring back the taste of whisky when whisky was taken as medicine. Don't let that put you off.

Just the Facts

Mash Bill	Corn: 72% Rye: 18 % Barley: 10 %
Proof	Proof: 115 ABV: 57.5%
Age and Char Level	No Age Statement; #4
Chill Filtered?	No

TASTING NOTES

From: Old Forester Distillery website

https://www.oldforester.com/products/old-forester-1920-style-prohibition-whisky/

Aroma: An intense medley of cherry preserves, drippy caramel, dark chocolate, thickened maple syrup and seasoned oak spiciness.

Palate: Dark caramel coats layers of malt nuttiness and sweet graham cracker all warmed by green peppercorn and coriander spice brightened with a hint of cedar.

Finish: Tart apple crispness gives way to a long smoky finish full of toasted marshmallow, chocolate and graham cracker sweetness.

From: The Whiskey Shelf (Reviewer: Alexander Wei Wang)

https://www.thewhiskeyshelf.com/old-forester-1920

Aroma: . . .fragrant and alcohol-soaked maraschino cherries, brown sugar, and apple pie spices with a healthy dose of musty corn, dough, and wood. . .Lighter spritzes of effervescent lemon and pine. . .additional wood and mint follow the initial sweetness. The alcohol constantly reminds me that it's there, but it's not terribly hot. Swirling ups the vanilla and buttercream scents mixed with darker charred wood, cinnamon, caramel, maple syrup, and other spices, but is bright and vibrant overall. The scents ebb and flow between sugar, orange, apple, cinnamon, mint, vanilla, and cocoa that sometimes give me baked apples with a spritz of orange and lemon, peppermint patties, or pecan pie. . . . Everything is very nice minus the noticeable raw dough smell that fades over time as you let the glass breathe.

Palate: . . .dark and rich dried oranges, caramel, and corn, mingling with the brighter alcohol flavors. There's a noticeable minty corn mash taste from the rye, with a little nuttiness. . . . Strong "chewing" releases a rush of brown sugar, mint, corn, and vanilla frosting followed by roasted wood, fuji apple peels, and a dash of orange juice.

Finish: . . .lingering cornbread sweetness with mint and charred wood. Lengthy chewing leaves more savory sugars, mint, and wood with a little nuttiness, cinnamon, and cocoa. It's a lightly sweet, savory, and boozy snickers bar.

Overall: . . .a delicious bourbon with a lot of character, but it isn't quite complex or interesting enough to receive a "Top Shelf" rating. The nose is very hot at first, spewing doughy alcohol and musty corn. After it settles, I finally get the 1920s rich, sweet, and savory traits.

From: The Over a Barrel Gang

Looks: Deep copper, amber.
Aroma: Robust. Chocolate, caramel, vanilla, cinnamon, cherry, grape, grass, campfire.
Flavor: Medium body. Bitter, sweet.
Mouth Feel: Sharp, heavy.
Going Down: Strong strength, long length.
Notes: She's strong.

Toast

George Herman "Babe" Ruth was the most famous baseball player with a reputation for drinking in the 1920s and 30s, but Jay Hanna "Dizzy" Dean wasn't far behind. Dizzy pitched in the 1930s and is enshrined in the Hall of Fame. He was old enough to drink when Prohibition ended, though Dizzy probably was far from a novice by then. Dean was a different kind of role model for American youth, maybe a little more forthcoming than Mom and Dad would have liked: "Sure, I eat what I advertise. Sure, I eat Wheaties for breakfast. A good bowl of Wheaties with bourbon can't be beat."

To Prohibition, may we never forget the lessons it taught us.

DINNER AT THE COTTON CLUB, MANHATTAN, NY, WITH DUKE, LOUIE, AND BILLIE

Speakeasy culture has one iconic dish. The repast of fried chicken and waffles has a special kind of origin story.[12] Legend has it that this yummy pairing of dinner and breakfast originated in Harlem's Wells Supper Club.[13] After the speakeasy would close, the club would serve breakfast to the musicians, staff, and lingering patrons. Breakfast often consisted of waffles topped with what was left over from the favorite dinner entree the night before.

Today, you can get chicken and waffles at franchise restaurants. At home, you can make fried chicken using Ava Gardner's recipe from Chapter 13, with its roots deep in the South. Silver dollar size waffles work perfectly if you are tasting from lots of eras, but they are hard to make at home. You can find a wide variety available at your local grocery store. You can eat your chicken and waffles with syrup[14] or any fruit preserves you fancy.

Also first appearing in the 1930s, *The Joy of Cooking* is one of the most successful cookbooks of all time. It first was self-published by Irma S. Rombauer in 1931 and has sold more than eighteen million copies in nine editions since then. *The Joy of Cooking* has been in print for over seventy-five years. The first edition included twenty-two recipes for soufflés, with cream sauce and beaten egg whites as the principal ingredients.

Recipe: Corny Soufflé

From: https://en.wikibooks.org/wiki/Cookbook:Corny_Soufflé

Ingredients:
- 1 (16-ounce) package frozen corn
- 1 cup milk
- 3 eggs
- 2 tablespoons sugar
- 1/8 teaspoon salt
- 1 tablespoon butter, cut into 6 pieces

Directions:
1. Preheat oven to 325 degrees.
2. Put frozen corn, milk, eggs, sugar, and salt into a blender.
3. Blend on medium until ingredients are mixed thoroughly.
4. Pour into medium sized baking dish coated with cooking spray.
5. Dot the top with butter pieces.
6. Bake for 70 minutes.

---

12   www.pbs.org/food/the-history-kitchen/history-chicken-and-waffles/2

13   Others, with less of a taste for the romance of the time, suggest it is simply a Northern variation on the South's chicken and biscuit. What do they know?

14   Mrs. Butterworth's Pancake Syrup did not appear on store shelves until 1961.

Recipe: Boiled Shrimp

From: https://www.wikihow.com/Cook-Boiled Shrimp#Questions_and_Answers_sub

Ingredients:

I lb fresh, wild shrimp

¼ cup cider vinegar

I pinch salt

3 to 4 tablespoons Old Bay Seasoning, or to taste

Ice water

I lemon, sliced in half, for garnish

Directions:

1. Bring a large pot of water just to a boil. You want enough water to comfortably hold all the shrimp. There should be about I to 2 inches (2.5 to 5.I cm) more water than there is shrimp.

   To the water, add:

   ¼ cup cider vinegar

   Pinch of salt

   Seasoning. Zatarain's Shrimp Boil seasonings may be used, or Old Bay seasoning, or a combination of both. Either use a small box of Zatarain's, 3 to 4 tablespoons of Old Bay, or a box of Zatarain's with I tablespoon of Old Bay.

   Shrimp Cocktail.
   Does the design look familiar?

2. Boil the water for a few minutes to season well. This helps turn the water into more of a broth or brine, which you'll then sink the shrimp into.

3. Drop the fresh shrimp into the water. Most chefs agree that cooking the shrimp with the heads and shells on, while annoying to peel, makes the shrimp tastier and more flavorful. If desired, de-vein the shrimp before you place them in the pot to cook.

4. Boil the shrimp until a few start floating on top of the water. There is no set time for boiling shrimp, but smaller shrimp (50+ per pound) will take around 2 to 3 minutes, while larger shrimp (~30 per pound) will take around 5 to 7 minutes. This is only a guideline however. If you feel like you want to check for doneness, shrimp is cooked when the thickest part of the flesh is opaque. Take care not to overcook the shrimp. Overcooked shrimp become tough and rubbery. Remove the shrimp from the heat as soon as a few begin popping up to the top of the water.

5. Drain the shrimp in a colander and shock immediately in an ice-bath. Just submerge the colander in the ice bath and take out immediately. This will more or less stop the shrimp from overcooking.

6. Drain all water from shrimp, set on platter, and garnish with a half of a lemon. Enjoy!

MUSIC THAT TAKES US BACK TO THE TIME BETWEEN THE WORLD WARS

The time between the World Wars saw the arrival of the mass-produced automobiles, motion pictures, and radios. Much radio content was classical music and opera, meant to help different ethnic groups retain a tie to home. But it also provided a platform and new opportunities for forging a common culture. This culture included jazz combos, big bands, and dance marathons (see the movie, *They Shoot Horses, Don't They?*)

How Are You Going To Wet Your Whistle (when the whole darn world goes dry)?, performed by Billy Murray (1919)

Billy Murray, a star of vaudeville, recorded this song expressing growing public anxiety in 1919. The idiom *"wet your whistle"* dates back to a 14th century poem written by Geoffrey Chaucer, the same guy who wrote *The Canterbury Tales.*

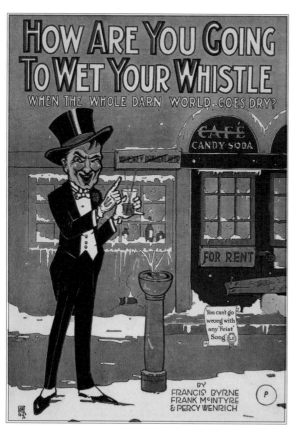

An image of dystopia?

Stars and Stripes, by the John Phillip Sousa Orchestra (remastered 2004)

John Phillip Sousa was the son of a Portuguese trombonist who played in the US Marine Band. He directed the Marine Band for twelve years and *Stars and Stripes* became the national march of the US. Sousa wrote over 130 marches.

My Mammy, performed by Al Jolson (re-issued 2001)

This song is from *The Jazz Singer*, the first full-length talking motion picture, released in 1927. *Singer* tells the story of Jakie, the son of a Jewish father who wants his son to be a cantor, or singer in a synagogue. Jakie wants to sing popular songs and jazz. While the picture delved into the conflict between parents' desire to maintain their immigrant traditions and their children's desire to assimilate, its content was tone deaf with regard to other matters; Jolson sang in blackface.

Summertime, performed by Billie Holiday (1936)

Summertime was written by DuBose Heywood for George and Ira Gershwin's American opera, *Porgy and Bess.* Although best known today for her version of *Summertime,* Holiday's biggest selling song was *Strange*

Fruit in 1939. The song was about the lynching of African Americans.[15] It put her on the radar of law enforcement officials. Holiday suffered from alcohol and drug addiction for many years. In 1959, she entered a New York City hospital for treatment of liver and heart disease. The Federal Bureau of Narcotics had her arrested, handcuffed, and placed under police guard while she lay in bed. She died later that year at age forty-four. She had been swindled out of her money and passed away with seventy cents in the bank and $750 in cash.

Sweet Georgia Brown, performed by California Ramblers (1997)

This song has lyrics but this is an instrumental version. If it sounds familiar but you can't place it, that's because it was adopted by The Harlem Globetrotters basketball team as their theme song.

Minnie the Moocher, performed by Cab Calloway (1931)

Written and sung by Cab Calloway, *Minnie* is based on a real person. She was a homeless woman known throughout Indianapolis, IN, for her begging. Calloway was famous for his distinctive dance moves, skat lyrics, and call-and-response with the audience. He sung this song for audiences until he was past the age of eighty. Callaway published a *Hepster's Dictionary* in 1938, supposedly compiled by his press agent. *Minnie* contains the slang terms *kick the gong around* (smoke opium) and *cokey* (an opium or cocaine user).

Get Happy/Happy Days are Here Again, performed by Barbra Streisand with Judy Garland (1963)

Happy Days celebrates the World War I armistice, but it didn't appear until over a decade later in the play, *Chasing Rainbows*. It was written and released just as the Great Depression began. Franklin D. Roosevelt used it as his campaign song. As for the singers, maybe Garland and Streisand arrived on the scene later, but who's gonna argue about listening to these two voices together?

Barbra Streisand and Judy Garland.

---

15   The term lynching was coined after Colonel Charles Lynch of Virginia, who took up the practice of lashing loyalists thirty-nine times. The association with hanging came later.

Brother, Can You Spare a Dime, performed by Bing Crosby (1932)

Was this song, lamenting the fate of the working man during the Great Depression, anti-capitalist propaganda? Some people thought so. It was written for a musical revue with a melody from a Russian-Jewish lullaby.

It Don't Mean a Thing if It Ain't Got That Swing, performed by the Duke Ellington Orchestra (1932)

The music for this number was composed by Ellington during the intermission of a show. An anthem to jazz, it was inducted into the Grammy Hall of Fame in 2008.

Charleston, performed by Paul Whiteman and His Orchestra (1925)

Named after the city, the Charleston was the biggest dance craze of the Prohibition Era.

You Are My Sunshine, performed by Carly Simon (2007)

Sunshine was first published in 1939 by Jimmie Davis, a country singer. It has been recorded by Gene Autry, Johnny Cash, and Willie Nelson, but lost its country twang in versions by Doris Day, Chuck Berry, and this one by folk singer Carly Simon.

Bread and Roses, performed by Dawn Landes (2017)

Bread and Roses derives its lyrics from a speech given by Helen Todd, a suffrage activist. Todd's words were inspired by a poem by James Oppenheim, first published in 1911, then set to music in 1917. Dawn Landes grew up near Louisville, KY, and spent many years in Brooklyn, NY.

This Land is Your Land, by Woody Guthrie (1945)

How can you think about popular music during the Great Depression without thinking of this song? Guthrie wrote it in 1940. Some folks, including the late Robert Kennedy, think it oughtta be the national anthem. Verses of the song dealing with hunger, poverty, and private property are often omitted from sung and published versions. But you can still hear Woody's son, Arlo, sing them in concert.

Chapter 11
BOOTLEGGERS AND MOONSHINERS, YOU AIN'T NEVER HEARD OF

*When I sell liquor, it's called bootlegging; when my patrons
serve liquor on Lake Shore Drive, it's called hospitality.*
—Al Capone

The story of Al Capone, the gangster and *bootlegger*[1] during Prohibition, is part of American history and folklore known by most. But there were other folks, in the big city and the backcountry, whose stories may not be as well-known (nor quite as bloody) but they are equally worthy of retelling.

GEORGE REMUS: THE REAL JAY GATSBY?
George Remus was a criminal defense lawyer with a background in pharmaceuticals, a perfect combination of expertise to make a fortune distributing illegal liquor. Even though he had a license to sell medicinal whiskey legally, the profit wasn't enough for him. He began hijacking truckloads of his own legal whiskey and then reselling it on the black market. He bought the storehouses of distilleries as his profits increased.

Remus was also the inspiration for F. Scott Fitzgerald's Jay Gatsby, in *The Great Gatsby*. Remus made a huge fortune as a bootlegger of bourbon whiskey. Like Gatsby, Remus threw lavish parties; at one, the party favors for female

George Remus.
King of the Bootleggers (and Slayer of Imogene).

---

1   The origin of the noun "bootlegger" seems straightforward; that is, deriving from someone who used a tall boot to conceal a flask of whiskey. Or a knife. But the term "to bootleg" appears to connote any use of trickery.

guests were new automobiles, which George had lined up on the front lawn of his mansion.

You couldn't do business during Prohibition on the scale of Remus's operation without *greasing some palms* (this idiom is from a time long ago), or even maybe providing alcohol to the White House (for Warren Harding). As his enterprise grew, so did his need to bribe government officials. Remus's plans included an attempt to buy off the attorney general, Harry Daugherty. When the government finally caught up with Remus, he was indicted for thousands of violations of the Volstead Act (which he had memorized). He was convicted by a jury in no time flat (about two hours) and sentenced to two years in prison.

Before Remus went to jail, he turned over the power of attorney for his assets to his wife, Imogene. Smart move, but maybe not too smart. Imogene had started *canoodling* (18th century slang but popular in the thirties) with Franklin Dodge, the federal agent who brought her husband to justice. Dodge quit his

Imogene Remus.
Getting ready to visit her husband in prison or her lover in the warden's office?

government job and began using George's legal permits to sell booze with Imogene.

The two fell in love. Remus found out (the story goes that Dodge and Imogene spent their first night together in his warden's office) and upon his release, Remus tracked down Imogene and Dodge. Remus shot Imogene in the gut in public, sinking the gun barrel so deep in her stomach it could hardly be heard. No matter, Remus turned himself in. Being the best criminal lawyer he knew, he defended himself at trial. He pleaded "temporary maniacal insanity," won his case, and spent six months in a mental hospital. Remus lived another uneventful twenty years, dying in 1952 at age seventy-seven.

MOONSHINE

The only real requirement for a whiskey to be called *moonshine* is that it be made illegally. It's typically made from corn but, since it has no legal definition, it can be made from any grain or other sugar source. The term came into general use during Prohibition to describe the potion that rural folk cooked up by the light of the moon. They worked at night so that the smoke from their stills would not be detected by nearby revenuers. It would not be accurate to say that moonshining, to avoid the excise tax, was anything new during Prohibition, but the 18th Amendment to the Constitution certainly didn't hurt the trade. Today, if you see "moonshine" used on a label in a liquor store, it is probably corn (or white) whiskey with a marketing device glued on. It'll have a mash bill that contains 80% to 100% corn. Moonshine won't be aged at all; corn whiskey is a segment of the whiskey market like no other.

Let's meet a couple of real backwoods moonshiners. They weren't city slickers, like those *highfalutin* (this one also goes way back as well) speakeasy goers. Today they would be called "hillbillies."[2]

---

2   Lots of grocers and mercantile store owners during Prohibition made "bathtub gin." These stories ain't about them.

WHERE DOES THE TERM "HILLBILLY" COME FROM?

"Hillbilly" was a term used by English and Irish Catholics to belittle the Irish Protestants who lived in the hill country. William of Orange, an English royal from the Dutch Republic, was installed to rule Ireland and to convert its inhabitants to Protestantism. William became known as "Billy" to disparage him. His followers became "hillbillies."

Maggie Bailey: The Queen of the Moonshiners

Maggie Bailey was born in 1905 and lived to be 101 years old. For eighty of those years, starting when she was about age seventeen, Maggie made and sold moonshine from her home in the hills of Harlan County, KY. She often wore a T-shirt that read "National Distillery."

Maggie was a beloved citizen. She had no children of her own but did raise two nephews. When times were tough, Maggie gave food to neighbors and gave financial assistance so that the children of friends could go to college and law school. She spent two of her 101 years in a federal reformatory for women. Her friend and lawyer, Mr. Otis Doan, wrote about her court appearance:

> Well, they loved Maggie. You gotta remember, when Maggie walked into the courtroom, you'd see someone who reminded you of your grandmother. She had grayish hair. She wore a print dress with an apron, and that's how she came to court and that's how she dressed every day.

When Maggie passed away in 2005, she was eulogized in the *Lexington Herald-Leader*, on the Jimmy Buffett fan website, and on National Public Radio. The character Mag in the FX television series *Justified* is based on Maggie Bailey.

Popcorn Sutton: The Johnny Appleseed of Moonshine

Marvin "Popcorn" Sutton was born in 1946 and lived in western North Carolina and eastern Tennessee. He came from a long line of Scots-Irish ancestors who made their own *likker*. Marvin was dubbed "Popcorn" in his twenties when he got "three-thirds" drunk and attacked a popcorn machine with a pool cue.

Popcorn came from the hills; his appearance personified that of someone from the backwoods. But he was no *hick* or *scam*. In his lifetime, he wrote a self-published autobiographical guide to moonshining and also produced a home video depicting his moonshining activities. He was the subject of several documentaries. One film on Popcorn by Neal Hutcheson, *The Last One*, received a Southeast Region Emmy Award in 2009. Popcorn knew how to take advantage of his celebrity. He charged a fee for pictures and autographs, sold "hillbilly hats," ran an "antique" store, and, of course, sold moonshine.

Popcorn was convicted of illegal activities five times but never served a prison sentence. In 2007, a fire on his property led to the discovery of 650 gallons of untaxed alcohol. In 2008, an undercover agent for the Bureau of Alcohol, Tobacco, Firearms, and Explosives found another nine hundred gallons of moonshine owned by Popcorn. He was convicted of moonshining, parole violation, and illegal firearms possession. Popcorn

Popcorn at his still.

pled guilty and asked for house arrest; he was dying of cancer. At age sixty-two he said he would rather die than go to jail. The judge denied his request and sentenced him to eighteen months in federal prison. No way Popcorn was going to jail; he committed suicide in his car from carbon monoxide poisoning in March 2009. The epitaph on Popcorn's gravestone reads, "Popcorn says fuck you."

Hank Williams II attended Popcorn's memorial service. It may not simply have been to pay his respects to a fallen hero but also to discuss a business deal with Popcorn's wife, Pam Manning. Together they started producing *Popcorn Sutton's Tennessee White Whiskey*, claimed to be produced in stills designed by Popcorn and using his secret family recipe and techniques. In recent years, the distillery was sold, and the stills were replaced with new copper and brass ones.

But the story doesn't end there. Regina Sutton Chennault is a nationally known trauma surgeon[3] living in Anchorage, AK. She produced a birth certificate claiming she was Popcorn's only legitimate daughter and therefore the true heir to all his royalties.

WHAT DOES XXX ON A JUG OF MOONSHINE STAND FOR?

The XXX on a jug or bottle of moonshine stand for the number of times the contents had been run through the still before it was bottled. The more Xs, the purer the 'shine.

---

3   Chennault relates she discovered her interest in trauma surgery when, while watching TV at six years old, a man showed up at Popcorn's trailer door with a knife in his neck. After getting her medical degree at the University of Texas at Houston, she married Red Duke, another trauma surgeon. Red's greatest claim to fame is that he operated on Governor John Connally when he was injured at the assassination of President John Kennedy in Dallas, TX.

Chennault claimed that Popcorn had twelve children and four wives, none of whom he ever divorced.

OUTSMARTING THE REVENUERS AND THE BIRTH OF NASCAR

Henry Ford hated liquor, but it certainly helped make his fortune. Bootleggers needed fast cars and the Ford Coupe flathead V8 was one of their favorites, sometimes souped-up with a more powerful Cadillac engine and heavy-duty shock absorbers and springs. The bootleggers would use fake license plates and wear shoes with the bottoms fashioned to look like hoofs, so they left no human footprints in the woods.

Robert Glenn "Junior" Johnson

Robert Glenn Johnson Jr. claims that running moonshine was the hardest work in the world:

> . . .starting at about midnight, they'd [the bootleggers] be coming out of the woods in every direction. . .the roads was full of bootleggers. . .careening through the darkness, old Carolina moon. . .all the cars registered under phony names.

Hard work? Maybe so, but it also showed folks Johnson had a gift for driving—at the age of fourteen.

Of all Junior's family members, his mother was the only one never sent to prison. In 1955, Junior got caught at his father's still, not while he was driving (let's be clear) and before his stock car racing career was about to pick up speed. He was caught by Joseph Edison Carter who gave a humble assessment of the circumstances:

> You know I couldn't catch him in his souped-up hot rod liquor car [a Ford with Cadillac V8 ambulance motor] and me driving a goddamn government purchased Mickey Mouse mechanical miscarriage called an automobile.

Junior Johnson gets a (legit) job.

Junior served eleven months of a two-year sentence in jail. Junior took over his dad's moonshine business and at one point employed thirty-five people, ten freight trucks, and two tractor trailers in addition to his fleet of liquor cars.

By the late 1940s, Bill France Sr. had realized Americans had a need for speed, so he could organize car races and make them profitable. Certainly, the moonshine transportation industry could provide a ready-made farm system for race car drivers. France began the National Association for Stock Car Auto Racing (NASCAR) and was its first president. NASCAR is still a family-owned business today.

Luckily, France Sr. could spot talent when he saw it. In a telegram, he offered Junior Johnson a job as a race car driver, with only one stipulation; Junior would have a job with a major racing team and make $10,000 a year "provided he is placed on probation." Years later, President Ronald Reagan pardoned Junior.

Junior's accomplishments making fast left turns are the stuff of legend. He was a six-time Winston Cup Series winner, is a member of the International Motorsports Hall of Fame, and the NASCAR Hall of

Fame. In 1988, he was named one of NASCAR's 50 Greatest Drivers.[4]

WHISKEY IN THE WHITE HOUSE: THE FIRST HALF OF THE 20TH CENTURY

Theodore Roosevelt (26th president, 1901–1909). Roosevelt, called "a damn cowboy" by his political opponents, became president when William McKinley was shot. TR called himself "a temperate man." He even fought with newspaper reporters who claimed otherwise. While it may be true that Teddy eschewed whiskey served neat or on the rocks, he had a weakness for Mint Juleps made with rye whiskey instead of bourbon. When he settled down, the leader of the Rough Riders in the Spanish-American War—who would "speak softly and carry a big stick"—traded his big stick for a tennis racket and the favorite drink of the Kentucky Derby (over a hundred thousand Mint Juleps are served on Derby Day at Churchill Downs).

William Howard Taft (27th president, 1909–1913). William Howard Taft was a man of considerable size; he managed to top out at over three hundred pounds without the assistance of much alcohol. After six months of research, Taft authored the Taft Decision that defined for the first time the different varieties of whiskey; straight, blended, and imitation (which included Scotch and Irish whiskey).[5]

Woodrow Wilson (28th president, 1913–1921). Woodrow Wilson was president when the Volstead Act passed, after Congress overrode his veto. He had a wine cellar in the White House (presumably secured

---

4   It is alleged that the early NASCAR drivers kept a flask of whiskey in their cars as necessary equipment when they raced. Very bad idea. Alcohol may be "liquid courage" but it is also a Performance Inhibiting Drug.

5   Taft was also the first president to throw out the first pitch on opening day of the baseball season.

before the Volstead Act went into effect). Wilson suf-fered a debilitating stroke halfway through his second term and the country principally was run by his wife, Edith, for the remainder of his presidency. He also enjoyed Scotch as medicine in his later years.

Warren Gamaliel Harding (29ᵗʰ president, 1921–1923). Harding ran for office as a dry candidate, but his love of whiskey was well-known (as well as his affin-ity for chewing tobacco). He kept a bottle of whis-key in his golf bag. Theodore Roosevelt's daughter, Alice, wrote of the Harding White House: "The air heavy with tobacco smoke, trays and bottles contain-ing every imaginable brand of whiskey stood about, cards and poker chips ready at hand. . ." Harding died of unknown causes, perhaps heart failure; his wife refused to allow an autopsy.

Calvin Coolidge (30ᵗʰ president, 1923–1929). Silent Cal was not much of a drinker, and not much of a personality either. Social critic and writer Dorothy Parker supposedly said upon Coolidge's death, "How could they tell?"

Herbert Hoover (31ˢᵗ president, 1929–1933). Hoover was a proponent of Prohibition, whether he favored it or not, and kept liquor out of the White House. Oddly, he suggested to his son Herbert Hoover Jr., when Junior was appointed to the State Department during the Eisenhower presidency, to keep a bottle of whiskey in his bottom desk drawer. Hmm.

Franklin Delano Roosevelt (32ⁿᵈ president, 1933–1945). FDR ran for president on the platform plank that Prohibition should be abolished. Hoover, who he defeated, gave tepid endorsement to the 18ᵗʰ Amendment although he realized it was not working. Roosevelt loved mixed drinks, and loved mixing them for guests, mostly with gin (a martini), but occasion-ally with whiskey (a Manhattan).[6]

While moonshine was as simple and down home as whiskey could get, the native American spirit was about to reveal its more sophisticated side.

---

6   In addition to being fifth cousin to Teddy, genealogists believe FDR was related to ten other presidents, by blood or marriage. There are two fathers and sons who served as president, one grandfather and grandson, and a pair of second cousins.

WHAT DOES MOONSHINE TASTE LIKE?

Junior Johnson's *Midnight Moon Moonshine*
Piedmont Distillers, in Madison, NC, asked Junior Johnson to help them make a moonshine based on his celebrated recipe. It is crafted in small batches by a small batch of 'shiners but they use a state-of-the-art hybrid copper pot/column still. To get the distillate down to 80 proof (40% ABV), *Midnight Moon* is made with water filtered five times. There is no age statement, of course, because it ain't aged.

Just the Facts

Mash Bill	Corn: 100% Barley: a touch
Proof	Proof: 100 ABV: 40%
Age; Barrel Char	Unaged
Chill Filtered?	No, but triple distilled (XXX)

TASTING NOTES

From: The Piedmont Distillery website
https://www.juniorsmidnightmoon.com/spirits-index

The distillery's website provides a brief tasting note: "slightly sweet, ultra-smooth, and clean tasting."

From: The Over a Barrel Gang
Looks: Clear.
Aroma: Light. Corn, peach, black pepper, apple, apricot, maple.
Flavor: Medium body. Sweet, bitter, salty.
Mouth Feel: Delicate, round, sharp.
Going Down: Medium strength, medium length.
Notes: Pleasant on the palate; surprising after the nose.

Some Other Moonshine Choices

If you discover you enjoy unaged corn whiskey and want to try some other varieties, you will find that there is much more variation in their aromas, flavors, and finishes than you would expect from the relatively limited variations in mash bills and aging (none at all). Several websites contain lists of unaged corn whiskey that they deem the best.[7] Here are the consensus top selections:

1. *Troy & Sons Platinum* (Asheville, NC). ashevilledistilling.com/product/ts-platium
2. *Buffalo Trace White Dog Mash #1* (Frankfort, KY). https://www.buffalotracedistillery.com/our-brands/white-dog/white-dog-mash-1.html
3. Junior Johnson's *Midnight Moon Moonshine* (Madison, NC). https://www.juniorsmidnightmoon.com/moonshine
4. *Tim Smith's Climax Moonshine* (Culpepper, VA) https://www.timsmithspirits.com/climax-spirits
5. *Ole Smoky Tennessee Moonshine* (Gatlinburg, TN) https://olesmoky.com/
6. *Hudson New York Corn Whiskey* (Gardiner, NY) https://www.newyorkcraftspirits.com/products/hudson-new-york-corn-whiskey?variant=16331793670
7. *Popcorn Sutton's Tennessee White Whiskey* (Newport, TN). http://popcornsutton.com/
   [Sad to say, this corn whiskey may no longer be in production, though you might be able to find some online, at a cost.]

Toast

Who else but Popcorn Sutton could provide a toast for sippin' moonshine:

"Jesus turned water into wine; I turned it into likker. And I don't think there's anything wrong with it, 'cause they drunk wine back in Biblical times and any kind of shit like that. . . "

To Maggie Bailey, Popcorn Sutton, and all the folks down in the holler.

---

7   Here are the web addresses, if you want to further your study:

https://www.huffpost.com/entry/moonshine-taste-test-legal_n_4435347

https://www.southernliving.com/travel/best-legal-moonshine

https://swirled.com/best-moonshine-brands/

https://www.wideopencountry.com/legal-moonshine-10-best-brands-in-america/

DINNER AT THE SEELBACH HOTEL, LOUISVILLE, KY, WITH GEORGE AND IMOGENE REMUS

In Chapter 3 of *The Great Gatsby*, F. Scott Fitzgerald provides a description of the gatherings at the home of Jay Gatsby: "At least once a fortnight a corps of caterers garnished [buffet tables] with glistening hors d'oeuvres, spiced baked hams crowded against salads of harlequin designs and pastry pigs and turkeys bewitched to a dark gold." The two recipes below will let you eat like a big-time bootlegger or like the more modest folks in hill country.

Recipe: Hot Brown Sandwich

From: https://www.brownhotel.com/dining/hot-brown

The Hot Brown sandwich was created by Chef Fred Schmidt at The Brown Hotel in Louisville, KY, in the 1920s. It was served for breakfast to guests who were tired of traditional ham and eggs. It is an open-faced turkey sandwich with bacon, tomatoes, and a Mornay sauce.

Ingredients:

[This recipe serves 2; it is a big dish for a multi-course dinner, so adjust accordingly. Consider making this recipe and cutting the Hot Browns into smaller portions. Maybe make a bit more if people are yelling for an encore.]:

    2 ounces whole butter

    2 ounces all-purpose flour

    8 ounces heavy cream

    8 ounces whole milk

    ½ cup Pecorino Romano cheese plus 1 tablespoon for garnish

    Pinch of ground nutmeg

    Salt and Pepper to Taste

    14 ounces sliced roasted turkey breast, sliced thick

    4 slices Texas toast (crust trimmed)

    4 slices crispy bacon

    2 Roma tomatoes, sliced in half

    Paprika

    Parsley

Directions:

In a two-quart saucepan, melt butter and slowly whisk in flour until combined and it forms a thick paste (roux). Continue to cook roux for two minutes over medium-low heat, stirring frequently. Whisk heavy cream and whole milk into roux and cook over medium heat until cream begins to simmer, about 2–3 minutes. Remove sauce from heat and slowly whisk in Pecorino Romano cheese until the Mornay sauce is smooth. Add nutmeg, salt and pepper to taste.

    For each Hot Brown, place two slices of toast with the crusts cut off in an oven safe dish—one slice is cut in half corner to corner to make two triangles and the other slice is left in a square shape—then cover with 7 ounces of turkey. Take the two halves of Roma tomato and two toast points and set them alongside the base of the turkey and toast. Next, pour one half of the Mornay sauce to completely cover the dish. Sprinkle with additional Pecorino Romano cheese. Place the entire dish in the oven. Suggested bake time is 20 minutes at 350°F. When the cheese begins to brown and bubble, remove from the oven, cross two pieces of crispy bacon on top, sprinkle with paprika and parsley, and serve immediately.

Recipe: Wonder Beef Cups

From: Wonder. (2007). *The Wonder Bread Cookbook.* Berkeley, CA: Ten Speed Press. P. 41.

The *Hot Brown* might have been a choice of the more successful moonshiners and bootleggers. Here's one that was in everybody's reach. When *Wonder Bread* first appeared on grocery shelves in the early 1920s it was the best thing since, well, sliced bread. Come to think of it, it was one of the first pre-sliced breads on the market. But that's not all—it "helps build strong bodies in 8 ways."

Ingredients (serves 6):

3 tablespoons butter, at room temperature
12 slices Wonder bread
1¼ pounds ground beef
1 egg
1 small onion, chopped
1 (10¾ounce) can creamed mushroom soup
Salt and pepper to taste
¾ cup shredded cheddar cheese

Directions:

Preheat oven to 350°F. Butter one side of each slice of Wonder bread and press each slice butter side down into the cups of a muffin tin. In a medium bowl, mix together the ground beef, egg, onion, soup, salt, and pepper until well blended. Fill each bread cup with the mixture. Sprinkle shredded cheddar cheese over the top.

Bake for 30 minutes, or until the meat is cooked through. Gently lift out of the muffin tins and serve immediately.

MUSIC THAT WAS INSPIRED BY MOONSHINE

In the South during the Prohibition Era the places you drank socially might be called *nip joints* or *shot houses*. All these songs celebrate, or condemn, moonshine.

Copper Kettle, performed by Bob Dylan (1970)

This song's origin is disputed. What's for certain is that it'll teach you the recipe for making moonshine and how to drink it when it's ready ("in the pale moonlight").

Mountain Dew, performed by Willie Nelson (1972)

This number originated as an Appalachian folk song. This version was written by a North Carolina lawyer, Bascom Lunsford, who defended moonshiners in court. His lyrics included a chorus about such a court appearance. The words were changed by Scotty Wiseman, who bought the song from Lunsford in 1937 for $25, but Wiseman paid Lunsford half the royalties for the rest of his life. Does Willie Nelson's melody sound a little like *On the Road Again*?

Bootlegger Blues, performed by Mississippi Sheiks (1997)

The Sheiks were a country blues and popular music band of the 1930s, composed mostly of Chatmon family members from Mississippi. Their biggest hit, *Sitting on Top of the World*, was covered by the rock band *Cream*, on their third album *Wheels on Fire*, in 1968.

Chug-A-Lug, performed by Roger Miller (1964)

This was the second hit for the *King of the Road* (Miller's biggest hit). It relates the story of a youthful encounter with strong liquor. It was a kinda harsh experience, *dang me*.

White Lightning, performed by George Jones (1959)

Jones, who had a drinking problem, did eighty takes of this song and was almost decked by the upright bass player whose fingers became severely blistered. They ended up using the first take. The song was written by J. P. Richardson, better known as "The Big Bopper" (and performer of *Chantilly Lace*).

George Jones.
Lobby card for Country Music on Broadway, 1964.

Ballad of Thunder Road, performed by Robert Mitchum (1967)

Mitchum wrote the lyrics for this song, which was the theme song for the movie *Thunder Road* that he starred in.

Moonshiner's Life, performed by Hank Williams III (2010)

This song contains a shout-out to Popcorn Sutton. Hank III is the third-generation Williams musician. He is channeling the bootleggers here, but he is equally well-known for punk rock and heavy metal music.

HOME FROM THE WAR AND READY TO PARTY

Chapter 12
AMERICA (AND BOURBON) TAKES FLIGHT

I drink to make other people more interesting.
—Ernest Hemingway

WHISKEY AND WORLD WAR II

Whiskey was certainly a part of American soldiers' gear during WWII; it provided courage, relief from pain, and celebration for victories hard fought. No single individual embodies the story of war and whiskey better (but maybe not for his better) than the great American writer, Ernest Hemingway. Hemingway, in his own way, defined what it meant to be a real man, or to be *macho*, for a generation of Americans.

Ernest Hemingway

Ernest Miller Hemingway, born in 1899, was a writer of fiction and nonfiction of no less stature than Mark Twain.[2] He would be a correspondent and sometime soldier in three hot wars and one cold war before his death in 1961. He loved being in war but was not able to enlist because of poor eyesight. Some have speculated that his love of conflict and his belligerent personality derived from his abusive father, who beat him with a barber's strop, but who also taught him to hunt and fish

Hemingway (on right) and friends
Likely outside the Ritz-Carlton in Paris. Hemingway's canteen is reputed to have contained pre-mixed martinis.[1]

---

1 Hemingway was an equal opportunity drinker, but his favorite whiskey was *Old Forester* bourbon.

2 Hemingway believed "all Modern American literature comes from one book by Mark Twain called *Huckleberry Finn*."

in northern Michigan, and his professed hatred for his mother, who made him wear girl's clothes until he was age six and tried to have him play the cello.

Hemingway became a Red Cross ambulance driver in WWI, at age eighteen. He won an Italian Medal of Honor for taking care of wounded soldiers while he was injured himself.[3]

As his fame as a writer grew, Hemingway penned his tribute to whisky:

> I have drunk since I was fifteen and few things give me more pleasure. When you work hard all day with your head and you know you must work again the next day what else can change your ideas and make them run on a different plane than whisky? When you are cold and wet what else can warm you? . . . The only time it isn't good for you is when you must write or when you fight.

In the Spanish Civil War, Hemingway served as a correspondent for a large syndicate of newspapers, the *North American Newspaper Alliance*. This is when he took on his anti-fascist leaning that would last his lifetime. He was one of the last journalists to leave the battlefield when the Republicans lost their final big battle to Francisco Franco and the Nationalists.

In World War II, Hemingway was present at the Allies' invasion at Normandy as a reporter, but he was not allowed to go ashore; his fame made him too important to risk his life. After the beach was taken and the troops moved inland, Ernest often acted as a soldier instead of as a chronicler of the war. Hemingway became the de facto leader of a small village militia and provided reconnaissance for the Office of Strategic Services (OSS) as it prepared for the invasion of Paris. A senior OSS officer concluded

Hemingway was a rare combination of "advised recklessness" and caution, he was "a born leader of men and, in spite of strong independence of character. . .a highly disciplined individual."[4] Ernest had his own jeep to move him around. His jeep driver may have most succinctly described what it was like to fight a war with Hemingway: "Best outfit I have ever been with. No [Army] discipline. Got to admit that. Drinking all the time. Got to admit that."

Having a civilian lead a militia was against the Geneva Convention and Hemingway was brought up on charges. He argued he was only giving advice and was acquitted. He was present at the liberation of Paris. He was present at the Battle of the Bulge but was too ill with pneumonia to be on the front.

Hemingway's WWI injury and WWII pneumonia were only the beginnings of a string of injuries thought to have contributed to his heavy drinking and ultimate demise. He:

- suffered a concussion from a car accident in London during WWII;
- had two car accidents that left him with a smashed knee and a visible scar on his forehead;
- suffered from headaches, high blood pressure, weight problems, and diabetes after WWII;
- was in two plane crashes while on safari in Africa; in one he used his head to push the door open (probably leading to a leakage of his cerebral fluid), suffered burns, two cracked discs, kidney and liver ruptures, and a dislocated shoulder;
- fell on his boat, *Pilar*, and hit his head on the gaff, leading to another concussion, this time with bleeding.

After WWII, Ernest shuttled between homes in Idaho, Wyoming, Florida, and Cuba, his favorite place of all. His politics were, well, confused. He hated the

---

3   Ernest was wounded by mortar fire and spent six months in the hospital. *A Farewell to Arms* is informed by this experience.

4   Hemingway is credited with having saved the life of another war correspondent, Andy Rooney (yes, the curmudgeon from the CBS television news show, *Sixty Minutes*).

way the veterans of WWI were treated after the war. He thought the West had been remiss in not aiding the Republican cause during the Spanish Civil War (the Russians did), and that Russia had not been properly recognized for its contributions, and losses, in the defeat of the Nazis. Hemingway referred to himself as a "premature anti-fascist;" he aided the Soviet Union for a while (he would bring caviar and whisky to his meetings with Soviet agents, two rare commodities they loved him for providing).

In 1947, Hemingway was awarded the Bronze Star. His friends thought this might have been a way to keep him from being investigated by the House on Un-American Activities Committee (HUAC). Ernest believed he was being followed by federal agents and his mail was being read. Yes, both HUAC and the

HEMINGWAY AND FIDEL CASTRO

Hemingway supported Fidel Castro in his fight again Fulgencio Batista for control of Cuba and before Fidel became a communist. During the cold war, Hemingway worked for the United States reporting on Spanish businessmen visiting Cuba and doing reconnaissance on his sailboat off the shores of Havana. His wife at the time, Mary Welch, thought his principal motivation was to get fuel during wartime so he could have a *blast* fishing and drinking with his friends. Hemingway met Castro only once, at a fishing tournament, and broke with him politically when Castro began nationalizing property. Ernest's home outside Havana, the *Finca Vigia*, where he slept on the floor with five dogs and eleven six-toed cats, was nationalized after the Bay of Pigs invasion and turned into a museum. His break with the communists was final when they thought his book, *For Whom the Bell Tolls*, was too politically even-handed.

Statue of *Barfly* Hemingway at his favorite seat at La Floridita, Havana, Cuba.
The picture of Hemingway and Castro hanging on the bar wall was taken the only time the two met.

HEMINGWAY'S MAJOR WORKS

The Sun Also Rises (1926)
This book portrays American and British expatriates who travel from Paris to the Festival of San Fermin in Pamplona to watch the running of the bulls and the bull fights. It presents Hemingway's notions of America's "Lost Generation," considered to have been decadent, dissolute, and irretrievably damaged by World War I. Not so, suggests Hemingway; the veterans were resilient and strong. The book also examines themes of love and death, the power of nature, and the notion of masculinity. *Sun* was later criticized for misogyny, anti-Semitism, homophobia, and racism.

A Farewell to Arms (1929)
Arms is based on Hemingway's experiences in WW I. Its focus is a love affair between an expatriate and an English nurse.

Snows of Kilimanjaro
Snows is a short story with four separate references to having a whiskey and soda.

For Whom the Bell Tolls (1940)
This is Hemingway's most famous novel. It tells the story of Robert Jordan, a young American in the International Brigades attached to a republican guerrilla unit during the Spanish Civil War.

Old Man and the Sea (1951)
Santiago, an aging Cuban fisherman, struggles with a giant marlin far out in the Gulf Stream off the coast of Cuba.

Federal Bureau of Investigation (FBI) had files on Hemingway. FBI Director J. Edgar Hoover had been keeping a close eye on him since WWII. You're not paranoid if they truly are out to get you, but there is no evidence the United States government ever did anything but surveil Hemingway.[5]

In 1954 Ernest was awarded the Nobel Prize for Literature for "his mastery of the art of narrative, most recently demonstrated in *The Old Man and the Sea*,

and for the influence that he has exerted on contemporary style."

After numerous bouts with depression and paranoia, Hemingway committed suicide in 1961 in Ketchum, ID. He had undergone electroconvulsive therapy over a dozen times. His father, sister, and brother had all committed suicide before him. His granddaughter, Margaux committed suicide thirty-five years after Ernest's death and became the fifth member of the family in four generations to take their own life. The actress Mariel Hemingway, known best for her performances in the movies *Lipstick* (1976) and *Manhattan* (1979), for which she received a nomination for Best Supporting Actress, is also a grandchild of Ernest.

---

5   In 1958, Ernest and a friend took half an hour to throw a cache of weapons from his fishing boat into the sea. His wife, Mary Welsh, who accompanied them, was amazed when she saw the heavy guns, rifles, sawed-off shotguns, hand grenades, mysterious canisters, and belts of ammunition thrown overboard. She hadn't known the weapons were on the boat and that she had been sleeping atop a small arsenal.

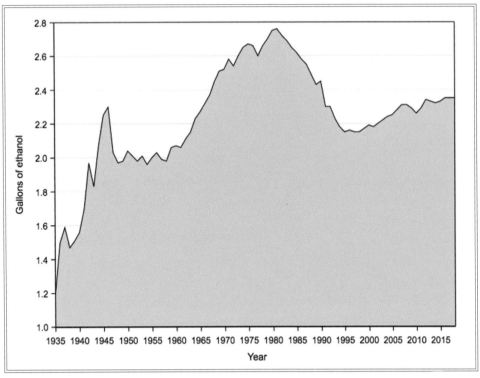

Total per capita ethanol consumption all types, United States, 1935–2017.[6]

THE POST-WAR BLUES[6]

Two developments conspired to diminish whiskey's place in American life immediately after the Second World War, especially the native spirits of bourbon and rye. First, Prohibition had served to decrease the amount of bourbon and rye being distilled in the United States. This gave a competitive advantage to Scotch, Irish, and Canadian spirits. Though these libations were still illegal in America during Prohibition, they were certainly more readily available (and probably of better quality) than their American brethren to quench the thirst of those speakeasy patrons. Second, distilleries in the

United States were converted to industrial alcohol to help the war effort. But not to worry, help was on the way, in the form of true American ingenuity and entrepreneurship. If there was a gentler 1950s counterweight to Hemingway's macho, it was exemplified by the family of William Samuels, Sr.

THE SAMUELS FAMILY

The Samuels family involvement with whisky spans many generations. Robert Samuels served in the Pennsylvania militia during the Revolutionary War; he was the company distiller. Taylor William (T. W.) Samuels was the owner of a distillery and sheriff of Nelson County, KY. Taylor's nephews Frank and Jesse James resigned from the Confederate Army and turned in their guns on T. W.'s front porch (they acquired new ones, however). Leslie B. Samuels kept the family distillery operating until Prohibition. After the 18th Amendment was repealed, the T. W. Samuels

6   From: Slater, M. E. and Alpert, H. R. (2019). Surveillance report #113. Apparent per capita alcohol consumption: National start, and regional trends, 1977–2017. https://pubs.niaaa.nih.gov/publications/surveillance113/CONS17.htm

Distillery, under the watchful eye of William Samuels Sr., barely survived. It was shuttered during World War II. Bill, Sr. "retired" at age thirty-seven.[7]

But retirement wasn't for Bill, Sr. or his wife, Margie. She told him to "get off his ass" and do something. Bill, Sr. wanted to start distilling again. Margie agreed under two conditions: He could not produce the same, harsh-tasting whisky his father produced ("that shit will blow your ears off") and she wanted to design the bottle.

Bill, Sr. put together an advisory committee to help him fashion a unique mash bill and distilling process. He called on a few friends with a bit of expertise in the whiskey business, including Jere Beam (the son of Jim Beam), "Hap" Motlow (the son of Jack Daniel's partner Lem Motlow), Ed Shapira (one of the masterminds that created the Heaven Hill distillery), and Julian "Pappy" Van Winkle.[8] Meanwhile in the kitchen, Margie was experimenting by baking 150+ loaves of bread in different combinations of the grains that give whisky its taste.

Bill, Sr. decided to make a bourbon with wheat as the second ingredient, as suggested by Pappy, instead of rye. This mash bill would produce a milder whisky with less of a bite. Samuels used a roller mill for his grain, as opposed to a hammer mill, to avoid scalding the wheat. He used relatively small fermenters and squatter pot stills to create more interaction

Margie Samuels.

between the liquid and the copper. As the business grew, the equipment was reproduced in the original size, not enlarged, so the flavor profile would not be altered. The barrels were left outside to be seasoned to reduce tannins before they were charred. They were rotated by hand in the rickhouse, so that the climate conditions were the same for all of the barrels over the life of the aging process, thus promoting consistency in taste. This is still the process used today.

Margie Samuels

Margie moved from the kitchen to the basement, along with her deep fryer. Using her expertise in chemistry, Margie went to work on a sealing wax for the whisky bottle. She experimented with different color pigments and viscosities until she hit on what struck her as perfect. She dipped the neck of the bottle into the wax, turned it upright, and let the wax drip down the bottleneck. And so was born the trademark look of the Samuel's distillery.[9]

Margie was not only a chemist (and bread baker) but she also had a great sense of design and had studied calligraphy. She molded a prototype bottle out of papier mâché. She drew the label by hand and used a tattered edging to resemble a bottle of French cognac.

Not all things went down so smooth. The Samuels family could not use their own name on the label because it was owned by the distillery that Bill, Sr. had quit when he "retired." Margie created the S[IV] logo and put it on her label. She named the whisky

---

7   There may be two earlier generations of Samuels distillers, but these have evaporated over time.

8   The Pappy Van Winkle line of whiskeys (now made at the Buffalo Trace Distillery) is the most sought-after brand of American whiskeys. Pappy shared recipes and technical tips with Bill, Sr. Kentucky distillers are a tight-knit group.

9   A six-week trial in the Sixth Circuit Court in 2012 versus the Diageo alcoholic beverage company resulted in the red dripping wax seal being ruled a valid trademark. The court concluded "*Maker's Mark* occupies a central place in the story of bourbon."

Maker's Mark; the logo stood for her husband who was the fourth generation of registered distillers in the Samuels family.

The Burks' Spring Distillery in Loretto, KY, was where *Maker's Mark* began operation in 1953. It released its first bottle in 1958. Margie believed the Victorian look of the distillery would appeal to history-minded visitors. She was right again. In 1980, Burks' Spring, renamed Maker's Mark Distillery, became the first distillery to be named to the National Registry of Historic Places and was the first stop on the Kentucky Bourbon Trail.[10]

William (Bill) Samuels, Jr.

The Samuels family wanted their business to remain small and produce a high-quality bourbon that would sell itself by word-of-mouth. That didn't last long. The family's fifth generation in the whisky business, William (Bill) Samuels, Jr. saw to that. He was, and is, a marketing genius.

In his teens, Bill Jr. worked as chauffeur and gofer for Harland Sanders, the Colonel Sanders who began the Kentucky Fried Chicken (KFC) fast food chain.[11] He received his bachelor's degree from Case Western Reserve, then a master's degree in engineering from the University of California at Berkeley. He worked as a rocket scientist for Aerojet General on the Polaris missile system but was fired after an engine he

designed fell off and caused much damage. Deciding that maybe engineering wasn't for him, Bill, Jr. went to law school at Vanderbilt.

Upon his return to the family business, Bill, Sr. put Bill, Jr. in charge of finding more customers. Though his father was skeptical, Bill, Jr. suggested that they hire an advertising agency. His intent was to position *Maker's Mark* for upscale consumers as a "premium bourbon whisky," a term that was an oxymoron at the time. In 1965, *Maker's* ran its first ad in the *New Yorker* magazine. It contained one of the most memorable and successful tag lines of all time: "It tastes expensive. . .and is."

Bill, Jr. wasn't done. His next master stroke was to get *Maker's* onto airline beverage carts. There, this American bourbon had a captive audience of upwardly mobile travelers who were more familiar with drinking expensive Scotch whiskies and other spirits. Bill, Jr. became *Maker's* Chief Executive Officer in 1975.[12]

In 1980, the "airline strategy" caught the attention of *Wall Street Journal* reporter, David Garino. Or maybe, Garino was hoodwinked into paying attention. Bill, Jr. had a friend, Sam Walker, who went to journalism school with Garino. Bill, Jr. also knew the bartender at The Brown Hotel in Louisville, KY, where the reporter was staying. Samuels arranged a celebration at the distillery and gave exclusive rights to broadcast it to a local television station. Walker made sure Garino was at the bar near a television when the story aired. He asked if Garino wanted to meet Bill, Sr. He said yes. Bill, Jr. told his dad that Garino was an old fraternity buddy, not a reporter. Garino ended up spending over two days touring the distillery.

Garino's article, headlined "*Maker's Mark* Goes Against the Grain to Make its Mark," explained how the rural distillery was finding success through a

---

10 Distilleries are not known for being environmentally friendly. At the Burks' Spring Distillery, however, the Samuels built a waste treatment plant that uses converted methane gas to power 25% of the operation. It also has an anaerobic digester that turns the spent grain into food for cattle and a solar array that offsets the power needs of the rickhouse complex.

11 In a famous episode, Bill, Jr. watched the Colonel rip a fryer out of the wall at one of his restaurants because the employees weren't following his recipe. When Bill, Jr. asked why he did it, the Colonel replied, "So I won't have to do it again." Lesson learned.

12 Even Fidel Castro became a fan. When the mayor of Frankfort, KY, visited Cuba in 1978 Castro asked him to send a case of *Maker's Mark*. He didn't.

strategy that most distillers considered folly. The story ran on the front page of the *Journal* on August 1, 1980. The story ignited double-digit increases in *Maker's Mark* sales over the next two decades.

In 2011, Bill, Jr. retired and turned the distillery over his son, Rob, named after that earlier Samuels relative who served in the Revolutionary War.

If the Samuels family exemplified how to mix heritage and innovation to make a great whiskey, would the broader popular culture also reward such creativity when it was fueled by the consumption of copious amounts of *gasoline* (alcohol)?

WHAT DOES AMERICA'S FIRST PREMIUM WHISKEY TASTE LIKE?

Maker's Mark Kentucky Straight Bourbon Whiskey

Maker's Mark is sweeter than most bourbons because it uses wheat in the mash bill instead of rye. *Maker's* also simmers its mash for four hours instead of the industry standard of thirty minutes. *Maker's Mark* states its water comes from "the limestone shelf where the distillery is located. . .the only distillery with its own water source and protected watershed" and that it uses an "heirloom yeast strain that's more than 150 years old. This highly guarded microorganism has been passed down to every bottle of *Maker's Mark* ever produced."

In 2010, *Maker's Mark* released *Maker's Mark 46* (named after "Project #46" in Bill, Jr.'s logbook). French oak staves are placed inside a finishing barrel and it is aged an additional nine weeks in the cooler temperatures of the industry's only limestone whisky cellar. It is bottled at 94 proof (47% ABV), not the 90 proof like the original *Maker's Mark*. There are now numerous *Maker's Mark* expressions.

Just the Facts

Mash Bill	Corn: 70% Rye: 0 Malt: 14% Wheat: 16%
Proof	Proof: 90 ABV: 45%
Age and Char Level	"When it's ready" at least 3 years, usually 6–7 years; #3
Chill Filtered?	No

TASTING NOTES

From: The Maker's Mark Distillery website

https://www.makersmark.com/makers-mark

Aging: The bourbon tells us when it's ready, and not the other way around. Barrels spend a minimum of three hot Kentucky summers in the top of the rackhouse where the whisky expands through the wood, gaining color and flavor. Unlike most distillers, Maker's Mark isn't satisfied simply setting a clock. That's why we age to taste, not time. It usually takes between six to seven years for the whisky to be ready.

Aroma: Woody oak, caramel, vanilla and wheat prevail in the nose

Palate: Sweet and balanced with caramel, vanilla and fruity essences

Finish: Smooth and subtle

From: Modern Thirst (Reviewer: Bill)

https://modernthirst.com/2016/03/25/makers-mark-bourbon-review/

Packaging: There's no denying that Maker's Mark has the most distinctive bottle in the business. They own a trademark on the red wax, and any advertisement for any product dripping with the iconic red wax is instantly recognizable as a Maker's Mark promotion. Aside from the screw-top under the wax, this is a recognized classic packaging.

Appearance: Maker's Mark pours a light straw into a Glencairn Glass.

Aroma: Light woody flavors greet the nose. There are hints of vanilla, cinnamon, and caramel just underneath. It's a light aroma, very sweet.

Flavor: True to the nose, this is light and sweet. It's heavy on baking spices- cinnamon, nutmeg, cloves. Oak plays only a small part on the mid palate, while sweet simple syrup and vanilla finish off the back of the palate. Only mildly viscous on the tongue, this lacks a little of the creaminess one might hope for with an older wheater.

Finish: Short to medium in length, but pleasant. There are some sweet spices that linger on the rear palate, namely cloves and cinnamon, but by and large, this is a crisp finish.

Synopsis: The real complaint most bourbon geeks have with Maker's Mark isn't really what's in the bottle. It's overexposure. Being a rabid fan of Maker's Mark is like being a rabid fan of Coca Cola. It's sort of the popular baseline for bourbon, not a diamond in the rough or a rare gem.

Nonetheless, it's a solid sip. It's sweet, light, and extremely easy to drink. It makes a fine cocktail, and it's affordable. As far as other wheaters in its price range, it's very competitive, perhaps even superior to standard Weller Special Reserve, and clearly superior to the 90 proof Old Fitzgerald. If you're not into sweet whiskey, you'll want to look elsewhere. There's no spiciness to this (you might consider Maker's 46 if that's what you're looking for). But if wheaters are your thing, Maker's Mark is perfectly suitable as an everyday sip.

From: The Over a Barrel Gang

Looks: Amber, gold.

Aroma: Light. Corn, black pepper, clove, orange, caramel, campfire, wood.

Flavor: Heavy body. Sweet, salty, bitter, sour.

Mouth Feel: Creamy, sharp, round, heavy.

Going Down: Medium strength, medium length.

Notes: A bourbon's bourbon, middle of the road.

Toast

In addition to his advice that one should not drink before writing or fighting, Ernest Hemingway gave this piece of advice to imbibers: "Always do sober what you said you'd do drunk. That will teach you to keep your mouth shut."

To Margie Samuels, and the lessons she taught us about innovation and entrepreneurship.

DINNER AT MAKER'S MARK DISTILLERY, LORETTO, KY, WITH BILL, SR. AND MARGIE SAMUELS AND BILL, JR.

The 1950s provided many iconic images that remain recognizable today. The *Mad Men* series captured the era for a new generation. "Hot or cold? Swedish meatballs or chicken salad?" queries Betty Draper when husband Don arrives home. When it came to style, in the 1950s Scandinavia ruled—think IKEA—especially smorgasbords. Swedish meatballs became a dinner staple of many American households in the 1950s.

Recipe: Swedish Meatballs

Gelman, J. & Zheutlin, P. (2011). *The Unofficial Mad Men Cookbook*. Dallas, TX: Smart Pop. P. 197.

Ingredients (makes 24 meatballs):
- I cup soft bread crumbs
- ⅓ cup milk
- I pound ground beef
- ½ cup finely grated onions
- I egg, beaten
- ¾ teaspoon salt
- ⅛ teaspoon ground black pepper
- ¼ – ½ teaspoon ground nutmeg
- 2 tablespoons butter
- 2 tablespoons all-purpose flour
- I beef bouillon cube, dissolved in I cup of boiling water
- ½ cup light cream or half-and-half

Directions:
1. Soften bread crumbs in milk in a mixing bowl. Drain excess milk. Add beef, onions, egg, salt, pepper, and nutmeg and mix and combine with hands.
2. Shape into balls about I inch in diameter. Melt butter in large skillet; add meatballs and brown over medium low heat. Remove with a slotted spoon to a baking dish.
3. Whisk flour into pan drippings and blend well. Cook stirring constantly, until bubbly. Gradually add beef broth to the flour mixture, stirring constantly until smooth. Add cream or half-and-half. Continue cooking for approximately 3 minutes, stirring constantly, until sauce thickens.
4. Add meatballs to sauce, and simmer for 10–15 minutes, stirring occasionally until sauce is of desired consistency. Serve warm.

Recipe: Eisenhower's Orange and Tomato Salad

From: Eisenhower Library. (1995). *Eisenhower Recipes*. Abilene, KS: National Archives and Records Administration. P. 26.

This cookbook was compiled from the archives at the Eisenhower Library in Abilene, KS. The recipes come from Ida (Dwight's mother), Dwight D., and Mamie.

Ingredients:

    3 tbsp. melted shortening

    4 tomatoes

    4 oranges

    1 tbsp. chopped parsley

    Vinegar

    Salt

Directions:

Peel oranges and tomatoes, slice and arrange alternately in salad bowl. Mix juice of two oranges with equal amounts of tarragon vinegar, add shortening and salt to taste. Pour over fruit and sprinkle parsley over top.

Recipe: Picadillo

From: Goldberg, D. Kuhn, A. & Eddy, J. (2016). *Cuba! Recipes and Stories from the Cuban Kitchen.* New York, NY: Ten Speed Press. P.47.

Ingredients (makes about 3 cups):

    2 tablespoons olive oil

    1 yellow onion

    ½ green bell pepper, stemmed, seeded, and diced

    4 cloves garlic

    1½ pounds ground beef

    ½ cup tomato sauce

    ½ cup white wine

    Salt and freshly ground pepper

    ¼ cup raisins

    2 teaspoons capers

    ¼ cup sliced pimiento-stuffed green olives

Directions:

Heat the oil over medium heat until shimmering. Add the onion and pepper and sauté until just softened, 5–7 minutes. Add the garlic and cook until fragrant, about 2 minutes. Add the beef to the pan and stir, breaking up the big chunks. Cook until the beef is browned, 10–12 minutes. Add the tomato sauce and wine and season with salt and pepper. Mix well, cover, and simmer for about 25 minutes. Stir in the raisins, capers, and olives. Taste and adjust the seasoning to taste with salt and pepper. Allow to cool slightly before using to fill the Papa Rellenas.

[Picadillo can be served in many ways. In addition to filling the potato dish called Papa Rellenas (the recipe is available in this cookbook) it can served with tacos or white rice.]

MUSIC THAT WAS ON THE RADIO IN THE 1950s

Move It On Over, performed by Hank Williams (1947)

Williams is perhaps the most revered country music artist of them all. But his career spanned less than two decades; Hank was an alcoholic. At one performance, he fell off the stage and badly hurt his back. He died at twenty-nine years old from heart failure, probably brought on by drink and abuse of pain killers. Williams penned many country standards, including *Jambalaya*, and *I Saw the Light*. *Move It On Over*, released in 1947, is claimed by many to be the first rock & roll song.

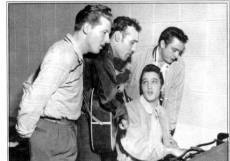

Jerry Lee Lewis, Carl Perkins, Elvis Presley, and Johnny Cash.
Sun Studios, Memphis TN, December 4, 1956.

Rock Around the Clock, performed by Bill Haley and His Comets (1954)

Rock is also a contender for the first rock and roll song. Haley and His Comets also gave us *Shake, Rattle and Roll* and *See You Later Alligator*. Haley starred in the first Rock & Roll musical film named for this song. Alcoholism contributed to his death as well.

At Last, performed by Etta James (1960)

Twenty years after this song was written, James recorded the version of *At Last* known to all. It has been on the soundtrack of over a dozen movies and television shows. Beyonce sang it to Barack and Michelle Obama at Barack's inaugural ball.

Love Me Tender, performed by Elvis Presley (1956)

How many movies can you name that got their title from a song? *Love Me Tender* is one of them. The movie was Elvis' acting debut. He got third billing behind Robert Egan and Debra Paget.

The Great Pretender, performed by The Platters (1955)

The Platters had forty singles make the Top 100 over a dozen years. The music style is doo wop, a type of rhythm and blues featuring tight harmonies. It was popular in New York City in the 1950s and was briefly revived in the 1970s by the band, Sha Na Na. You may still be able to catch The Platters on tour but don't expect to see any of the original members.

Fever, performed by Peggy Lee (1958)

Born Norma Deloris Egstrom, Lee was a blues-influenced singer. This is a torch song for the ages. She was a songwriter as well, contributing her songs (and distinctive voice) to Disney's *Lady and the Tramp*.

I Walk the Line, performed by Johnny Cash (1956)

This is Cash's first #1 hit. He has been inducted into the Country Music, Gospel, and Rock and Roll Halls of Fame. He also acted in eight films and had his own variety TV show, with wife June Carter Cash. When Cash sang this song at San Quentin Prison on January 1, 1958, he inspired a twenty-year-old inmate to pursue his dream of taking up country music singing as well. The inmate was Merle Haggard.

That'll Be the Day, performed by Buddy Holly and the Crickets (1957)

Born Charles Hardin Holley in Lubbock, TX, Buddy was the first rockabilly artist to hit the mainstream. He was inducted into the Rock and Roll Hall of Fame in 1986. In 1959, Holly was killed in a plane crash. Another passenger was J. P. Richardson, then known as The Big Bopper (he wrote *White Lightening*). Richardson, who was too ill to ride the tour bus, asked Waylon Jennings if he could have his seat on that fatal plane ride.

La Bamba, performed by Richie Valens (1958)

Valens was on that plane too.

Dedicated to the One I Love, performed by the Shirelles (1959)

Girl groups and Phil Spector didn't hit it big until the 1960s. But the Shirelles were around from the beginning and stayed around until the mid-1970s. The folk rock group the Mamas and the Papas covered this hit in 1967.

Monument in front of the Surf Ballroom, Clear Lake IA.

Johnny B. Goode, performed by Chuck Berry (1958)

The first rock and roll hit about being a rock and roll star (can you name others?). This song was a tribute to Johnnie Johnson, Berry's piano player and frequent songwriting partner.

The Twist, performed by Chubby Checker (1960)

The Twist was originally released in 1959 as a B-side. Checker's cover version was #1 for only one week. However, it set a record by being the only song to reach #1 twice, in 1960 and when it topped the charts again in 1962. *The Twist* is #1 on *Billboard* Magazine's Greatest Singles of All-Time.

Hit the Road Jack, performed by Ray Charles (1961)

Hit the Road was written by Percy Mayfield, a rhythm and blues singer and song writer (*Please Send Me Someone to Love*). Ray Charles (Robinson) didn't record this song until 1961. It's still quintessential 1950s music and this number is quintessential Ray. *Rolling Stone* magazine named Charles #10 on its list of the greatest artists of all time.

In the Still of the Night, performed by the Five Satins (1956)

This doo-wop number was a flop, peaking at #24 on the pop charts when it was first released. However, in 2020 SiriusXM radio ran a poll of listeners of its fifties station; it came out on top.

Chapter 13
"LADIES AND GENTLEMEN, DIRECT FROM THE BAR. . ."

I'm here to kick ass and drink whiskey. And, pilgrim, I'm all out of whiskey.
—John Wayne

THE 1950s ON STAGE: THE RAT PACK

Five guys walk into a bar: Two Italian Catholics, a Jew from the Bronx, NY, an English "Aristocrat," and an African American with a glass eye. Hey, wait a minute . . . they rule this bar! It's the early 1950s and these *bar flies* are about to go onstage at the Sands Hotel in Las Vegas, NV. Known as the Rat Pack, this quintet was the hottest singing, dancing, joking, and drinking stage show of the 1950s: Frank Sinatra, Dean Martin, Sammy Davis, Jr., Joey Bishop, and Peter Lawford. They also personify the increasing ethnic diversity of the American population, the melting pot (or tossed salad, if you will) of diverse cultures, and the social classes and clashes this mixture would cause.

The Rat Pack (Peter Lawford, Sammy Davis, Jr., Frank Sinatra, Joey Bishop, Dean Martin).

Frank Sinatra

Frank Albert Sinatra was born in Hoboken, NJ, in 1915. His mother, Natalie "Dolly" Garavente, was the neighborhood midwife and that rare woman who got involved in ward politics in the early twentieth century.

His father, Marty Sinatra, was a sometime-boxer[1] when he wasn't running a speakeasy. Frank was an only child whose mother babied him long after his infancy, often dressing him up in fancy clothes not to his liking. Frankie heard Bing Crosby sing on the radio and knew immediately what he wanted to do. He could not serve in World War II because of a punctured eardrum.[2] By the end of the war he was the biggest star in the world, grossing millions of dollars by the late 1940s.

But Frank fell from popularity due to trouble with his voice, bad song choices, and bad press tying him to mobsters and communists. A promising film career also lost steam when he made a sarcastic remark about the mistress of Louis B. Mayer, the film producer and founder of Metro-Goldwyn-Mayer (MGM) studios. Frankie got *canned*.

Sinatra made a comeback in the mid-1950s. He changed his clothing style, donning fancy suits and a fedora. He won an Academy Award and Golden Globe for Best Supporting Actor for his performance in *From Here to Eternity*, starring Burt Lancaster, Montgomery Clift, and Deborah Kerr.

Frank also found a prop that became a part of his image: a bottle of *Jack Daniel's Old No.7 Tennessee Whiskey*. Have you heard the rumor that Sinatra was buried with a bottle of *Jack*? That's true. If you think he made a fortune promoting *Jack*, that's not true. His love of *Jack* was real; there was no endorsement deal. Sinatra would drink two fingers of *Jack* with three ice cubes, and a splash of water.

A doctor once asked Sinatra how he felt in the morning, after a night of drinking. Frank allegedly responded, "I don't know, I'm never up in the morning."

Dean Martin

Dino "Dean" Paul Crocetti was born in Steubenville, OH, in 1917. His father, Gaetano Crocetti, became a barber rather than work in the coal mines. By his early teens, Dean was involved with the mob and had quit school to become a boxer. He was a better singer than *palooka* so he became a singing card dealer (can you imagine playing Blackjack or Twenty-one while Dean Martin sang and shuffled cards a few feet away?).

After joining a traveling orchestra, Dino sold portions of his future earnings to raise cash.[3] When he was done selling shares, he had sold 105% of himself. No matter, he never paid back the *bread*. In 1944, Dean teamed up with Jerry Lewis and they became one of the biggest comedy acts in show business, including making sixteen hit movies. The duo came to hate each other, once trading *knuckle sandwiches* in public. Lewis was ambitious and Martin was laid back. Once on his own, Dino perfected his relaxed and carefree stage act (*menefreghismo* in Italian) so he didn't have to rehearse and could flub lines and still be greeted by the audience with *bust-a-gut* laughter instead of consternation. The glass he was holding on stage was as likely to contain apple juice as whiskey. He pursued a solo career but also teamed up with Sinatra.

Sammy Davis, Jr.

Sammy Davis, Jr. could do it all. It is generally agreed he was the most complete performer in the Rat Pack. He sang, danced, joked, did impressions. Born in Harlem in 1925 to a Puerto Rican mother, Elvera Sanchez, a showgirl, and Sammy, Sr., a song and dance man. Elvera soon *split* to pursue a career on her

---

1   Dolly would sneak into Marty's fights (he fought under the name Marty O'Brien) dressed as a man.

2   Sinatra married his first wife, Nancy, in 1939 and they had two kids before 1944, Little Nancy and Frank Jr. You might remember Nancy Sinatra as the singer of *These Boots are Made for Walking*. You might remember Frank Jr. (or might not) as the singer of *His Way!*

3   One of his investors was Lou Costello, of Abbott & Costello fame.

SAMMY DAVIS, JR. AND RACE RELATIONS

Life was not easy for black entertainers (or any racial minorities for that matter) in the still-segregated South of the 1950s. The Chitlin Circuit was a series of performance venues that encompassed the Civil War South but ranged up the east coast and into the Midwest. It provided a stage and spotlight for black performers to entertain and make a living doing it. A good living it wasn't; the performers met with discrimination wherever they went, most notably in restaurants, hotels, other public places, and from the police. Further, their music and acts were often "appropriated" by white performers.

Sammy, Jr. didn't escape from prejudice when he entered the army. He put up with racism and even physical abuse. George M. Cohan, whose statute now graces Time Square on Broadway (and who wrote the songs *Over There, Give My Regards to Broadway*, the modern version of *Yankee Doodle Boy, and You're a Grand Old Flag*) also was in the army at the time. He saw Sammy, Jr. perform and put him in touring army shows.

When Sammy, Jr. became famous, he created much fodder for the gossip columns by dating white women and marrying May Britt, the Swedish daughter of a Nobel laureate. The marriage got him dis-invited from singing at John Kennedy's inaugural ball. Sammy, Jr. was nominated for an Emmy for his performance on Broadway in *Golden Boy*, a play that was written with him in mind in which he acted opposite a white woman.

own. Sammy, Sr. took Junior with him on the road where Senior, along with Will Mastin, performed a vaudeville act on the Chitlin Circuit. Like many fabled rags-to-riches stories, Sammy, Jr. was raised in dressing rooms, boarding houses, and on tour buses. Sammy, Sr. watched Junior imitate the acts he saw on stage and realized his son was a born entertainer.

In 1941, "Will Mastin's Gang featuring Little Sammy" was called to substitute as the opening act for Tommy Dorsey's band featuring Frank Sinatra. The North was little more hospitable to Black performers than the South. Sinatra recognized Sammy, Jr.'s talent and insisted Mastin's trio open for him at the Capitol Theater in New York. Frankie told Sammy, Jr., "If anybody hits you, let me know."

Joey Bishop

Joseph Abraham Gottlieb was born in the Bronx, NY, in 1918 to Anna and Jacob Gottlieb, two Polish immigrants. Jacob was a machinist and bicycle repairman.

Joey quit high school and wanted to be a performer. His father wouldn't let him. Joey worked in a hat factory but then emceed at a Chinese restaurant on Broadway. He was drafted for the army and spent four years in the special services. His dry humor caught Sinatra's attention in 1952 and Frank then guided Joey's career. Bishop would later become known as "a comedian's comedian." But while he was a certified member of the Rat Pack, Joey would never be as close to Frank as were the other members—he was as dry as his humor.

Peter Lawford

Peter Lawford's mother was eccentric, to say the least. She hated babies because they smelled like sour milk and urine; her idea of *pillow talk* was "don't" and "hurry up." Perhaps it is not surprising that Peter, born in London, England, 1923, was her only *ankle-biter*. His father, Lieutenant General Sir Sydney Turing Barlow Lawford (May's third husband) had been knighted for valor during World War I.

Peter wanted to be an actor, but his father would not let him. No matter, destiny is destiny: Peter's family had to move to Los Angeles, CA, when Peter nearly lost his arm in an encounter with a window and needed the dry air to ward off stiffness. He started to get bit parts in the movies. His good looks led to liaisons with some of Hollywood's most famous leading ladies (including Lana Turner, Rita Hayworth, Ann Baxter, Judy Garland, June Allyson). In 1959, Sinatra asked Peter to join the Rat Pack. But then Peter and Frank had a falling out when Sinatra thought Peter was *birddogging* his ex-wife, Ava Gardner.[4]

Lawford married Patricia Kennedy, the sixth offspring of one of America's most famous bootleggers, Joseph P. Kennedy Sr., whose second child, John, would become the 35th president of the United States. Politics and Peter's connection to the Kennedys was what brought Frank and Peter back together again. But once John became president, the Kennedys *brushed off* Frank because of his mob ties and Frank jettisoned Peter because his in-laws had ditched him.

"NEVER RAT ON A RAT"

It was Lauren Bacall who came up with the *handle* "The Rat Pack." Bacall, an actress and the wife of Humphrey Bogart, saw her husband drinking with Sinatra and a bunch of other 1950s superstars. She passed judgement on their appearance: "You look like a goddamn rat pack." The group thought the label worth keeping and drew up a coat of arms and adopted a motto, "Never rat on a rat." It was supposed to be a joke, but a newspaper reporter wrote a story about the Rat Pack. Sinatra, with a different line up, made it something real.

Frank was a part owner of the Sands Hotel, along

with some mobsters who had given him a share of the property. The show he created for the venue was called "The Summit." Much of the show was improvised. The five Rat Pack members would perform at the Sands at night and filmed *Ocean's Eleven* during the day, before they started drinking (heavily). Their shows would be considered the quintessential entertainment of the 1950s, an amazing coming together of the diverse cultures in America then trying to negotiate a truce. By today's standards though, their shows were also exceedingly politically incorrect, including putdowns of ethnic minority groups (which most of them were members of) and women.

THE 1950s ON SCREEN: A REAL MAN AND A REAL BOMBSHELL

John Wayne

Marion Robert Morrison, better known as John Wayne, was born in 1907 in Winterset, IA. He played football for the University of Southern California until he was injured and got a summer job on the set of Tom Mix movies in exchange for football tickets. His rugged good looks were spotted by director Raoul Walsh.[5]

John drank many different kinds of liquors, but bourbon was his favorite. His movie directors tried to do their filming before noon so Wayne would not be drunk. He also smoked up to six packs of cigarettes a day. He was a tough guy, having a lung removed surgically before playing Rooster Cogburn in True Grit, for which Wayne won an Academy Award in 1969.

---

4 A newspaper photographer took a picture of Lawford and Gardner having dinner with his manager and Ava's sister. The paper airbrushed the manager and sister out of the picture.

5 Many of Wayne's stunts were done by Enos Edward "Yakima" Canutt, a rodeo star turned stunt man and stunt director. It was Canutt who did the famous scene in *Stagecoach* in which he stops a team of runaway horses. Yakima was also the stunt double for Clark Gable in *Gone with the Wind* and second director on *Ben-Hur*; the chariot race Canutt directed is probably the most remembered film stunt of all time. Canutt received a special Academy Award in 1966.

He eventually died of lung cancer in 1979.

Ava Gardner

In 1999, the American Film Institute unveiled a list of the greatest twenty-five male and twenty-five female screen legends. Ava Gardner was included on that exclusive list of stars. She also ranks among the most famous (though not necessarily in excess) whiskey drinkers in American history: "For someone of my naturally irreverent temperament, playing a sassy, tough-talking playgirl who whistles at men, [and] drinks whiskey straight from the bottle. . .was a gift from the gods."

Ava was born on Christmas Eve, 1922 in Grabtown, NC. Of Scots-Irish descent, she was the youngest of seven children. Her mother was religious and strait-laced. Now comes the Hollywood Dream story. As a high school graduation present, Ava's mother let her visit her married sister in New York City. Her brother-in-law was a photographer (you can see where this is going). He thought she was *the most*, took her picture, and put it in the window of his studio. An employee of MGM pictures walked by, saw Ava's photo, and inquired about her. All this led to a screen test. The test was a disaster, mostly because Ava's thick Southern drawl made her incomprehensible to Northern ears. Still, Louis B. Mayer saw the test and proclaimed "She can't sing, she can't act, she can't talk. She's terrific! Sign her!" MGM sent her to a voice coach.[6]

Ava Gardner in *The Killers*.
The film was based on a short story by Ernest Hemingway.

Ava married three times: to the multi-talented Mickey Rooney; bandleader Artie Shaw; and a guy named Frank Sinatra. Her marriage to Frank lasted about six years (1951–57). Ava wrote of Frank and their relationship:

> Our phone bills were astronomical, and when I found the letters Frank wrote me the other day, the total could fill a suitcase. Every single day during our relationship, no matter where in the world I was, I'd get a telegram from Frank saying he loved me and missed me. He was a man who was desperate for companionship and love.

After her separation from Frank, Ava moved to Spain where Ernest Hemingway introduced her to bull fighting. They became close friends; she starred in

---

6   When Ava played the part of Julie LaVerne in the 1951 film *Show Boat*, she had to relearn a Southern accent. In the movie, Gardner plays an actress in the 1880s who is part African American. When Julie confesses to this, she must leave the company of white actors.

JOHN WAYNE'S POLITICS

John Wayne was a staunch anti-communist in the 1950s and remains a conservative icon to this day. He was the President of the Motion Picture Alliance for the Preservation of American Ideals and a big supporter of Richard Nixon and Ronald Reagan. He especially disapproved of the movie *High Noon*, starring Gary Cooper. Wayne thought it presented the American West in an un-American way because the townspeople refused to help Marshall Will Kane; in the last scene Kane throws his badge in the dirt.

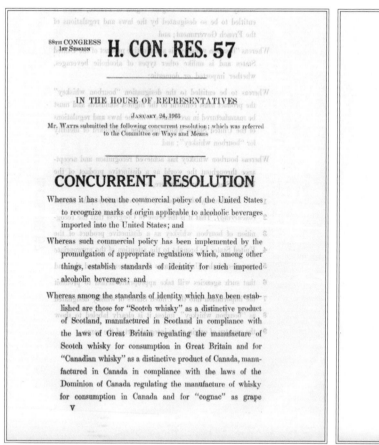

Congressional Declaration 1963.
If it ain't made in America, it ain't bourbon.

three movies based on his writing (*The Killers*, *The Snows of Kilimanjaro*, and *The Sun Also Rises*[7]).

It should be obvious that Gardner was a quote machine, tossing out gems like, "Women's liberation as a movement makes some valid points. But in the final analysis, it doesn't matter who wears the pants— as long as there's money in the pockets," and "Deep down inside, I'm pretty superficial."

AMERICA MOVES ON

The end of the Rat Pack arrived from Liverpool, England, in the form of four *mop-tops* (The Beatles) and from Hibbing, MN, in the guise of a curly haired folk singer (Bob Dylan). The times they were a changin'. But as the 1960s began, an act of Congress enshrined bourbon as a "distinctive product of the United States" (as Champagne must come from France). Bourbon finally was recognized as being as American as apple pie (maybe more so, since mom's pie cooling on the windowsill has no similar legal status).

As the music of the 1950s and its larger-than-life movie stars would pass to history, would American whiskey also become a casualty of the rebellious 1960s?

---

7   Ava said about Lady Brett Ashley, her role in *The Sun Also Rises*: "Papa [Hemingway] said [Lady Brett] 'was as charming when she is drunk as when she was sober.' I also felt close to Papa's women."

WHAT WHISKEY REMINDS US OF THE 1950s?

Jack Daniel's Sinatra Select

Sinatra Select pays tribute to Old No. 7's biggest fan. The process for making Sinatra Select is identical to Old No. 7's except that grooves are cut into the inside length of the aging barrels so there is more interaction between the wood and whiskey.

Just the Facts

Mash Bill	Corn: 80% Rye: 8% Barley: 12%
Proof	Proof: 90 ABV: 45%
Age	No age statement
Chill Filtered?	Filtered through sugar maple charcoal

TASTING NOTES

From: Jack Daniel's Distillery website

https://www.jackdaniels.com/en-us/whiskey/sinatra-select

Made with our unique "Sinatra Barrels" that have deep grooves specially carved into their staves to expose the whiskey to extra layers of toasted oak. This added exposure imparts a rich amber color, bold character, and pleasant smokiness, punctuated by an incredibly smooth vanilla finish. Much like Frank, this Tennessee Whiskey is one of a kind.

From: Adventures in Whiskey (Reviewer: Bobby Childs)

https://adventuresinwhiskey.com/2014/07/09/jack-daniels-sinatra-select-tennessee-whiskey/

Aroma: There's overwhelming oak and vanilla on top of the traditional Jack Daniel's sweet nose.

Palate: Jack's always been a sweet whiskey, but here that sweetness is held in check by the oak. I don't find it overly oaky, but if you're not a fan of oak in your whiskey you're probably not going to like this one. Look past the initial sweet oakiness and there's a little fruit and spice.

Finish: Nowhere near as rough as Old No. 7, but is about as sweet. How should I describe this whiskey? It's almost like putting a tuxedo on Jack Daniel's Old No. 7.

Overall: It's definitely more refined than their standard black label. However, it's not a super-complex whiskey. . .but I don't think they were aiming to make a super-complex whiskey. That being said, there's lots more happening here than in a glass of their Old No. 7 black label.

From: The Over a Barrel Gang
Looks: Amber, gold.
Aroma: Light. Dried leaves.
Flavor: Medium body. Salty, bitter, sweet.
Mouth Feel: Rich, round, sharp, creamy.
Going Down: Medium strength, medium length.
Notes: Fruit forward on the nose, unexpected taste, almost gin-like, brine.

Russell's Reserve 10-Year-Old Straight Bourbon Whiskey

Sinatra Select is a hard whiskey to come by. So, let's look in John Wayne's liquor cabinet and see what we find. When John Wayne shot films in remote locations, he would have cases of *Wild Turkey* shipped to him. *Russell's Reserve* is a small batch bourbon produced by the Wild Turkey Distillery.

Just the Facts

Mash Bill	Corn: 60% Rye: 35% Barley and spelt: 5%
Proof	Proof: 90 ABV: 45%
Age and Barrel Char Level	Aged at least 5 years; #4
Chill Filtered?	Filtered through sugar maple charcoal

TASTING NOTES

From: Wild Turkey website
https://wildturkeybourbon.com/product/russells-reserve/

The Wild Turkey website describes Russell Reserve as "rich, caramel and vanilla taste and a uniquely smooth finish."

From: The Whiskey Cowboy (Reviewer: John)
https://thewhiskeycowboy.wordpress.com/2017/01/30/russells-reserve-10-year-old-bourbon-whiskey-review/
Color: Rich amber with a glint of gold when light hits it. Coats the glass thin but then holds for a bit before forming long thin legs. Slight beading at the upper edge forms with time.
Aroma: . . .vanilla, toffee, and a hint of burnt caramel. . ..some light spices and oak, with a trace of cinnamon. Keep smelling and cherries and sweet nuts emerge. . .then the sweet vanilla busts back in. . .

Palate: Very smooth and a bit oily. Sweet dominates the entrance, with vanilla, almonds, cane sugar, and a hint of toffee. Then cinnamon and spices slide in. . . and then a slightly smokey oak finishes it off. . .

Finish: Not a lot of heat, but it is pleasant. Sweetness from the vanillas and cane sugar linger for quite a while. And some more sweet nuts also linger, like almond and pecans.

Overview: . . .I think it is a well-balanced pour and offers what a nice bourbon should offer, if not a bit "gentlemanly." If you are a Wild Turkey lover, go ahead and add this one to your list. It does not blow me away, but I do enjoy it. . . With oxidation it becomes (to me) smoother and sweeter.

From: The Over a Barrel Gang

Looks: Amber, pale straw.

Aroma: Light. Maple, banana, caramel, butterscotch, clove, tobacco.

Flavor: Medium body. Sweet, salty, sour.

Mouth Feel: Creamy, round, rich, heavy.

Going Down: Medium strength, medium length.

Notes: Crowd pleaser, everything it needs, no bells or whistles.

Toast

The comedian Joe E. Brown attributed this gem to Dean Martin: "You're not drunk if you can lie on the floor without holding on." But a toast to the 1950s has to include Frank's lament for the abstainers: "I feel bad for people who don't drink. When they wake up in the morning that's as good as they're going to feel all day."

To the Rat Pack, Ava, John, and the way they *lit up* the 1950s and showed us how not to behave.

DINNER AT THE SANDS HOTEL, LAS VEGAS, NV, WITH FRANK SINATRA AND AVA GARDNER

Marjorie Child Husted.
The real Betty Crocker.

Rumor has it that the Rat Pack loved to eat and drink. But Sinatra, for all his glitz and glamor, was a man of simple tastes. And Ava Gardner began life as a North Carolina country girl. Recipes from Italian American and down-home Southern kitchens best reflect who they were when it all began.

Among several 1950s food icons was a fictional character named Betty Crocker. Ann Pillsbury, Aunt Jemima and Uncle Ben were also born of corporate imagination.[8] "Betty" was the most successful of the bunch. She answered letters and hosted both radio and television shows (the TV show was a flop). Betty was created and her presence sustained by Marjorie Child Husted. At the time, Husted got little credit and was paid much less than a successful salesman. She became an advocate for women's rights.

Recipe: Spaghetti, Italian Style

From: Corporate Author. (1950). *Betty Crocker's Picture Cook Book*. Minneapolis, MN and New York, NY: General Mills and McGraw Hill. P. 385. [You can purchase this cookbook today in a facsimile edition.]

Serves 12

Cook until browned in 2 tablespoons hot olive oil. . .
1 pound ground beef or beef and pork
Add and simmer slowly for ½ to one hour (long cooking improves flavor)
3½ cups cooked tomatoes (#2 ½ can)
2 cloves garlic, finely cut
1 bay leaf, crumbled
1 teaspoon salt
⅛ teaspoon pepper
Pour over hot drained boiled spaghetti (1 pound uncooked) on hot platter. Sprinkle with grated Parmesan cheese (serves 12).

---

8   Aunt Jemima's look was based on a former slave named Nancy Green. In summer 2020, in response to protests calling for an end to racial bias and injustice, Quaker Oats promised to discontinue the brand—421 years after slaves first arrived in the United States and 132 years after the brand first appeared on grocery store shelves. The image on Uncle Ben's Rice was based on a Chicago maître d'hôtel named Frank Brown. Uncle Ben was supposedly a real-life African American rice grower. In 2007, an advertising campaign promoted Uncle Ben to Chairman of the Board. But, also in summer 2020, Mars, Inc. stated, "we recognize that now is the right time to evolve the Uncle Ben's brand, including its visual brand identity."

Recipe: Fried Chicken

From: Ava Gardner Museum. (1996). *Cooking with Ava: Recipes from her family, fans & friends*. Kearney, NE: Morris Press.

This recipe is directly handed down from the Gardner family.

Ingredients:
   Chicken pieces
   Salt and pepper
   Self-rising flour
   Water
   Crisco or oil

Directions:
   Salt and pepper chicken pieces. Coat with flour. Sprinkle enough water over chicken in a bowl to make a paste when patted with dampened hands. (May need to add more flour.) Put in iron skillet with hot grease. Chicken should not touch sides of pan or another piece of chicken or the crust will come off. Brown and turn, lower heat. Cover with lid for about 10–15 minutes, so steam can tenderize chicken. Take lid off for last few minutes to make crust crisp. Watch constantly.

Recipe: Fried Green Tomatoes

From: Corporate Author. (1950). *Betty Crocker's Picture Cook Book*. Minneapolis, MN and New York, NY: General Mills and McGraw Hill. P. 381. [Facsimile edition, 1998, Houghton Mifflin Harcourt and General Mills.]

Dip firm tomato slices (¼ inch thick) into slightly beaten egg. . .then into fine cracker crumbs. Sprinkle with salt and pepper. Brown in melted butter.

MUSIC THAT WAS ON THE STAGE AND SCREEN IN THE 1950s

The House I Live In, performed by Frank Sinatra (1945)

"Wouldn't we be silly if we went around hating people because they combed their hair different from ours?" Sinatra asks this question to a group of kids harassing a boy outside his studio where he was recording this song. It appears in a 10-minute RKO Radio Picture meant to combat fascism and anti-Semitism.

Everybody Loves Somebody, performed by Dean Martin (1964)

Everybody was added to the *Dream with Dean* album at the last minute when the record was one song short. It was co-written about seventeen years earlier by Ken Lane, the pianist on the album.

I've Gotta Be Me, performed by Sammy Davis, Jr. (1968)

From the Broadway show *Golden Rainbow* starring the married couple Steve Lawrence and Eydie Gormé. The musical was kind of a flop (running for less than a year) but this version was Davis Jr.'s third biggest hit.

Diamonds Are a Girl's Best Friend, performed by Marilyn Monroe (1953)

This song is from the movie *Gentlemen Prefer Blondes*. Monroe was paid $500 a week for appearing in the film, as stipulated in her studio contract. Jane Russell, who played opposite Monroe, was paid $200,000.

What Kind of Fool Am I, performed by James Brown (1970)

Fool was one of Sammy Davis Jr.'s biggest hits (*Candyman* was biggest; he hated it). *Fool* is a cover of an Anthony Newley song from the Broadway musical *Stop the World—I Want to Get Off*. This version is a real genre-bender by the "Godfather of Soul."

Can't Help Lovin' Dat Man, performed by Ava Gardner (1927)

This song was written by James Kern and Oscar Hammerstein II for *Show Boat*. Gardner was not known as a singer.

America, performed Chita Rivera (1957)

The play *West Side Story* was Romeo and Juliet redone for Broadway by Arthur Laurents (book), Leonard Bernstein (music), and Stephen Sondheim (lyrics). This homage to America is sung on a rooftop in Manhattan.

Singing in the Rain, performed by Gene Kelley (1952)

The movie by the same name tops the American Film Institute's list of the greatest movie musicals of all time. Kelley (as Don Lockwood) is smitten with Debbie Reynolds (as Kathy Selden). After an encounter, Kelley can't help dance down the street, regardless of the weather. He had a 103° fever and flu when the scene was shot.

My Way, performed by Frank Sinatra (1960)

This song was written by Paul Anka (a teen idol in the 1950s with songs like *Diana, Lonely Boy, Put Your Head on My Shoulder*) based on a French song titled *Comme d'Habitude.*

IT'S HIP TO BE SQUARE

Chapter 14
MAYBE DAD WAS HIPPER THAN I THOUGHT

You can handle just about anything that comes at you out on the road with
a believable grin, common sense and whiskey.
—Bill Murray

BOURBON HITS A DRY SPELL

The 1960s, 1970s, and early 1980s were not good to the whiskey industry.
Sales were in a stupor. There were several reasons for the tailspin. One major
cause was changing tastes; clear spirits (mostly gins and vodkas) took center
stage as a rebellious generation didn't want to be like dad. A health craze also
kicked up. VCRs were jammed with tapes of Jane Fonda leading exercisers
through a home workout while down the street fitness centers flexed their
muscles.

The government also got involved. The Nixon administration joined a
worldwide *War on Drugs*. First Lady Nancy Reagan championed the "Just Say
No" campaign during her husband's presidency. While these initiatives were
aimed primarily at use of hard drugs, they also targeted alcohol and cigarettes. Increases in advertising fees and taxes on alcohol depressed the spirits
market and led to greater consumption of wine and beer. Mothers Against
Drunk Driving (MADD) started rolling in 1981. In schools, the Drug Abuse
Resistance Education (DARE) program was founded in 1983 and kids were

Jane Fonda's Workout Book
was a New York Times Best-
Seller in 1981.
You can now see her with glass
in hand in *Grace* and *Frankie* on
Netflix.

"A DRINK IS A DRINK IS A DRINK"

Every good bartender knows this rough measure of the alcohol content that fills most of the glasses they pour. Here are the equivalents for America's favorite libations:

Potion	Equivalent	% ABV	Calories
Whiskey (e.g., *Jim Beam*)	1 ounce	40%	65
Wine	2.9 ounces	14%	60
Beer (e.g., *Budweiser*)	8 ounces	5%	100*

The alcohol in your blood will be a function of your metabolic rate, your sex, your physical size, the food in your stomach and small intestines (remember to eat and drink water), and your health (and any medications you are taking). It will also be a function of how quickly you are drinking. Men metabolize alcohol more efficiently than women because they have a greater amount of the enzyme alcohol dehydrogenase (ADH) in their stomach and liver. People who are physically large will have a lower alcohol concentration in their blood than skinnier folks who drink the same amount (but this calculation excludes body fat). Whatever you drink, learn to be a sipper, not a chugger. Eat, sip, drink water, eat some more, and repeat. Be careful about how merry you get.

For more information see:

https://alcohol.stanford.edu/alcohol-drug-info/buzz-buzz/factors-affect-how-alcohol-absorbed

*Lite beer has fewer calories than regular beer but generally not much less alcohol.

told, "alcohol is a gateway drug that can lead to other, stronger chemical dependencies."[1]

But the whiskey world wouldn't stay flat for long. Keeping an eye on the phenomenon that was *Maker's Mark*, other whiskey distillers followed suit with *choice* brands of their own.

C. Everett Koop was Surgeon General from 1982 to 1989.
The first SG to dress like a general in a while.

THE COMEBACK: *BLANTON'S ORIGINAL SINGLE BARREL BOURBON WHISKEY*

Albert Blanton

Kentucky Colonel[2] Albert B. Blanton started working at the O.F.C (Old Fashioned Copper) Distillery in Frankfort, KY, as an office boy in 1897. He worked his way up to plant manager in 1912, when the distillery

---

1   DARE's effectiveness is yet to be established. If anything, much research suggests it was ineffective, though it still carries on and has been revised many times.

2   In Kentucky, the title "Colonel" is bestowed as an honorific (e.g., Colonel Harland Sanders of KFC fame); no military service required.

was rechristened George T. Stagg, and then he became president in 1921. You might think that was bad luck given that his promotion came during Prohibition, but Albert obtained a federal license to produce whiskey for medicinal purposes and the distillery stayed open. Albert worked at the distillery for around fifty-five years. In 1953, when he retired, the distillery was renamed the Albert B. Blanton Distillery.[3]

Given his dedication to the distillery, it is little wonder that in 1984 Elmer T. Lee,[4] the first Master Distiller at the now rechristened Buffalo Trace Distillery, named the first super-premium, single-barrel bourbon after Blanton. Its cost put it on the shelf right next to the most expensive Scotch whiskys.

The Bottle

The *Blanton's* bottle is round, squat, and easy to spot on a shelf. Each bottle is marked with the warehouse and barrel that the whiskey came from. The bottle's cork stopper is topped with one of eight figurines depicting a racehorse and jockey in different action poses. Look closely and you will see that each stopper also has on it a different letter from the name Blanton's. Collect 'em all! They're *totally tubular!*

Blanton's versus *Maker's Mark*

According to Michael Veach, the gurus at *Blanton's* marketing corps came up with the idea of running tasting contests against *Maker's Mark*. Tasters unaware of which brand they were drinking would pick their favorite. A local business magazine held the event and *Blanton's* won every time. It was discovered that the *Maker's* bottles were being picked off liquor store shelves at random while *Blanton's* was selecting its bottles. *Maker's* objected and *had a cow*; the tests were halted.[5]

Blanton's in Popular Culture

The popularity of *Blanton's* has climbed sharply in recent years. The wonderful taste and unique bottles have been accompanied by appearances in some of the most popular films and television series. This has put *Blanton's* in front of large audiences. For example, you can catch a glimpse of that bottle in the:

Netflix drama *House of Cards;*

HBO comedy *Bored to Death;*

Cinemax drama *Banshee;*

FX drama *Justified* (the United States Marshalls drink *Blanton's* in their offices);

2014 movie *Gone Girl;*

NBC crime series *Blindspot;*

Spike Lee's (2006) crime film *Inside Man;*

Fox sitcom *Last Man Standing;*

Netflix comedy *Grace and Frankie;*

2014 movie *John Wick* (after a tough fight, Wick nurses a bottle of *Blanton's*. When the doctor asks, "Do you need anything for pain?" Wick responds, "No, I've got that covered")

No wonder *Blanton's* is one of the more difficult whiskeys to find on the store shelf.

---

3   The distillery was renamed Ancient Age in 1962 and Buffalo Trace in 2001. It has changed ownership several times.

4   Do you recognize the names George T. Stagg and Elmer T. Lee from the bourbon shelf at your local liquor mart? They have also been so honored.

5   Except from a marketing point of view (think Coke versus Pepsi), the idea of taste tests was ludicrous. Both of these bourbons have an exceptional, unique taste and it wouldn't take long for anyone to tell them apart with their eyes closed.

THE BIRTH OF THE WHISK(E)Y WIZARDS

F. Paul Pacult

In 1988, Paul Pacult, a wine writer and class instructor, was approached by the *New York Times Sunday Magazine* to write an article for a supplement on Scotch whisky. Pacult knew nothing about whisky; he thought it was an old man's drink. A foodie writer friend suggested he think twice: ". . .it won't do much to advance your wine-tasting career. Whisky is. . .unfashionable and, well, brown."

Despite his preconception and the warning of his friend, Pacult was not dissuaded. He took up the gauntlet and went on a tour of Scotland. He was enamored with the Scotland scenery, the charm of the distilleries, as well as the remarkable range of tastes that all came under the umbrella of "Scotch whisky." In December 1989, the *Times Sunday Magazine* published his article, *Scotch Whisky: A Consumer Guide*, a four-part, ten thousand-word advertising supplement that rivals the front-page *Wall Street Journal* article on *Maker's Mark* for its impact on making whiskey drinking acceptable and, indirectly, on the American industry. In 1991, Pacult launched *Spirit Journal* that provides instructions on how to drink as well as reviews of many types of spirits, including American whiskeys.

Michael Jackson [no, not the singer]

Michael Jackson was an Englishman who wrote *World Guide to Beer* and then started to take an interest in Scotch whisky. It wasn't a great leap from the brewery to the distillery; after all, beers and Scotch whiskies both start out as a malted barley mash (beer has a bittering agent).[6] In 1989, Jackson published *World Guide to Whisky* in England, and it appeared in the United

States in the 1990s. Jackson passed away in 2007 but his guide to world whiskies lives on, now in its seventh edition, written by others.

Today, you can find several monthly and quarterly magazines devoted to whiskey, and at least three, *Bourbon Review*, *American Whiskey*, and *Bourbon+*, specific to the American spirit. Each of these feature numerous pundits. There are too many blogs, newsletters, and tasting sites to mention them all. You can also become a whiskey expert yourself by attending seminars at one of the many whiskey events held throughout the world.

WHISKEY IN THE WHITE HOUSE: SECOND HALF OF THE 20TH CENTURY

Harry S. Truman (33rd president, 1945–1953). Harry S. Truman (the "S" stands for only that; it was the first initial of both his grandfathers) was a devoted bourbon drinker. He had his first daily encounter with bourbon shortly after a brisk 5 a.m. walk, one that led his Secret Service detail to return to the White House out of breath. When HST thought a looming labor strike in the steel industry might hinder the United States war effort in Korea, he wanted the government to take over steel production. The Supreme Court said "no" to the takeover. Not long after, Chief Justice Hugo Black invited Truman to a BBQ and poured bourbon. Truman declared: "Hugo, I don't much care for your law, but, by golly, this bourbon is good." Warm feelings flowed.

Truman was president during the Red Scare of the 1950s. Joseph McCarthy led this ill-conceived anti-communist movement. As chair of the House Un-American Activities Committee, McCarthy was incensed when Truman removed General Douglass McArthur from his command and accused Truman of being a drunk. He shouldn't have thrown that stone. McCarthy died of acute hepatitis, believed to have

---

6   What did the distiller call the brewer? "Quitter."

been caused by cirrhosis of the liver.

John Kennedy (35th president, 1961–1963). Kennedy's father, Joe, built at least a portion of his fortune on bootlegging and stockpiling Scotch in England to rush to the United States when Prohibition was repealed. JFK was a drinker but not a guzzler. His real passion was Cuban cigars (and women). Pierre Salinger, his press secretary, wrote that before establishing the Cuban trade embargo, Kennedy asked Salinger to find out how many Cuban cigars he could rustle up for him. Salinger returned to say he could get hundreds. Kennedy signed the embargo.

Lyndon Baines Johnson (36th president, 1963–1969). LBJ used alcohol to help get legislation passed in Congress. He would have legislators over for a drink. His staff was told to keep his Scotch and soda weak but make everyone else's drinks strong. Republican Senator Everett Dirksen was a favorite target; his glass of *Jack Daniel's Old No. 7* bourbon might contain three times the liquor LBJ was drinking.

Gerald Ford (38th president, 1974–1977). Gerald Ford's father was an alcoholic and physical abuser. Ford changed his name (from Leslie King Jr.) when his mother divorced his father and remarried. Ford was known for being clumsy but likely this was rarely due to too much drink (except, captured on film, maybe when hitting his head exiting Air Force One). He was, however, a practitioner of the three-martini lunches that seemed to lubricate all of Washington, DC, at the time. But it was First Lady Betty Ford who took the spotlight. She developed a drinking problem in Michigan while Gerry was at the nation's capital.

Lillian Carter and her son.
Jimmy didn't have a beer named after him.

The problem progressed to an addiction to pain killers. What was remarkable about First Lady Ford was that she went public with her problem, a rarity at that time for a so prominent a figure. Her obituary in the *New York Times* said of her: "Few first ladies have been as popular as Betty Ford, and it took her frankness and lack of pretense that made her so." The first nonprofit Betty Ford Center for helping people recover from addiction opened in 1982. There are now over a dozen centers located around the country, from Oregon to New York.

James Earl "Jimmy" Carter (39th president, 1977–1981). Jimmy Carter is a religious man who teaches Sunday School in his hometown of Plains, GA, and rarely drinks. His wife, Rosalynn, follows suit. So, let's skip over them and get to the real drinkers in the family. Carter's mother, "Miss Lillian," was a lover of bourbon. To get an idea of how much she drank bourbon, she once said it helped her sleep. Hubert Humphrey sent her a bottle of bourbon when Miss Lillian was a Peace Corp volunteer in India. Then there was President Carter's brother, Billy. He became a national curiosity because of his homespun ways and his drinking beer for breakfast. He was a big fan of *Pabst Blue Ribbon* but that didn't stop him from trying to cash in on his celebrity. *Billy Beer* appeared in 1977. It was a flop.

Ronald Reagan (40ᵗʰ president, 1981–1989). Like Gerald Ford, Reagan grew up with an alcoholic father. This taught him the awful things alcohol abuse can cause. It was during the Reagan years that a nationwide age limit of twenty-one for the legal consumption of alcohol became law. In his folksy manner, Reagan defended this law by speaking about what he learned from his father's disease.

William Jefferson "Bill" Clinton (42ⁿᵈ president, 1993–2001). Bill Clinton was impeached for some well-documented extra-marital affairs but drinking to excess was never claimed to be one of his vices. Born William Jefferson Blythe III, his father died when he was an infant and his mother married Roger Clinton. Roger was an alcoholic with abusive tendencies when drunk. Clinton learned to drink in moderation.

OTHER SUPER-PREMIUM WHISKEYS JOIN IN THE FUN

As the scales began to tip back in favor of the golden clixir, other distillers began to follow *Maker's Mark*'s lead by turning out their own super-premium varieties. Several of these have already been in the spotlight on these pages. Others included *Booker's Bourbon*, a collection of barrel strength bourbons that is uncut and unfiltered, and the Jim Beam Distillery's *Baker's Small Batch Bourbon*. Whiskeys from Four Roses, Heaven Hill, and Evan Williams joined the parade.

With so much choice appearing on whiskey shelves, the only thing missing was some interesting people to drink it with.

WHAT DOES SUPER PREMIUM WHISKEY TASTE LIKE?

Blanton's Original Single Barrel Bourbon Whiskey

If a bourbon is labeled "single barrel" it means, not surprisingly, that the content of the bottle comes from one barrel; there is no mixing of spirits from different barrels. As with all premium bourbons, there is also no added neutral spirits, colorings, or flavorings. *Blanton's* lays claim to being the "original" single barrel bourbon.

Blanton's is aged in Warehouse H at the Buffalo Trace Distillery in Frankfort, KY. This unique warehouse is clad in metal, not the brick that forms the exterior of most rickhouses, so that more extreme temperatures would promote more interaction between the whiskey and the barrel.

Just the Facts

Mash Bill	Corn: at least 51% Rye: 12–15%? Other: ?%
Proof	Proof: 91 ABV: 46.5%
Age and Barrel Char Level	6–8 years; #4
Chill Filtered?	Yes

TASTING NOTES

From: Blanton's Bourbon website

The Blanton's website says this whiskey's nose evokes vanilla with hints of butterscotch and caramel, as well as baking spices. The taste is "sweet, with notes of citrus and oak."

From: Honest Booze (Reviewer: John Andrews)

https://honestboozereviews.com/blantons-the-original-single-barrel-bourbon-whiskey-750ml/

Aroma:. . .some spice and heat to it. There's a singe of burn . . .

Palate:. . .nice complexity of sweetness and spice . . .really enjoyable.

Finish:. . .the burnt caramel you would want from a single barrel whiskey. I do wish there was a bit more complexity here.. . .the burn is minor, but the warmth and overall smoothness make this fantastic.

From: The Over a Barrel Gang

Looks: Amber, deep copper.

Aroma: Delicate. Black pepper, vanilla, cherry, tobacco.

Flavor: Medium body. Sweet, bitter.

Mouth Feel: Creamy, round, rich.

Going Down: Medium strength, medium length.

Notes: Short and sweet; pleasant mouth feel long after, though taste goes pretty quick.

Toast

There are many legendary distillers, but none is more revered than Julian P. Van Winkle. He began as a traveling salesman for the distiller William Larue Weller and ended up fashioning some of the most sought-after bourbons in America. But he was also known as a gentle, kind, and honest man.[7] His ethic, short and simple, is most appropriate for celebrating the emergence of bourbon as a first-class product: "At a profit if we can, at a loss if we must, but always fine bourbon."

To Pappy Van Winkle and the reinvention of American whiskey.

---

7   You will pay dearly for any bottle of whiskey with the Van Winkle name on it.

DINNER AT STONY HILL MANSION, FRANKFURT, KY, WITH ELMER T. AND LIBBY LEE & ALBERT BLANTON

In addition to bread bowls, seven-layer salad, and potato skin appetizers, quiche was appearing on many dining tables in the 1980s. A slice of quiche along with fresh salad and warm bread made for an easy meal preparation. And in the 1980s easy dinners gained popularity with the increasing number of women joining the workforce. Ironically, the best-selling book *Real Men Don't Eat Quiche*, by Bruce Feirstein, helped quiche establish itself as an American staple.

Recipe: Swiss Cheese and Mushroom Quiche

From: Molly Katzen. (1977). *Moosewood Cookbook*. Berkeley, CA: Ten Speed Press. P. 111.

> 1 hour to prepare. 4–6 servings.
> This recipe makes one 9" pie. It can be an appetizer or main dish.
> - Follow pie crust recipe for Spinach-Ricotta pie, or your own favorite for a single crust. [See page 123 in cookbook.]
>   - Cut together 1 cup flour (⁴/₅ white plus ¹/₅ whole wheat is nice) (that's approximate of course) and ¹/₃ cup cold butter. Use a pastry cutter or two forks, or food processor fitted with a steel blade.
>   - When the mixture is uniformly blended, add about 3 tbs. cold buttermilk (or water. But buttermilk really. Specialness is worth it.) ~ or enough so that mixture holds together enough to form a ball.
>   - Chill the dough at least one hour.
>   - Try to work quickly so ingredients stay cold.
> - Cover bottom of crust with 1½ cups grated Swiss. (Gruyere is best.)
> - Cover cheese with: 1 medium onion, ¼ lb. mushrooms: chopped; sautéed in butter with salt, paper, dash of thyme.
> - Make a custard: Beat well together: 4 eggs, 1½ cups milk, 3 tbs. flour, ¼ tsp. salt, ¼ tsp. dry mustard.
> - Pour custard over mushroom layer.
> - Sprinkle with paprika. Bake at 375°F 40–45 minutes, or until solid in the center when jiggled.

Variations:
- Substitute cheddar cheese for Swiss.
- Use fresh tomato slices instead of mushrooms. (Tomatoes don't need to be sautéed first.)
- Substitute 1 cup scallions for the onions.
- Add 1 tsp. prepared horseradish.

Unlike Betty Crocker and the other products of corporate imagination, Fannie Farmer was a real person. She learned to cook at age sixteen, while recovering from a paralytic stroke that left her an invalid her entire life. Her cookbook, *The Boston Cooking-School Cookbook*, was published in 1896. The title of the book was changed to *The Fannie Farmer Cookbook* in 1965. Marion Cunningham, a cookbook author who championed home cooking (not Richie's mother on *Happy Days*), revised Fannie's book in 1979. Chicken Fricassee was a favorite dish in the

1980s. This recipe comes from the 14th edition that celebrated the 100th anniversary of the cookbook's first appearance.

Recipe: Chicken Fricassee

From: Marion Cunningham. (1996). *The Fannie Farmer Cookbook.* New York, NY: Alfred A. Knopf. P. 237.

A great old-fashioned dish, the essence of chicken in a creamy sauce.

Ingredients (serves six):

    5 pound chicken, in large pieces
    ¼ pound butter
    2 tablespoons oil
    1 small onion, sliced
    2 stalks celery with leaves in pieces
    1 carrot, sliced
    1 bay leaf
    4 tablespoons flour
    1 cup heavy cream
    2 tablespoons lemon juice
    Salt
    Freshly ground pepper

Directions:

Rinse the chicken and pat it dry. Heat 4 tablespoons of the butter with the oil in a Dutch oven, and brown the chicken on all sides. Lower the heat, pour on boiling water to cover the chicken, and add the onion, celery, carrot, and bay leaf. Cover and simmer 40–45 minutes. Remove the chicken to a platter and keep warm. Strain the broth and remove any surface fat. Bring the broth to a boil and reduce to 1½ cups. Melt the remaining 4 tablespoons of butter in a saucepan. Stir in the flour and simmer for 4–5 minutes until thickened and smooth. Add the lemon juice and salt and pepper to taste, spoon over the chicken, and serve.

Chicken Fricassee with Mushrooms: Add 1 cup mushrooms sautéed in 2 tablespoons butter to the sauce just before adding the lemon juice.

Recipe: Succotash with Sausage

From: Linda Bauer. (2010). *Capitol Hill Cooks: Recipes from the White House, Congress, and all the Past Presidents.* Lanham, MD: Taylor Trade Publishing. New York, NY. P. 344

This was Jimmy Carter's entry in the *Capitol Hill Cooks: Recipes from the White House, Congress, and all the Past Presidents.*

Ingredients (serves 4):
- 1 pound sausage links
- 2 tablespoons butter
- ½ cup onions, finely chopped
- 3 large ripe tomatoes, peeled and seeded
- 2 cups fresh or frozen lima beans
- 1½ cups fresh or frozen corn kernels
- 1 cup tomato juice
- 1½ teaspoons salt
- ¼ teaspoon freshly ground white pepper
- 1 tablespoon parsley, chopped

Directions:
1. In a large skillet, cook sausages over medium-high heat until they are cooked thoroughly. Brown for 10 minutes. Drain fat, cover, and keep warm.
2. In a separate skillet, melt butter and sauté onions over medium heat for 3 minutes or until transparent. Do not brown.
3. Dice tomatoes and add to sautéed onions. Stir in lima beans, corn, tomato juice, salt, and pepper.
4. Cover and simmer for 25 minutes. Stir occasionally.
5. Transfer to a deep serving dish. Arrange sausage links across the top.
6. Sprinkle with chopped parsley and serve immediately.

[If you are interested in honoring Ronald Reagan, put out a bowl of Goelitz Mini Jelly Beans. Ronald used them to help break his pipe smoking habit. The company shipped three and half tons of red, white, and blue jelly beans to Reagan for his Inauguration in January, 1981.]

MUSIC THAT WAS ON THE RADIO IN THE 1980s

Born in the USA, performed by Bruce Springsteen (1984)

Springsteen wrote this as a post-Vietnam War protest song, or more precisely a portrayal of the plight of veterans returning from that war.

Bette Davis, her eyes, and Gary Merrill. Co-stars in *All About Eve*, 1950.

Bette Davis Eyes, performed by Kim Carnes (1981)

Jackie DeShannon (you may remember her for her song *What the World Needs Now is Love*) co-wrote this song and recorded it in 1974. Carnes's synthesizer-based version spent nine weeks at #1 on the *Billboard* magazine chart and was the biggest hit of 1981.

Power of Love, performed by Huey Lewis & The News (1985)

If it's Huey Lewis & the News, this must be the 1980s (but Lewis is still touring today). Huey sued Ray Parker Jr. over the similarity in melody between *Power* and the title song to the movie *Ghostbusters*. They settled out of court. In 2018, Lewis was diagnosed as suffering from Meniere's disease, an incurable condition that affects his hearing. In 2020, he and the News released their latest album, *Weather*.

I Wanna Dance with Somebody, performed by Whitney Houston (1987)

Houston is one of the most celebrated pop singers of all time. Her version of the *Star-Spangled Banner* at Super Bowl XXV was a Top 20 hit, the only time the national anthem has been on the popular music charts. Her performance was steeped in controversy though, because the microphone was turned off as a recorded version played. Her spokesperson reminded folks this was not an unusual procedure at large, noisy outdoor events.

Don't Stop Believin', performed by Journey (1981)

When originally released, *Believin'* never made it passed #8 on the *Billboard* charts. The song is ubiquitous now and is the #1 paid download among songs appearing before 2000. Steve Perry (lead singer) has left the group but *Journey* found an incredible voice clone, Arnel Pineda. The song was used in the movies *Monster* and *House of Rock*, and on TV in *Family Guy, Glee,* and the final episode of *The Sopranos*. It also has the dubious honor of having been covered by *Alvin and the Chipmunks*.

Material Girl, performed by Madonna (1985)

Compare this song to Marilyn Monroe's *Diamonds Are a Girl's Best Friend*. The two songs not only share a sentiment, but Madonna's video of *Material Girl* pays homage to the Monroe performance in *Gentlemen Prefer Blondes*, down to the costuming and set design. The TV show *Glee* did a mash-up of the two songs.

Jack & Diane, performed by John Cougar (Mellencamp) (1982)

The Recording Industry Association of America named this *ditty* one of the Songs of the Century. The record company made Mellencamp use "Cougar" for a last name because his real name didn't seem hip. He didn't use his real last name until his seventh album for which he used both names. Mellencamp drop the "Cougar" completely for his ninth album. He was inducted into the Rock and Roll Hall of Fame in 2008. He now focuses mainly on Americana music.

I Love Rock 'n Roll, performed by Joan Jett (1979)

Jett was a founding member of the Runaways, an all-female rock band (also one of the first punk rock bands) in the 1970s, a rarity for the times. She is best known for her solo career, and this rock anthem.

Streets of Bakersfield, performed by Dwight Yoakam and Buck Owens (1988)

Owens sang this song in the 1970s, but this version became its biggest hit, topping the country music charts. Yoakam grew up in Kentucky and Ohio but moved to Los Angeles, CA, after high school intent on becoming a country music artist. His brand of hillbilly honkytonk pays homage to Buck and Merle Haggard, two Bakersfield residents who preceded him.

Chapter 15
WHO TO DRINK WITH? RENOWNED WHISKEY DRINKERS OF YESTERDAY AND TODAY

There is no bad whiskey. There are only some whiskeys that aren't as good as others.
—Raymond Chandler

STEVE ALLEN AND *MEETING OF MINDS*

Steve Allen was a comic genius. He also had a sunny disposition and the common touch. He became one of the most familiar faces on that new-fangled device called a television set. Allen created and was the first host of *The Tonight Show*. He was an accomplished musician, composer, and lyricist who wrote songs recorded by Ella Fitzgerald, Judy Garland, and Ringo Starr, to name a few. He was the author of over fifty books, many of them murder mysteries. Allen was also the inventor of a time machine, kinda.

For many, Allen's crowning achievement was the Public Broadcasting System series, *Meeting of Minds*. He had the inkling for the show's concept in the 1950s, but it didn't come to fruition until 1977. On the shows, famous figures from different historical eras sat and talked to one another in the talk show format that he had created. Allen's "guests" included Plato, Socrates, Aristotle, Thomas Aquinas, Martin Luther, Cleopatra, Marie Antoinette, Florence Nightingale, Thomas Paine, Francis Bacon, Thomas Jefferson, Voltaire, Karl Marx, Charles

Jane Meadows and Steve Allen.

Darwin, and William Shakespeare (who appeared with characters from Shakespeare's own writing). Allen personally financed production of twelve two-part episodes.

As closely as possible, the scripts for *Minds* used words spoken or written by the guests but the conversations were woven together to sound as if they were talking to one another. Of course, there is no record of the actual words some of the guests might have spoken (Cleopatra, for instance) so their words were scripted to be as historically accurate as possible. Allen's wife, Jayne Meadows, appeared in eighteen segments, and played nine different characters.

The show was nominated for four Emmys, winning one, and also won a Peabody Award for outstanding achievement in media, a TV Critics Circle Award, an Encyclopedia Britannica Award, and a Film Advisory Board Award. Allen said of the show's audience, "What appealed to the thousands who wrote [to me], I believe, was that they were actually given the opportunity to hear *ideas* on television, a medium which otherwise presents only people, things, and actions."

The show ran until 1981.[1]

THE GUEST LIST

Imagine that Allen had created an episode of *Meeting of Minds* with famous personalities from American history who were also famous whiskey drinkers, both past and present. Who would he have invited? Many potential

William Faulkner.

guests have already graced these pages: George Thorpe, U. S. Grant, Mark Twain, W. C. Fields, Frank Sinatra, Ernest Hemingway, Ava Gardner, and John Wayne, to name a few. But a few names from the past are missing. For instance:

William Faulkner. William Faulkner was a high school English teacher who hailed from Oxford, MS. His specialty was writing about the South. He was a Nobel Laureate who wrote *The Sound and the Fury* (1929) and *As I Lay Dying* (1930) among other acclaimed novels. Here is some advice from Faulkner on writing you didn't get from your *nerdy* high school English teacher: "My own experience has been that the tools I need for my trade are paper, tobacco, food and a little whisky."

Raymond Chandler. Chandler was the pipe smoking creator of Philip Marlowe, the quintessential private detective and protagonist in his novels, including *The Big Sleep* (1939), *Farewell, My Lovely* (1940), *The Little Sister* (1949), and *The Long Goodbye* (1953). A whiskey drinker by preference, he is credited with the quotation that opens this chapter, correcting anyone who thinks anything like bad whiskey even exists.

Humphrey Bogart. In 1999, the American Film Institute named Humphrey Bogart the greatest male actor in classic American cinema. He was *butter*, as smooth as they come. He played Sam Spade in *The Maltese Falcon* and Phillip Marlowe in the movie version of Chandler's *The Big Sleep*, opposite his wife, Lauren Bacall (William Faulkner was the lead screenwriter). "Bogey" was an Academy Award nominee three times, for *Casablanca*, *The African Queen* (he won), and *The Caine Mutiny*. Were his last words truly "I never should have switched from scotch to martinis"?

Johnny Carson. Carson was the third host of *The Tonight Show*, after Steve Allen and Jack Paar. He was its longest running host, occupying the seat for thirty years. He won numerous awards, including a Presidential Medal of Freedom. He helped Americans and their dogs go to sleep with smiles on their faces: "Happiness is having a rare steak, a bottle of whisky, and a dog to eat the rare steak."

There is a glaring inequity revealed by the list of guests so far; only one woman, Ava Gardner, is on it. Whiskey drinking was a man's activity for most of American history.[2] Or at least, if you were a woman, a taste for whiskey was not something you advertised. This began to change in the 1930s when cocktails made whiskey, in particular in the Old Fashioned and Manhattan mixed drinks, a gender-neutral way to imbibe.

So, to make your dinner more interesting today, let's turn Allen's time machine to the decades after the 1980s and include some women on the whiskey guest list, including some we can forgive for favoring Scotch.[3]

Hillary Clinton. Clinton was caught on video in 2008 drinking *Crown Royal Canadian Whisky*, apparently not a one-time occurrence. During her campaign for the presidency in 2016, she made a stop at the Maker's

Chandler wrote the book, Faulkner wrote the screenplay, Bogart and Bacall starred.
A whiskey lover's dream of a movie.

Mark Distillery and dipped her own bottle to create the red wax seal.

Lady Gaga. Stefani Joanne Angelina Germanotta, a.k.a. Lady Gaga, is a big fan of *Jameson Irish Whiskey*. She credits their "friendship" with inspiring her multi-platinum hit album "Born This Way." In front of a crowd of forty thousand fans, she pulled out a bottle and said, "I have made so much of my music with Jameson. I'm not being paid a cent to advertise the whiskey. . .I should be. The whiskey has made my new songs."

---

2   Calamity Jane could be added to the list of early female drinkers, in her case to excess. She also was known for hanging out with Wild Bill Hickok, for wearing men's clothes, swearing a blue streak, and nursing ailing miners and cowboys.

3   Thanks to https://www.supercall.com/spirits/whiskey/women-who-drink-whiskey

NOAH "SOGGY" SWEAT

Noah "Soggy" Sweat was a judge, law professor, and Mississippi state legislator at the end of the 1940s. He is most famous—perhaps only famous—for a speech he gave before the legislature in which he took a firm stand on both sides of the whiskey controversy:

I had not intended to discuss this controversial subject at this particular time. However, I want you to know that I do not shun controversy. On the contrary, I will take a stand on any issue at any time, regardless of how fraught with controversy it might be. You have asked me how I feel about whiskey. All right, here is how I feel about whiskey.

If when you say whiskey you mean the devil's brew, the poison scourge, the bloody monster, that defiles innocence, dethrones reason, destroys the home, creates misery and poverty, yea, literally takes the bread from the mouths of little children; if you mean the evil drink that topples the Christian man and woman from the pinnacle of righteous, gracious living into the bottomless pit of degradation, and despair, and shame and helplessness, and hopelessness, then certainly I am against it.

But; If when you say whiskey you mean the oil of conversation, the philosophic wine, the ale that is consumed when good fellows get together, that puts a song in their hearts and laughter on their lips, and the warm glow of contentment in their eyes; if you mean Christmas cheer; if you mean the stimulating drink that puts the spring in the old gentleman's step on a frosty, crispy morning; if you mean the drink which enables a man to magnify his joy, and his happiness, and to forget, if only for a little while, life's great tragedies, and heartaches, and sorrows; if you mean that drink, the sale of which pours into our treasuries untold millions of dollars, which are used to provide tender care for our little crippled children, our blind, our deaf, our dumb, our pitiful aged and infirm; to build highways and hospitals and schools, then certainly I am for it.

This is my stand. I will not retreat from it. I will not compromise."

Looking back on his famous speech, Sweat later recalled, "The drys were as unhappy with the second part of the speech as the wets were with the first half."

Mila Kunis. Milena Markovna Kunis came to America from Ukraine with her parents at age seven. She played Jackie Burkhart, girlfriend of Ashton Kutcher's Kelso, on *That 70s Show*. She then was a Golden Globe nominee for her performance in *Black Swan* opposite Natalie Portman, who won the Academy Award for Best Actress. Her role as Jim Beam's spokesperson is credited with helping create a huge increase in the brand's sales, especially amongst younger women. But all was not *hunky-dory* when Mila confessed to making anonymous donations to Planned Parenthood in the name of Vice President Mike Pence, a staunch pro-lifer. Attempts at a boycott of Beam products never took hold. A long-time whiskey drinker, Mila will tell you "I like a little *Jim Beam* (Black Label) on the rocks. . .ice, for sure. A big chunk of ice."

Halle Berry. Legend has it that while promoting her movie *Kingsman: The Golden Circle* at a comic-con event, Berry outdrank the rest of the cast by downing a half-pint of whiskey. *Old Forester Statesman Straight Bourbon Whiskey* was "inspired" by the characters in the movie.

Christina Hendricks. Some other women whisky drinkers had a bit more business savvy. Hendricks, a star of *Mad Men* and *Good Girls* on TV, will always remember *Johnnie Walker Scotch* as the drink she ordered on her first date with her husband. She returned the favor by appearing in several Johnnie Walker ads.

If your time-traveling whiskey friends weren't impressed with what had happened to American whiskey through a quarter millennium of change, you might ask them to stick around—some big shots were about to appear.

Christina Hendricks.

WHAT WHISKEY SHOULD YOU SERVE YOUR DISTINGUISHED GUESTS?

Jim Beam Kentucky Straight Whiskey (White Label)

In 1980, some of the guests at your *Meeting of Minds* will have yet to be born. Others will be long gone but they may still be sipping in the great beyond. How do you know what to serve them?

You won't be able (quickly) to have them taste whiskeys from many of the different distilleries operating today, much less the different labels. Trying to find the right whiskeys to serve will lead to a seemingly endless series of decisions. Do you want to serve the top selling brands? If you go for top selling, internationally or domestic? Sales by volume, caseloads, cost? How about picking according to which whiskeys have won awards or other judgments of taste? You can pick from dozens of arbiters, sometimes with explicitly different criteria, for example, best for the price, or most unheralded gems.

You will notice, if you examine lists based on lots of different criteria, there are three or four mass market labels that appear with the greatest frequency. They appear on lists based on both sales and taste tests. For your guests traveling from different times, these will inform them most clearly about what's going on in the whiskey market today. Two of these distilleries you have already sampled, Jack Daniel and Maker's Mark. The one missing is Mila Kunis' favorite, Jim Beam. All three distilleries are enormously popular today and have multiple expressions to choose from. If you want to keep it simple, choose the flagship labels: *Jack Daniel's Old No. 7 Tennessee Whiskey*, *Maker's Mark Kentucky Straight Bourbon Whisky*, (you have sipped these already) and/or *Jim Beam Kentucky Straight Bourbon Whiskey* (White Label). All have a claim to great taste and domestic and world-wide popularity. If you want two selections (you'll need more than one bottle for this crowd anyway), consider the *Jim Beam Kentucky Straight Bourbon Whiskey* (White Label) and another selection from the Jim Beam Distillery, one of its top-shelf bourbons, *Knob Creek Kentucky Straight Bourbon Whiskey*.

Just the Facts

Mash Bill	Corn: 77% Rye: 13% Malt: 10% Wheat: 0% Other: 0%
Proof	Proof: 80 ABV: 40%
Age; Barrel Char	# Years: 4; #4
Chill Filtered?	Yes

TASTING NOTES

From: The Jim Beam Distillery website
https://www.jimbeam.com/bourbons/jim-beam

The distillery's tasting wheel that suggests the most prominent flavors will be grain and oak, with some sweetness, char, and fruit.

From: Sour Mash Manifesto (Reviewer: Jason Pyle)

https://sourmashmanifesto.com/?s=jim+beam+white

Color: Lighter—Deeper Golden

Aroma: Baked red apple, corn syrup, vanilla nougat, and wet oak. The aromas are soft and sweet, but also flat.

Palate: Not as cloyingly sweet as the nose gave hints to, but once again it's as flat as pancake. There's a vanilla, corn, and caramel party with a bit of dried apple adding fruit character. Towards the end of the sip we finally get some moderately warming cinnamon spice for a welcomed shake-up. The wood begins to emerge as well.

Finish: It continues to liven up with some bitterness from the wood adding interest. The caramel and warming spices fade into a rather clean and tidy finish.

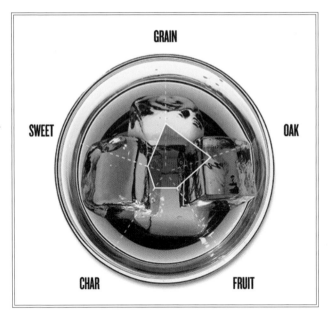

Jim Beam tasting wheel.

Overall: Here's the thing—this is a Good/Solid entry level whiskey. If you know someone that's new to whiskey or bourbon and looking to dip their toe in the water—this would be a great introduction. It's quite pleasant, mildly spiced, and has traditional bourbon flavors. Even though it's only 4 years old, it doesn't taste its youthful age. Jim Beam White Label is a nice casual sipper in a pinch or a versatile mixer, but not a whole lot more.

From: The Over a Barrel Gang

Looks: Gold, pale straw.

Aroma: Delicate. Clove, leather, caramel, apple, grape, tobacco.

Flavor: Medium body. Sweet, salty.

Mouth Feel: Round, creamy, sharp, light.

Going Down: Soft strength, short length.

Notes: Good for getting you there, nothing fancy.

Knob Creek Kentucky Straight Bourbon Whiskey

Knob Creek is one of the Jim Beam's small batch expressions. It is pricier than the *Jim Beam* (White Label). Its mash bill is the same as the White Label, but it has been aged five years longer and bottled with 50% more alcohol. It has won numerous awards in tasting competitions, including a "Best Bourbon" award.

Just the Facts

Mash Bill	Corn: 75% Rye: 13% Malt: 12% Wheat: 0%
Proof	Proof: 100 ABV: 50%
Age; Barrel Char	9 Years; #4
Chill Filtered?	Probably not

TASTING NOTES

The Knob Creek website describes the color of its straight bourbon whiskey as "copper to medium amber," its taste as "sweet, woody, full-bodied, almost fruity" and its texture as "rich."

From: Beverage Testing Institute[4]

https://www.tastings.com/Spirits-Review/Knob-Creek-Kentucky-Straight-Bourbon-Whiskey-USA-100-Proof-10-01-2017.aspx

Amber color. Aromas and flavors of crushed peanuts, coconut frosting, bruléed banana, chocolate sponge cake, allspice, and molasses with a velvety, crisp, dryish medium-to-full body and a warming, complex, long finish. A bold and coating Bourbon that delivers rich flavors and velvety texture.

From: The Over a Barrel Gang

Looks: Amber, deep copper.
Aroma: Delicate. Maple, butterscotch, cinnamon, apple, wood.
Flavor: Heavy body. Sweet, bitter.
Mouth Feel: Round, creamy.
Going Down: Medium strength, medium length.
Notes: Hot but not overwhelming, easy drinking; a rye lover's go-to.

Toast

Steve Allen said on the first telecast of *The Tonight Show*, September 27, 1954, "This is *The Tonight Show*. I can't tell you too much about it, other than the fact that this program is going to go on forever."

To Mr. Steve Allen. This quote suggests he could clearly use his time machine to travel to both the past and future. And to the history of ideas.

---

4   The Beverage Testing Institute uses trained panelists unaware of the product they are tasting and a proprietary methodology (http://trade.tastings.com/info/methodology).

DINNER AT KCET-TV, HOLLYWOOD, CA, WITH STEVE ALLEN, JANE MEADOWS, AND THEIR GUESTS ON *MEETING OF MINDS*

In the 1950s, fast food joints were sprouting up around the country to accommodate the new suburban commuters and their young families. But a few decades later on the West Coast a movement emphasizing locally sourced, fresh, and sustainable ingredients was taking root. Alice Waters opened *Chez Panisse* in Berkeley, CA, in 1971. Wolfgang Puck opened *Spago* in Los Angeles, CA, in 1982. These chefs were destined to become media celebrities.

California was the epicenter of a *bodacious* culinary revolution. Pizza recipes challenged diners to go beyond tomato sauce, cheese, and spicy meats. Toppings including fruits and vegetables were among the first California innovations to break through on the national scene. As well, the West Coast was a garden of multicultural delights and its culinary contributions reflected its diversity. Recipes that fused cooking traditions, especially ones that were variations on Mexican and Asian dishes, were part of the California movement as well. Your table of dishes for your whiskey-drinking guests could reflect this assortment of traditions.

Recipe: Easy Chipotle Chicken Tacos
From: America's Test Kitchen. (2015). *The Best Mexican Recipes*. Boston, MA: America's Test Kitchen. P. 95.

Ingredients (serves 4):
    3 tablespoons unsalted butter
    4 garlic cloves, minced
    2 teaspoons minced canned chipotle chili in adobo sauce
    ¾ cup chopped fresh cilantro
    ½ cup orange juice
    1 tablespoon Worcestershire sauce
    1½ pounds of boneless, skinless chicken breasts, skinned
    1 teaspoon yellow mustard
    Salt and pepper
    12 (6-inch) corn tortillas, warmed
    Lime wedge

Directions:
1. Melt butter in 12-inch skillet over medium-high heat. Add garlic and chipotle and cook until fragrant, about 30 seconds. Stir in ½ cup cilantro, orange juice, and Worcestershire and bring to simmer. Nestle chicken into sauce. Cover, reduce heat to medium-low, and cook until chicken registers 160 degrees, about 10 to 15 minutes, flipping chicken halfway through cooking. Transfer chicken to plate and cover.
2. Increase heat to medium-high and cook liquid left in skillet until reduced to ¼ cup, about 5 minutes. Off heat and whisk in mustard. Using 2 forks, shred chicken into bite-size pieces and return to skillet. Add remaining ¼ cup cilantro and toss until well combined. Season with salt and pepper to taste. Serve with warm tortillas and lime wedges.

Recipe: Pineapple Fried Rice

From: Kuan, Diana. (2012). *The Chinese Takeout Cookbook.* New York, NY: Ballantine Books. P. 151.

The secret to making delicious fried rice is stir-frying with cold leftover rice. Rice that has been cooled is firmer and has less moisture, and it develops the signature crisp texture more easily in the wok [or large skillet].

Ingredients (serves 4 as part of a multicourse meal):

    3 cups leftover cooked white rice

    2 tablespoons peanut or vegetable oil

    2 shallots, finely chopped

    ½ red bell pepper, finely chopped

    1 tablespoon oyster sauce

    1 tablespoon soy sauce

    1 tablespoon Chinese rice wine or dry sherry

    1 cup fresh pineapple, cut into ½-inch bite-size cubes

    ¼ cup chopped thickly sliced ham

Directions:

1. Break up the cold cooked rice into small clumps.
2. Heat a wok or large skillet over medium-high heat until a bead of water sizzles and evaporates on contact. Add the peanut oil and swirl to coat the bottom. Add the shallots and bell peppers and stir-fry until fragrant and the edges of the shallots begin to crisp, about a minute. Move the shallots and bell peppers to the side, creating a well in the middle. Toss in the rice and break up any remaining clumps with a spatula.
3. Stir in the oyster sauce, soy sauce, and rice wine. Continue to stir-fry until the rice starts to turn golden, about 2 minutes. Add the pineapple and ham. Give everything in the wok a few quick stirs so that the pineapple and ham are heated through. Transfer to a large bowl or plate and serve hot.

MUSIC FROM THE 1980s THAT YOUR TIME TRAVELING GUESTS MIGHT LIKE TO HEAR

Footloose, performed by Kenny Loggins (1984)

Footloose was written for the movie by the same name. Lori Singer (as Ariel) is a high school student rebelling against her minister father John Lithgow (as Rev. Shaw Moore) who has banned dancing in the town. Who better for Ariel to *bust a move* with than Kevin Bacon (as Ren)? Dad comes around in the end.

Rapper's Delight, performed by Sugarhill Gang (1999)

Delight is #2 on *Rolling Stone* magazine's greatest rap songs of all time. It was the first rap song to get play-time on Top 40 radio stations. Its crossover appeal sent it to #36 on the pop charts. This is a 7-minute version, shortened from the original 15-minute version released as a twelve-inch single.

9 to 5, performed by Dolly Parton (1980)

From the movie by the same name, Dolly Parton, Jane Fonda, and Lily Tomlin exact revenge on their sexist, skinflint boss played by Dabney Coleman. Is this the first pop culture rumblings of the equal pay movement? Parton has written over three thousand songs.

Billie Jean, performed by Michael Jackson (1982)

Jackson is as controversial as they come. Charges of sexual abuse have followed him until today, well after his death in 2009. Radio stations around the world still refuse to play his music. Remember, this is a history book.

Sugarhill Gang, 1980.

Goodbye Earl, performed by the Dixie Chicks (2001)

The Dixie Chicks' music was banned from most country music stations in 2003 after Natalie Maines openly criticized George W. Bush and the impending invasion of Iraq during a concert in London. Their anti-war ways shouldn't have been a surprise though; Maines's remarks preceded their song *Travelin' Soldier*. In 2020, the group changed its name to The Chicks, removing the allusion to the Old South. And defiance was always a subtext of their songs, as Earl knows.

It's Still Rock and Roll to Me, performed by Billy Joel (1980)

William ("Billy") Martin Joel, the Piano Man, was born in the Bronx, NY, and was forced to take piano lessons by his mother. In his youth, he won twenty-two boxing matches in the Golden Gloves. Then he got his nose broken and gave up the sport.

Jessie's Girl, performed by Rick Springfield (1981)

A 1980s teen heartthrob, Springfield went on to a successful acting career, most notably as Dr. Noah Drake on the daytime soap opera, *General Hospital*. (He got a shout-out on the TV show *Friends*, when Matt LaBlanc, as Joey Tribbiani, an aspiring actor, played Dr. Drake Ramoray on *Days of Our Lives*). Springfield is now in his seventies and is touring again, singing the blues.

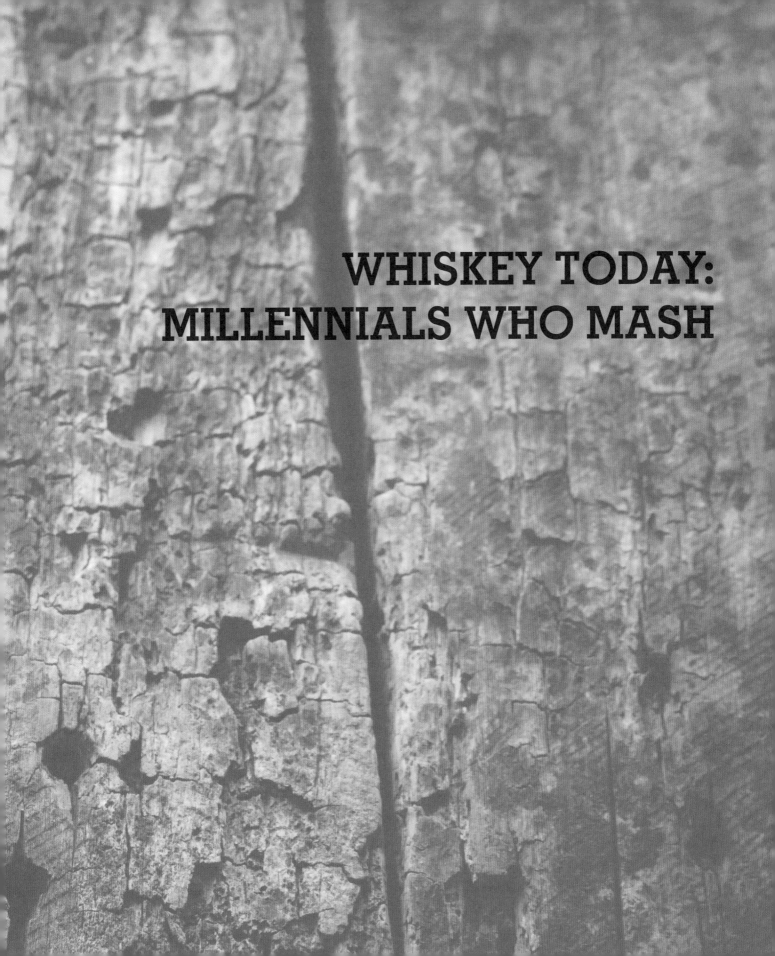

WHISKEY TODAY: MILLENNIALS WHO MASH

Chapter 16
MAKING FRIENDS WITH THE GOLIATHS

. . . all bourbon is handmade; bourbon, unlike coffee or orange juice,
cannot be grown in the wild.
—Florida Court Judgement, Salter v. Beam Suntory, Inc.
Case No. 4:14CV659-RH/CAS, 2015 WL 2124939

CORN AND RYE MAKE A COMEBACK

In the mid-1990s, the consumption of spirits per person in America may have hit its lowest point in decades. But things were about to improve. The turn of the century saw an upswing in the fortunes of American whiskey producers. Between 2002 and 2006, sales of bourbon and Tennessee whiskey rose by more than double digits. Sales of premium whiskeys rose more than 25% and super-premium brands doubled that rate of increase. As more whiskey products got placed on the top shelves at liquor stores, demand went up with price. And whiskey's image changed; it was no longer that *rot gut* people associated with a cowboy draining a shot in one gulp. Whiskey was now something to sip and savor. It was *lit*.

What led to the renaissance? Certainly, the success of premium and super-premium labels convinced distillers that the demand was there if their product was geared to the taste of a connoisseur. Flavored whiskeys also came into fashion. These could be used to introduce the spirit to imbibers not ready for the straight stuff. Among the favorite flavorings were honey, apple, and cinnamon. But distillers tried all sorts of added touches, including peanut butter (with due respect to Dave Barry, I'm not making this up). Another innovation involved moving aging whiskey from one barrel to another originally used to hold a different liquor. This technique is called "double casking." It can soften or sweeten the whiskey's flavor profile or add the hint of a new taste. The second barrel might have originally contained port, sherry, or another spirit. Finally, while the whiskey renaissance trailed behind the boom in craft beers and wines, spirits did benefit from the increasing

MORE AMERICAN WHISKEY CATEGORIES*

More definitions, not (yet) defined by law.

Small Batch: "Small batch" describes a whiskey distilled in limited quantity or chosen from a limited number of barrels. "Limited" typically means a quantity of around one thousand gallons or less, and fewer than 20 barrels (a full-sized whiskey barrel contains about 53 gallons), with a mash bill of under "200 bushels of grain." Small batch whiskeys are typically aged from six to nine years. It is not a legal term though, so what small batch means can vary from distiller to distiller.

Single Barrel: "Single barrel" whiskey comes from a single barrel. Typically, these will be chosen by tasters or will rest in a spot of a warehouse known to produce whiskey with a special taste. (Whiskeys that have no single barrel designation are typically comprised of whiskeys from multiple barrels that are mixed together.)

Cask Strength: A whiskey that is not diluted or only slightly diluted with water when it is transferred from the cask to the bottle will be called "cask strength" or an equivalent term, such as "barrel strength" or "barrel proof." This means it will have a higher alcohol content, typically 120 proof (60% ABV) or greater.

Finished or double matured or double cask: These terms denote a whiskey that has been moved from one barrel to another. The first barrel will be charred oak. The second barrel can be new or can have previously contained something the distiller thinks will contribute to a unique flavor. For example, the second barrel might have contained sherry. The label will say what first filled the second barrel. There is no standard for how long the whiskey has to rest in the second barrel, but the label may tell you this. The whiskey's time in the second barrel does not count toward the claimed age of the whiskey.

---

*   https://www.ecfr.gov/cgi-bin/retrieveECFR?gp=&SID=9b2a0a59ad7bdd15023465091823490c&n=27y1.0.1.1.3&r=PA
      RT&ty=HTML#27:1.0.1.1.3.3.25.1

---

popularity of the more general embrace of craft everything.

And then there was *Mad Men*.

The *Mad Men* Effect

The AMC television series *Mad Men* premiered in 2007, ran for seven seasons, and was viewed by more than a million pairs of eyes for each of its ninety-two episodes. Taking place in and around a Madison Avenue advertising agency, alcohol consumption was (accurately) portrayed as an integral part of this emerging subculture. While many of the accoutrements of the time are still with us, the liquor cart or credenza bar in an executive's office has faded into history, sometimes replaced by the much less conspicuous bottom drawer of the desk. Still, to viewers in the first decade of the twenty-first century, the fact that executives once openly displayed alcohol in their offices was a revelation.

Barbie Dolls fashioned after Betty Francis (formerly Draper), Don Draper, Joan Holloway, and Roger Sterling from *Mad Men*.
Over one billion Barbie Dolls have been sold since they first appeared in 1959.

Don Draper, *Mad Men*'s central character, favored drinking whiskey, especially an Old Fashioned, but he seemed like an equal opportunity imbiber. The show was hugely popular with audiences in advertisers' target demographic of young adults. The series received coverage in newspapers, magazines, and websites, and it instigated water cooler conversations around the country.

Women got involved in the alcohol culture as well. *Sex and the City* was an HBO series that ran from 1998 to 2004. It lasted for over ninety episodes and had two follow-up movies and a spinoff TV prequel. It was centered on the lives of four women living in New York City. Spirited drinks were prominently featured at meals shared by the women, especially mixed drinks. Many bartenders reported noticeable increases in requests for whiskey cocktails.

THE INDUSTRY RESPONDS TO THE NEW DEMAND

Distillers raced to keep up with the new consumer demand. One way they could increase their output was by lowering the amount of alcohol in their product.

This could be done by adding more water when a barrel was taken off the rack before bottling. In 2004, Jack Daniel's Distillery lowered its whiskey to 80 proof (40% ABV) from 86 proof and saw about a 30% increase in sales.[1] *Maker's Mark* also tried to lower its proof, from 90 to 84, but a revolt by loyal drinkers resulted in a return to the old formula.

Like any aged product, barreling whiskey and committing to let it sit for years meant distillers who expanded their capacity were making a bet with an uncertain outcome. Aging whiskey for two years, or four years, or ten years, meant they were gambling that the boom would go on; today's investment would not pay off for many years, and by then the demand for whiskey may have slackened.

Blenders and Sourcers

Blended whiskeys have always been around. Some of the iconic brands of Scotch whisky are blends, for example, *Dewar's Scotch*. But American whiskey blends arrived en masse at the beginning of the twenty-first century. Blended Scotch whisky mixes different ages. Some blended American whiskeys mix whiskeys of different ages or mash bills, but these can also mix whiskey with clear spirits, flavorings, and colorings. These might also contain additives to give the concoction a golden color, but you don't see additives too much anymore.

Many distilleries source their spirits from third parties. The aging process can be completed before the bottlers purchase it or the purchaser can add other whiskeys and ingredients and age it further. Because a whiskey is sourced does not mean it is of

---

1   There is more to it than simply getting more product. At the time, Jack Daniel's Distillery was selling whiskeys of different proofs in different markets worldwide. Making all *Old No. 7* have the same proof simplified matters.

lesser quality. For example, *WhistlePig* rye whiskeys from Goamericago Beverages in Shoreham, VT, is a much sought-after whiskey that was created by one of the industry's most renowned craftsman, Dave Pickerell. But it is sourced from Canada, at least until its own distillery can produce and age its own product. *Templeton Rye,* out of Templeton, IA, first appeared during Prohibition and was resurrected in the early 2000s by the son of one of the original moonshiners. However, the new *Templeton Rye* blend was not an original. In a lawsuit, the company admitted so. Besides acknowledging that *Templeton Rye* was sourced from another distillery and then processed and bottled at their plant, the company had to change its label from stating it was a "Prohibition-era recipe" and "small batch" to read that it was "based on" a Prohibition-era recipe with no claim about being small batch. That said, *Templeton Rye* has won many honors as an American straight whiskey. High West Distillery whiskeys also contain blends using their own distillate and other high-end whiskeys that vary in age, categories, and taste profiles. They are blended in-house. Many highly regarded whiskeys have one thing in common: they source their whiskey from the same sourcer, though they use different mash bills.[2]

GOBBLE, GOBBLE

Consolidation of the whiskey industry began with the end of Prohibition, but it has taken on renewed momentum in recent years. To meet the increasing demand, the need was great for capital to expand production. A consolidation of the industry seemed inevitable, and it happened. Today many of the iconic whiskey brands are a division of a larger corporation that finances their expansion and owns many different distilleries. Four corporations control well over half of the production of American bourbon and rye: Beam Suntory, Brown-Forman, Heaven Hill, and Sazerac. Even craft whiskeys are being gobbled up by the big beverage corporations, following in the footsteps of the beer and wine industries. As this has occurred, whiskey aficionados keep a watchful eye on their favorite brands and protest at the slightest suggestion that the taste of the product is being compromised. Meanwhile, billions of dollars are being spent to increase production and storage capacity.

Midwestern Grain Products (MGP)

Operating out of Atchison, KS, and Lawrenceburg, IN, Midwestern Grain Products (known as MGP) began as a small distiller of grains in 1941 and has since evolved into a leading supplier of premium distilled spirits, as well as specialty pasta, frozen dough, and other grain and dairy products. It is situated about one hundred miles north of Louisville, KY, and thirty miles west of Cincinnati, OH. It provides whiskeys and other spirits for companies both large and small.

MGP's image as a mass producer led premium whiskey drinkers to *throw shade* (say something nasty) regarding how it would taste. It didn't help that some distilleries were less than forthcoming on their labels and websites about their spirit's origin. Craft distilleries might use MGP whiskeys until their own stills were producing a unique product and while their whiskeys were aging. They would order custom mash bills made to their specifications, using the same mash bill of grains in the same proportion as they were cooking up and aging themselves, for the future.

Maybe the size of the distilling operation doesn't matter that much. The master distillers at MGP have decades of experience and are well-respected among

2   At big whiskey events today, seminars are given on how to blend whiskey. You can taste several varieties of whiskey, mix the ones you like in your own proportions, and go home with a bottle of your own concoction.

their peers. MGP has won accolades in contests where judges were unaware of where a whiskey came from. In 2015, MGP won *Whisky Advocate* magazine's award for Distiller of the Year. Now MGP is beginning to come out from behind the curtain. Moral: Try lots of whiskeys and drink what you like. It's as simple as that.

One thing is certain: industry consolidation and the proliferation of small, craft distilleries make it that much more important that buyers be as knowledgeable as possible of exactly what they are purchasing.

CAVEAT EMPTOR: THE FIRST IMPRESSION OF YOUR WHISKEY IS NOT IN YOUR NOSE OR MOUTH

The first impression of a whiskey comes not from its aroma or taste. It comes from something you hear in an ad, from a store clerk, or from a friend or bartender. Before you pop open a bottle, your most proximal impression will come from the shape of the bottle, the whiskey's color, and the design, prose, and poetry written on the label.[3] Don't rush past these clues; they will help you understand your experience. At the same time, don't let them alter your experience too much unless you come across something on a label that makes you suspicious of what might be hidden from you or you feel like you are being *sold a bill of goods*.

The Bottle Shape

Whiskey bottles come in a wide variety of shapes, so they appear more distinct to the eye on a liquor store or bar shelf. Most contain 750 ml of liquid, though 375 ml is not unusual (you can even find 1.75ml bottles in larger liquor stores). When you calculate how premium your premium whiskey is, be sure to make the price calculation to equivalent ounces.[4]

Color

All whiskey bottles use clear glass. This lets you inspect the color of the liquid before you buy or pour it. The color should be a shade of golden brown. All else equal, the darker the color, the longer the content has been aged (or had coloring added to make it look older). Hold the bottle up to the light. If you can see cloudiness from impurities floating around, it is not necessarily a bad thing; it means the whiskey has not been chill-filtered (that is, passed through a filter at a near freezing temperature before it is bottled). Chill filtering takes certain esters, proteins, and fatty acids out of whiskeys. Some distillers think the "impurities" give their whiskey a unique and desirable taste. Typically, if the whiskey was not chill-filtered it will be stated on the label but there is no legal requirement to do so.[5]

What's on the Label?

Most whiskey labels strive for technical accuracy, but some not so much.[6] Labels on a whiskey bottle will contain lots of information that will help you understand what is in the bottle and how, where, and by whom it was manufactured. Let's look at the reading material.

---

3   This is the marketing genius of *Maker's Mark's* red wax covering the cork. It stands out and is easily identifiable on any shelf.

4   Scotch and Irish whisky bottles are typically more uniform in size and shape than American whiskeys. Tradition must be upheld.

5   If nothing is stated about chill-filtering on the label you might assume that whiskey above 46% ABV has not been chill-filtered; clouding is not an issue when the alcohol content is that high.

6   In 2018, the government posted a notice of proposed changes to label regulations described in this section. If adopted, there will be more transparency in advertising but not much described in the regulations would change.

WATERFILL AND FRAZIER KENTUCKY STRAIGHT BOURBON LABELS

As the label states, *Waterfill and Frazier* whiskey has been around for over 200 years. It secured its place in whiskey history when the Prohibition Era began. Its owner, Mary Dowling dismantled the plant with the help of Joseph L. Beam (the founder of Heaven Hill Distilleries). It was moved to Juarez, Mexico, then the whiskey was smuggled back into the United States. The distillery was reopened in Kentucky when Prohibition ended. These labels are from the brand's third incarnation; it's a good example of what a whiskey label might look like, as well as an interesting episode in whiskey history.

Product Brand. The name of the product will be in the largest font on the front of the label, of course. There will typically be a unique picture or logo that identifies the product, such as the buffalo on *Buffalo Trace*, the S$_{IV}$ on *Maker's Mark*, or an old guy's picture for *Old Grand-dad* or *Old Rip Van Winkle*, among many others.

Whiskey Type. The type of whiskey usually appears below the brand. If the label says "bourbon (corn)" "rye," "malted barley" (or "single malt")," or "wheat," this tells you that at least 51% of the mash bill came from that grain. If it says "whiskey" it is likely a potion with a mash bill that contains no single grain in the majority (the label might even say "multigrain"). Labels rarely provide the complete mash bill but most of these can be found online (you can find many mash bills at https://modernthirst.com/home/bourbon-whiskey-mash-bills/).

If the label says "Kentucky" or any other state, it should be that all the steps in the manufacturing process happened in that state alone. The label might also say "straight" or "bottled-in-bond." If so, the whiskey meets the legal requirements for that designation. The label will also be sure to report whether the whiskey has come from a small batch or single barrel; it's an indication the stuff is "premium" that the producer does not want to hide.

Also on the label may be terms like "reserve," "special reserve," or "select." These terms have no standard meaning so if you are curious, read more on the label or ask before you buy. Sometimes, distillers will have their favorite or high-volume purchasers come to the distillery and select a barrel or barrels for their establishment. The label or the bar's menu will let you know it is "select" when this has happened, sometimes with an additional sticker placed on it.

A label might also say that the whiskey was "handcrafted." This is another term with no standard definition. Every whiskey has some hands-on moments. If you are curious about what handcrafted means on the label you are trying to decipher, you will likely have to try to find out on the brand's website, or through an inquiry.

Age Statement. The label may or may not contain a statement of how long whiskey was aged. If any of the whiskey that has gone into the bottle was less than four years old, the label must say so. If the whiskey is a blend, the statement of the age must refer to the youngest of the component whiskeys. The label may contain a statement of the year the spirit was barreled or the year it was bottled. Unlike wine, once whiskey is barrel-aged its properties will not change in the bottle unless it is poorly sealed or stored improperly. (Spirits are stored upright so there is no contact between the liquid and the cork.)

Site of Distilling, Aging, and Bottling. There are multiple stops that the contents of a bottle of whiskey has made before it reaches a bar or store shelf. These should be detailed on the label. It should tell you where the whiskey was distilled. If it says "produced," that's an ambiguous term; that whiskey may have been sourced and then blended or somehow transformed at the stated location. This can be different from where the whiskey was aged. The city and state of each stop in the process should also be stated.

Proof and Alcohol by Volume. On the front or back label, there should be a statement of the content's proof and alcohol by volume (ABV). If the whiskey was not reduced in strength between when the barrel was emptied and before it was bottled (or hardly so), there should be some verbiage that tells you it is "barrel strength," "cask strength," or even "navy strength." This will also be reflected in the statement of proof.

Government Warning. A government warning should be on all labels. It tells you not to drink alcoholic beverages if you are pregnant, not to drive or operate heavy machinery while under the influence, and that alcohol can cause health problems.[7]

Other Stuff. Most labels include a website address or phone number to call if you have questions about the brand. To impress you, some premium whiskeys might tell you the rickhouse it came from and the batch and bottle number. The label might also tell you the bottle's value for recycling (in some states).

Labels may also contain fun stuff to read, such as some history of the spirit's brand, how it was distilled (e.g., use of a copper pot still is a selling point nowadays), and the type and char of the barrel. You might see a quote or the signature of the

---

7   You'll rarely see tax strips across the tops of most whiskey bottles anymore. The stamps were used in the 1800s through to the 1980s to ensure that distillers paid their taxes. They were meant to make it harder for distillers to scam the government by reusing bottles and paying taxes only once. If you buy an unopened bottle of vintage whiskey that claims to be pristine, the first thing you should do is carefully examine the tax stamp for tampering.

master distiller or a historical figure associated with the brand.

A good reason for whiskey labels to remain honest is that federal laws require accuracy. A whiskey label cannot:

- contain false and misleading statements;
- disparage competitors;
- be obscene or indecent;
- make misleading statements about testing, analysis, or standards of production;
- make false promises;
- claim a connection with prominent individuals or organizations (unless consent was given);
- use government symbols, pictures, and such.

Of course, a description of the whiskey's history or its marvelous taste on the label can be selective, even hyperbolic, but it can't be fraudulent. The written description of a whiskey's characteristics can be straightforward or border on the poetic.

As the giants grew bigger and bigger, was there still room in the whiskey world for the little guys?

WHAT DOES A GOLIATH WHISKEY TASTE LIKE?

George Remus Repeal Reserve Straight Bourbon Whiskey

While MGP has distributed its own labels on a limited basis, *George Remus Repeal Reserve Straight Bourbon Whiskey* is its first venture into creating its own brand of whiskey available nationally. MGP bought the name from a small company that was sourcing its whiskey from MGP. Given that George Remus ran his bootlegging operations out of Cincinnati, OH, about thirty miles east of Lawrenceburg, IN, where MGP is located, the name had an historical appeal. *Remus Repeal Reserve* is being issued as an annual series. *Series III* (issued in 2019) uses a medley of four different bourbons barreled in 2007 and 2008, meaning it is aged ten to eleven years. The corn content varies for the two years.[8]

---

8 The label and bottle do not acknowledge the whiskey's MGP pedigree, but it does say that it was distilled in Lawrenceburg, IN.

Just the Facts

Mash Bill	Corn: 60–75% Rye: 21–36% Malt: 4%
Proof	Proof: 100 ABV: 50%
Age; Barrel Char	# Years: 10–11; #4 on the staves, #2 on the heads
Chill Filtered?	No

TASTING NOTES

From: George Remus Distilling Company

https://georgeremus.com/the-bourbon/remus-repeal-reserve-series/

. . .the 2019 limited edition of Remus Repeal Reserve features layers of caramel, candied fruit, chocolate, baking spice, smoke and leather, leading to a smooth finish with notes of caramel, and a hint of rye.

From: Bourbon Guy (Reviewer: Eric Burke)

https://www.bourbonguy.com/blog/2019/1/15/remus-repeal-reserve-series-2

Aroma: Crisp apple, black pepper, cinnamon candies and old, weathered wood.

Mouth: Spicy and warm in the mouth with a nice thick mouthfeel. Black pepper, baking spices, honey and a bit of fruit as it moves back.

Finish: Long and warm. Lingering apple, oak, baking spice and brown sugar.

Thoughts: Once again this is a delicious bourbon. It's hard to imagine that it could be otherwise when you consider the vast stocks of bourbon that are sitting in Lawrenceburg, Indiana. This is rich and thick and coats the mouth. So, now what about those differences *Inside* the bottle? The first thing you notice is that 2017 is much richer on the nose. Both have a lot of spice, but 2018 hits you with more fruit and more sweetness. On the palate where 2017 was dry, 2018 is much sweeter. It has a thicker mouthfeel and just feels more complicated. Continuing on the theme, the finish of 2018 is longer and sweeter than that of 2017. Overall, I'd say that though both of these are good bourbons, I much prefer 2018's Series II. It is much more in line with this Bourbon Guy's tastes.

From: The Over a Barrel Gang

Looks: Deep copper, amber, gold.

Aroma: Robust. Maple, caramel, apple, vanilla, clove, cherry, tobacco.

Flavor: Heavy body. Sweet, sour, bitter.

Mouth Feel: Creamy, rich, sharp, heavy.

Going Down: Strong strength, medium length.

Notes: Pretty even keel on the palate, really robust, classic nose, classic sipping.

Toast

Since we are approaching the end of our journey through time, let's make sure we acknowledge what matters most. Here's an old toast of unknown origin that reminds us of what to ask for in life:

May we never want for friends to cheer us, or a bottle of whiskey to cheer them.

WHAT DESSERT SHOULD YOU SERVE YOUR BEST WHISKEY FRIENDS TO KEEP THEM HEALTHY?

It's time for a healthy dessert.

In the early 2000s, artisanal food became even more hip; consumers began to show greater interest in locally grown and handcrafted foods (and spirits). Eating more healthy foods gained in popularity. Different culinary philosophies abounded. Here are three.

Vegan Diet

Vegans not only eschew meats but they avoid all animal products, including dairy and eggs. While vegetarianism has been around for almost a century (probably longer but not labelled such), veganism is a relatively recent movement. People can become vegans for several different reasons, most notably for its health benefits (for example, to avoid heart disease and diabetes) and out of concerns about animal welfare and the environment.

Recipe: Vegan Cheesecake

From: EatingWell, Inc. http://www.eatingwell.com/recipe/272204/vegan-cheesecake/

Ingredients:

Filling

1½ cups raw cashews or macadamia nuts

8 ounces silken tofu

1 cup coconut cream

1 tablespoon cornstarch

2 teaspoons pure vanilla extract

¾ cup sugar

2 teaspoons lemon zest

1 tablespoon lemon juice

⅛ teaspoon salt

Crust

1 cup pecans, toasted

1 cup gluten-free oat flour (see Note)

⅓ cup melted coconut oil

3 tablespoons pure maple syrup

½ teaspoon salt

Directions

1. To prepare nuts for filling: Place cashews (or macadamias) in a heatproof medium bowl. Cover with boiling water by 1 inch and let soak for 1 hour.

2. Meanwhile, preheat oven to 350°F. Coat a 9-inch springform pan with cooking spray.

3. To prepare crust: Process pecans in a food processor until finely ground. Add oat flour, coconut oil, maple syrup and ½ teaspoon salt; pulse until just combined. Firmly press into the bottom of the prepared pan.

4. Bake the crust until set but not browned, about 15 minutes. Let cool on a wire rack for 15 minutes.

5. Drain the cashews (or macadamias) and transfer to a blender or food processor. Add tofu, coconut cream, cornstarch, vanilla, sugar, lemon zest, lemon juice and salt. Blend until very smooth. Scrape into the crust. Place the cheesecake on a rimmed baking sheet.

6. Bake the cheesecake until the edges look very slightly dry and the center appears only slightly jiggly but not liquidy, 50 minutes to 1 hour. Cool on a wire rack until room temperature, about 1 hour. Refrigerate, uncovered, until very cold, at least 3 hours.

7. To serve, run a sharp knife along the edge to loosen the pan sides and remove.

Ingredient Note: People with celiac disease or gluten sensitivity should use oats and oat products, such as oat flour, that are labeled "gluten-free" as oats are often cross-contaminated with wheat and barley. To make ahead: Refrigerate for up to three days.

Keto Diet

Keto diets are a new variation on an old standard. They are low in carbohydrates and high in fats. Low carbohydrate diets have been around for some time, but keto diets and recipes are fairly new. The term "keto" derives from "ketone" or "ketosis." Ketone is produced by the body for energy when its supply of carbohydrates is low. Keto diets are meant to force the body to make ketones and to reduce the consumer's weight.

Representative ketones, from the left: acetone, a common solvent; oxaloacetate, an intermediate in the metabolism of sugars; acetylacetone in its (mono) enol form (the enol highlighted in blue); cyclohexanone, precursor to nylon; muscone, an animal scent; and tetracycline, an antibiotic.

Recipe: Paleo (or Keto) Apple Crumble

From: Healthy Recipes, https://healthyrecipesblogs.com/apple-crumble/

Ingredients:

Fuji apples: Or any other sweet apple variety that's suitable for baking (see details below).

Chopped raw walnuts: Pecans also work. Make sure they're unsalted.

Melted unsalted butter: European butter tastes best, but any unsalted butter will work.

Cinnamon: Make sure it's fresh. It's such an important part of this recipe, and a stale spice can easily ruin a dish.

Vanilla extract: It's best to use pure vanilla and not the artificial stuff. There's a difference.

Sweetener: This is optional and not really needed, in my opinion. But if you wish, you can use a small amount of granulated sugar-free sweetener or a syrupy one.

Directions:

1. Start by prepping the apples: peel, core, and slice them.
2. Arrange the apple slices in a baking dish. One layer is ideal, but two layers are OK too.
3. Mix together the remaining ingredients and pour over the apples.
4. Bake for about 30 minutes at 375°F. You'll know it's ready by the amazing smell!
5. Divide into plates, drizzle with the pan juices, and serve.

Plain Old Healthy Desserts

EatingWell emphasizes balanced nutrition for healthy eating; everything in moderation and no strict rules or fad dieting. They profess that healthy eating should be "a way of life, it should be accessible, sustainable, inspiring and-above all-delicious."

Recipe: Watermelon Fruit Pizza

From: EatingWell, Inc., http://www.eatingwell.com/recipe/254624/watermelon-fruit-pizza/

Ingredients:

½ cup low-fat plain yogurt

1 teaspoon honey

¼ teaspoon vanilla extract

2 large round slices watermelon (about 1 inch thick), cut from the center of the melon

⅔ cup sliced strawberries

½ cup halved blackberries

2 tablespoons torn fresh mint leaves

Directions:

1. Combine yogurt, honey, and vanilla in a small bowl.
2. Spread ¼ cup yogurt mixture over each slice of watermelon. Cut each slice into 8 wedges. Top with strawberries, blackberries, and mint.

MUSIC THAT MILLENNIALS LISTENED TO AS THE 21ST CENTURY BEGAN

Two themes emerged in the popular songs of the 21st Century: songs by men that are laced with profanity (e.g., Tupac Shakur) and songs by women about female empowerment (with some mild profanity thrown in). Let's focus on the latter. Popular music has splintered into so many genres that dozens of Grammy categories have resulted. While perusing this playlist, you may proclaim, "Yeah, but what about . . ." You are correct. Still, the most compelling story told by modern popular music is its evolution from colonial times, when a female voice was hard to find, until today, when the airwaves are filled with anthems sung by women.

Britney Spears, on stage, 2016.
Not a Mouseketeer anymore.

Oops! I Did It Again, performed by Britney Spears (2000)

Britney's life has been a national obsession since she was eleven years old and debuted as a Mouseketeer on *The Mickey Mouse Club*. Stadium tours, movies, the Las Vegas Strip.

Beautiful, performed by Christina Aguilera (2002)

Aguilera is another *Mickey Mouse Club* alum. She was also the first female judge on TV's singing competition show, *The Voice*.

It's Five O'clock Somewhere, performed by Alan Jackson and Jimmy Buffett (2003)

Two of country music's biggest stars collaborate on a song about every whiskey drinker's favorite excuse. Their duet was the Country Music Association's Musical Event of the Year.

Single Ladies, performed by Beyonce (2008)

Born in Texas but now the premier Brooklyn Nets fan, Beyonce Knowles-Carter is the most awarded artist in Grammy and Black Entertainment Television (BET) history. Queen Bey.

California Gurls, performed by Katy Perry (2010)

Perry grew up in the church and began her career singing gospel. Her first record, a Christian-themed endeavor, failed. She struck gold with her album, *One of the Boys*. Her breakout single, *I Kissed a Girl* was decried by both the Christian and LGBT communities. Snoop Dogg (a chef in Chapter 17) sings backup on *Gurls*.

Stronger (What Doesn't Kill You), performed by Kelly Clarkson (2011)

Clarkson was the first winner on another TV singing competition show, *American Idol*. In addition to singing, she went on to host a talk show.

Tik Tok, performed by Kesha (2010)

Kesha's first hit. The 2010s saw Billboard magazine finally include streaming in its chart calculations. It resulted in greater recognition of younger artists, and rap and hip hop music.

Born This Way, performed by Lady Gaga (2011)

Lady Gaga, née Stefani Joanne Angelina Germanotta, has become a musical chameleon with a right to sing about being different. From her "monsters" days, to duets with Tony Bennett, to an Academy Award for the song *Shallow* in the movie remake *A Star is Born* (2018), there's something for everybody in Gaga's repertoire.

Sprawl II (Mountains Beyond Mountains), performed by Arcade Fire (2010)

This number by indie rock band Arcade Fire comes off their album *Suburbs*, winner of a Grammy for Album of the Year. The group represented the genre on *Billboard* magazine's list of the ten most "defining" artists of the 2010s.

Chapter 17
MAKING ROOM FOR THE DAVIDS

It's a good time to be a glass of whiskey in America.
—Colin Spoelman & David Haskell

BOURBON WITH A MAN BUN: WHAT IS CRAFT WHISKEY?

In the wake of the whiskey industry's consolidation there arose a *youthquake* of whiskey crafters. These entrepreneurs value distilleries with small capacity, the use of ingredients grown nearby and perhaps organically, hands-on attention throughout the production and bottling process, and experimentation with ingredients (for example different varieties of corn), fermenting, distilling, and aging. To these innovators everything was testable, nothing sacred. In 2005, you could count about sixty craft distilleries in the US. In 2018, the number was nearly 1600, each turning out a unique product. Every state boasted at least one craft distillery. California had the most crafters, but New York, Washington, Texas, and Colorado also had impressive numbers.

Still, a problem loomed. It hovered around the edges of the definition of a craft whiskey. "Craft" was a selling point for whiskey, as it was for beer. So, given that calling a product "craft" gave distillers cachet, how would you as a consumer know a craft whiskey when you saw the claim? Which producers could use the term?

We can all agree that the small distillery in the industrial park three miles from your home qualifies as turning out a craft whiskey. It may use a copper pot still (or hybrid), grow grains on its own plot or source them from a small farm elsewhere in your state, age and bottle its product in a warehouse behind a tasting room that is jammed full of people on weekend nights, and have a limited kitchen or a

INDUSTRY DEFINITIONS OF CRAFT DISTILLED SPIRITS

The *American Distilling Institute* (ADI) is the largest trade association representing craft distillers. It opened its doors in 2003. It represents small-batch distillers. It defines a craft spirit as one that:

- has been run through a still identified on the label that says "Distilled by" followed by the name of the distillery;
- comes from a distillery that is less than 25% owned or controlled by alcoholic beverage industry companies who are not craft distillers;
- has maximum annual sales of less than 100,000 proof gallons; *
- is "produced to reflect the vision of their principal distillers using any combination of traditional or innovative techniques including fermenting, distilling, re-distilling, blending, infusing or warehousing."

The American Craft Spirits Association (ACSA) is a non-profit trade association. It acknowledges that the definition of "craft" is open to interpretation and debate. Thus, it doesn't provide a definitive definition. Instead, it offers a preferred definition. For a distillery to be called "craft" ACSA offers the same ownership guideline as *ADI* but has a 750,000-gallon (liquor gallons, not proof gallons) guideline and adds that a craft spirit should be "produced by a distillery who values the importance of transparency in distilling, and remains forthcoming regarding the spirit's ingredients, distilling location, and aging and bottling process."

The *Distilled Spirits Counsel of the United States* represents the larger producers of spirits. It agrees that craft distillers should be defined by size and ownership.

* A US liquid gallon contains about 3785 milliliters of liquid, or about five 750ml bottles. A proof gallon is a gallon of spirits containing 50% ethanol.

food truck or two parked outside. *B4YKI,*[1] if you are impressed with the whiskey, the distillery's owner might "lease" a barrel to you and put your name on it. You can visit your barrel on Friday night (and other days of the week). The owners—who are now on your holiday card list—might give you bottles from other barrels while you wait for your barrel to mature.[2]

We can also agree that the whiskey that comes out of MGP's Indiana plant is not a craft whiskey, however good it may be.

Between these extremes there is no generally agreed-upon definition of what qualifies as a craft distillery and whiskey. The government has no standard. Among the characteristics of a whiskey and its production that might be considered in classifying distilleries as "craft" include: who owns the distillery (a large corporation could have recently bought that distillery in the industrial park); how many barrels or bottles it

1 Before you know it.

2 Don't be surprised if your local distillers are millennials who graduated college with degrees in engineering. Don't be surprised if they made a good deal of money in a different profession (or had friends who did) and walked away to

follow a dream. Don't be surprised if you can buy a beanie with the distillery logo on it in the tasting room.

turns out; the type of stills used; the kind and origin of the ingredients, as well as other factors. Different distilleries might meet some parts of the definition but not others.

The solution to the problem of defining "craft" is far from simple. Consumers will disagree on a definition and this will lead to spirited conversations among friends. It will also keep producers in the industry going to seminars at their gatherings for years to come. This is good. If the arguments lead you to be more convinced that how much you like the aroma and taste of a whiskey is more important than its pedigree, you're the winner.

"Frankenwhisky"

For craft distillers, experimentation is the name of the game. Creating a product with a unique flavor profile is how you find your niche with consumers. Crafters are using atypical strains of yeast and corn to make their product distinct. They are expanding the types of grains that you will find in the mash bill. Are you ready for oat, millet, quinoa, rice, sorghum, amaranth, or triticale (yes, the grain the Starship Enterprise was carrying in *The Trouble with Tribbles* episode) whiskey? Don't answer until you've tried it.

And necessity is the mother of invention, especially when it comes to "speeding up" the aging process. Using smaller barrels than the standard fifty-three-gallon capacity is practiced by many distillers. You may also find crafters who use stainless steel tanks that are pressurized and have grooved oak staves inside. Some crafters take a page from the teabag playbook and immerse mesh bags with wood chips in their barrels. A sound wave generator placed inside a barrel can stimulate interaction between the whiskey and wood. Too technical for you? How about blasting heavy metal music in your rickhouse to shake the barrels? Led Zeppelin might be worth a try. Or, put your whiskey on a boat, journey it across the equator, and let the swaying

sea and change in temperature mature your whiskey (*Jefferson's Ocean Aged at Sea Bourbon* does this).

Older methods to speed up aging involve using shakers, electrical charges (careful), steam coils in the barrel, and ultraviolet exposure. But the prize for chutzpah goes to some Australian and Scottish distillers who in 1961 tried using isotopes and irradiation to speed up the aging of barrels of whiskey. Chris Middleton of *Whisky* magazine called this "Frankenwhisky." This experiment didn't last long, thank goodness.

FAKERY

It is not unusual for a new, small craft distillery to first bottle gin and/or vodka (which do not have to be aged) while sourcing the whiskey it offers under its own label until its own stuff reaches the desired maturity. Crafters will tell you they must do this in order to create a cash flow until their own whiskey can be marketed.

There's no problem with this practice as long as the crafter is honest with the consumer. Government regulations try to draw the line between a bit of hyperbole and fraud. Industry groups try to impose advertising rules. But brows furrow when the distillery keeps sourcing, never states this on the label, and never switches to its own product. For example, Wayne Curtis, a whiskey writer, visited a "distillery" that he did not name. He found that the proprietors sourced alcohol in bulk and simply ran it through charcoal or some other filter to make it their own. The label boasted of an "artisanal origin." The careful reader could see that the label said "bottled in" not "distilled at." But an artisan whiskey distilled somewhere else? Maybe not.

SECONDARY MARKET

Along with the increase in craft whiskeys the new century saw a burgeoning interest in any whiskey that is in short supply. This includes limited edition whiskeys with unique mash bills, barreling, and aging procedures and limited commemorative bottles hitting the market for the first time. Most importantly, it also includes the whiskeys of yesteryear.

Some people collect old and rare whiskeys, put them on a shelf, show them off, and hope the dollar sign arrow points up. Similar to all antiques, the value of the whiskey is based on demand, driven most notably by its rarity, age, and the condition of the bottle. You can participate in auctions for rare whiskeys and follow bottle and shopping cart prices of whiskeys online or in *Whisky Advocate* magazine. Some people can't resist opening and tasting a bottle of fifty-year-old whiskey from a company long out of business. You can buy rare whiskeys on the secondary market, but be careful: reselling is *wack* in many places, and some bottles may be refilled and their seals doctored.

LOOKING INTO THE CRYSTAL GLEN-CAIRN GLASS

A glimpse into the future suggests that things look golden for whiskey in America. Still, like any market, ups and downs are to be expected, and sales and expansion will respond to broader economic conditions. For example, the pandemic caused by the Coronavirus that shattered the world economy in early 2020 caused an increase in bottle sales of whiskey, except in airport duty-free shops, but ruined restaurant sales. More than half of the craft distilleries fear the pandemic may put them out of business.

Can the expansion of craft distilling go on or is a contraction inevitable? In the name of economic development, many states lowered the fees for starting a distillery and many states now allow distilleries to sell directly to the consumer. These are certainly positive developments for the future health of the industry. But it seems the rate of new craft distilleries has to slow and the marketplace will separate the wheat from the chaff.

Barriers to the whiskey industry still exist. The excise taxes on spirits still exceed those on wine and beer, by far.[3] Federal regulations still do not require full transparency on labels (granted it is a moving target) underlining the importance of consumer education and necessitating self-policing by the industry. And there are several police—industry organizations—that don't necessarily agree with what the criteria should be.

The tariffs imposed on spirits in 2018 have also had an impact, making it more difficult for American distilleries to sell overseas. The tariffs depressed the expansion in sales to countries in the European Union. After a jump in sales by a third from the second half of 2017 to the second half of 2018, the tariffs caused a near 9% decline from July to November in 2018. This economic bite was felt by the large distillers but especially by crafters, whose sales to Europe made up about a quarter of their business.

---

3   Legislation that reduces the excise tax on distilled spirits is passed by Congress on an annual or bi-annual basis, complicating distillers' planning for future expansion, especially craft distillers, who are hit hardest by the government bite.

WHAT DOES A CRAFT BOURBON BORN IN THE BROOKLYN NAVY YARD TASTE LIKE?

Kings County Straight Bourbon Whiskey

Colin Spoelman's Misspent Youth. Although most of Kentucky is wet, Harlan County, KY, is "moist." To this day, you can only buy alcoholic beverages in the city of Cumberland and in restaurants of Harlan County that seat more than one hundred people.[4]

Colin Spoelman grew up in rural Harlan County where he bought moonshine from a trailer sitting on the side of a two-lane road. In 2005, living in Brooklyn, NY, Colin made a trip back home and returned with a gallon of moonshine. Sharing with friends, he soon ran out. He suggested to buddy David Haskell that they try to make their own moonshine and began experimenting with home distilling. Their experiment was a huge success. They soon had a license for Kings County Distillery, the first in New York City since the Prohibition Era. It wasn't a big operation—it was the smallest licensed distillery in the country—an eight-gallon stainless steel still in a 325-square foot room.[5] Kings County quickly outgrew its humble abode and now occupies the former Paymaster Building of the Brooklyn Navy Yard.

The Congressional Controversy. New York senator Chuck Schumer wanted to give a gift to his colleague across the aisle, Mitch McConnell of Kentucky. What better way to win a Kentuckian's heart than give him a bottle of whiskey distilled in Brooklyn, NY? *Widow Jane Bourbon* was Schumer's choice. The *Twitterverse* went crazy; *Widow Jane* at the time was bottled in New York but sourced from Kentucky.

The *Wall Street Journal*, again, weighed in on the world of whiskey. Charles Passy headlined an article about Kings County Distillery: "New York Bourbons Are Nipping at Kentucky's Heels." After that, the haters *dissed* (disrespected) Kings County, noting that Colin was born in Kentucky. So what? From grain to still to bottle, Kings County products are pure New York.

Kings County Distillery (right), current residence of the Paymaster Building in the old Brooklyn Navy Yard (left).

---

4   Lynchburg, TN, the home of the Jack Daniel's Distillery, is also dry.

5   Are you glad you didn't live upstairs?

Just the Facts

Mash Bill	Corn: 80% Rye: 0% Barley: 20%
Proof	Proof: 90 ABV: 45%
Age; Barrel Char	2 years; #3
Chill Filtered?	No

TASTING NOTES

From: Kings County Distillery website

http://kingscountydistillery.com/

Kings County Distillery's Straight Bourbon is made from New York State 80% organic corn and 20% English malted barley, is twice distilled in copper pot stills and then aged in new charred oak barrels. Rich in caramel, vanilla, and holiday spice, this bottle is cited frequently in lists of best non-Kentucky bourbons. Aged for at least two years, this is a precocious whiskey, surprisingly robust for its age.

The Flaviar Tasting Spiral™ for *Kings County Straight Bourbon Whiskey.*

From: Flaviar

https://flaviar.com/kings-county-distillery/kings-county-straight-bourbon/tasting-notes-reviews

Appearance/Color: Sunlit russet

Nose/Aroma/Smell: Bitter and young aromas with hints of vanilla and caramel reminiscent of a ready Manhattan cocktail.

Flavor/Taste/Palate: Sweet, loud and vanilla-forward palate with notes of cinnamon, fruits and butterscotch.

Finish: Short finish.

From: The Over a Barrel Gang

Looks: Mahogany, amber, gold.

Aroma: Robust. Vanilla, caramel, honey, peach, clove, apple, tobacco.

Flavor: Light body. Sweet, caramel.

Mouth Feel: Light, round.

Going Down: Soft strength, short length.

Notes: Surprisingly light for rich appearance; finish is gentle so good whiskey for someone new to the species.

A Toast Deferred
The final toast can be found in the concluding Chapter 18.

THE DISTILLERY AT THE END OF YOUR STREET

If Brooklyn is too far for you to get to by electric scooter or Uber, here are a few more craft whiskey choices that deserve a *swipe right* and might be closer to home. In addition to Kings County, you have already tasted a few other whiskeys that might qualify as "craft," depending on your definition: *George Washington Rye; Old Potero; Midnight Moon Moonshine.* The following distilleries can be found in each time zone:

Tuthilltown Spirits (Gardiner, NY) http://www.tuthilltown.com/. Ralph Erenzo was drawn to upstate New York because he was a rock climber and wanted to build a campground and hostel for climbers in the Shawangunk Mountains. When the neighbors protested, he did the next best thing; he found a water-powered grist mill from the 1870s that Hasidic Jews had used to make matzo. Farming was legit so with partner Brian Lee—neither of whom knew anything about distilling—converted the mill site into a distillery. Tuthilltown and its *Hudson Baby Bourbon Whiskey* have received numerous industry awards.

F.E.W. Spirits (Evanston, IL). http://www.fewspirits.com/. Owner and master distiller Paul Hlekto founded F.E.W. Spirits in a suburb of Chicago that was dry until the 1970s. He named his distillery after Frances Elizabeth Willard, a leader of the Women's Temperance Movement. Willard drew a crowd of thirty thousand people to hear her speak at the 1893 Chicago World's Fair. The bourbon label has a drawing of *The Republic*, a statue that stood at the event. The distillery is housed in a former laundry and the whiskey is aged in a cinder block warehouse that was once an icehouse.

Balcones Distillery (Waco, TX). https://balconesdistilling.com/. Head distiller Jared Himstedt whetted his appetite for distilling as a home brewer and manager of a craft beer

Tasting room at Lost Spirits Distillery.
Inspired by the novel and film *The Island of Dr. Moreau.*

pub. Balcones Distillery began in an old welding shop then moved to a former storage building in downtown Waco, TX. It uses a strain of corn that was almost extinct before the distillers found and fell in love with the taste of the whiskey it produced. The corn grows in New Mexico. Balcones also malts a barley that is grown in Texas. Balcones is a winner of numerous awards including *Whiskey Magazine*'s Distiller of the Year award (twice).

Distillery 291 (Colorado Springs, CO) https://distillery291.com/. Michael Myers was a fashion photographer living in lower Manhattan on the day the World Trade Center was attacked. He could not return to his apartment and eventually moved to Colorado Spring, CO. He disliked commuting to the coast, so he started a new life in Colorado making whiskey. But Myers knew nothing about distilling and couldn't afford a new still. With the help of a local handyman, Myers converted his copper photogravure plates into a 45-gallon finishing still. Today, Distillery 291 has a 300-gallon finishing still, but the original still is used as a "doubler" and all products pass through the original still. In a nod to Colorado, the whiskey is finished with aspen wood staves. Distillery 291 is also a winner of numerous industry awards.

Lost Spirits Distillery (Los Angeles, CA) https://www.lostspirits.net/. An article written for *Smithsonian Magazine* called the distillers at Lost Spirits "the madcap scientists of booze." Founder Bryan Davis built his own still when he was sixteen based on a design he saw in an episode of *The Simpsons*. Today he and his crew use a gas chromatograph mass spectrometer to pull apart and record the 500 chemicals that give aged spirits their flavor. *Lost Spirits* then uses raw spirits, pieces of oak, and intense light to create in six days spirits that taste like they have aged 20 years. Some people scoff, others don't; *Jim Murray's Whisky Bible 2018* gave *Lost Spirits* a 94 (out of 100) rating, placing it in the top 5% of whiskies worldwide. *The* Lost Spirits distillery tour has also won international awards. It is a cross between *Disneyland* and a H.G. Wells novel.

DESSERT AT YOUR FAVORITE TASTING ROOM CAFÉ
More desserts with that special something.

Recipe: Bourbon Chocolate Chip Cookies with Tarragon and Brown Butter
From: Spoelman, C. & Haskell, D. (2013). *Guide to Urban Moonshining*. New York, NY: Abrams. P. 202–203. (Recipe authors: Agatha Kulaga and Erin Patinkin.)

Ingredients:
- 1 cup butter
- 2½ cups flour
- ¾ teaspoon baking soda
- ¾ teaspoon salt
- 1 cup granulated sugar
- ¾ cup brown sugar
- 1 egg yolk
- 1 egg
- 1 teaspoon vanilla extract
- ¼ cup bourbon
- 1 cup dark chocolate chips
- 1 tablespoon tarragon

Directions:
1. In a saucepan over medium-low heat, melt the butter and continue to heat until it crackles and foams. Once the foam begins to subside, butter solids will quickly begin to brown on bottom of pan. At this point, stir continuously with a wooden spoon to scrape browned bits off the bottom of the saucepan. Once nutty brown in color, remove from the heat. Do not let the butter become black and burn. Set aside and let cool.
2. In a separate bowl, whisk together the flour, soda, and salt. Once the butter is at room temperature, add it to the bowl of a standing mixer. Add the sugar and brown sugar, and mix on medium until incorporated. Separate the yolk from the white of 1 egg and add it to a small bowl. Discard the white or save it for another use. Add the whole egg to the same bowl, and then, with the mixer on low, add slowly to the butter mixture. Raise the mixer to medium-high, and beat for 1 minute until smooth. Turn the mixer back to low, add the vanilla and bourbon, and beat until combined, about 30 seconds. Add the flour mixture and mix until barely incorporated, about 30 seconds. Then add the chocolate and tarragon, mixing until all the dry ingredients are incorporated, about 30 seconds more. Remove the bowl from the mixer, and chill for 30 minutes. Scoop with a small ice-cream scoop or form by hand into 1-inch balls onto parchment-lined sheet pans.
3. Preheat oven to 350°F. Bake until light golden, about 10 minutes. Cookies will look slightly under-baked and soft in center, but will set. Let cool before serving.

Recipe: Bow Wow Brownies

From: Snoop Dogg, *From Crook to Cook*. P. 110. © 2018 by Snoopadelic Pictures, used with permission of Chronicle Books LLC, San Francisco, CA. Visit chroniclebooks.com.

Ingredients:

⅔ cup all-purpose flour

¼ tsp baking soda

½ tsp salt

½ cup granulated sugar

3 tbsp unsalted butter

2 tbsp whole milk

2½ cups milk chocolate morsels

2 large eggs

½ tsp pure vanilla extract

Your favorite vanilla ice cream and chocolate sauce

Directions:

1. Preheat oven to 325°F with a rack in the middle position. Butter an 8 x 8-inch square pan and set aside.
2. In a small bowl, whisk the flour, baking soda, and salt. Set aside.
3. In a medium saucepan over medium heat, combine the sugar, butter, and milk. Bring to a boil. Remove the pan from the heat and add 1½ cups of the chocolate morsels. Stir until the chocolate is melted and smooth.
4. Add the eggs and vanilla to the chocolate. Stir until blended and smooth.
5. Gradually add the flour mixture to the chocolate, stirring until just combined. Spread the batter evenly into the prepared pan. Sprinkle the top of the batter with the remaining 1 cup of chocolate morsels.
6. Place the pan in the oven and bake for 25 to 30 minutes, rotating the pan about halfway through the baking time to ensure even cooking until the brownies are set and the edges looked baked.
7. Remove the brownies from the oven and place on a wire rack to cook in the pan.
8. Cut the brownies into 6 large squares. Serve topped with vanilla ice cream and chocolate sauce, if desired.

Snoop writes: "If I really want to take it up a notch, I might even add a dash of my secret ingredient—a sprinkle of Snoop's herbs and spices. . . .This is why you bought the book right? So what the hell you waiting on? Go get baked!"

Before You Let Your Guests Head Home

Recipe: Arbuckle's Coffee

From: https://www.arbucklecoffee.com/

It's coffee time, and time to tell the story of Wild West coffee.

John & Charles Arbuckle of Pittsburgh produced the first roasted beans for cowboy coffee. They patented a roasting and bean-grazing process (with egg and sugar) to preserve freshness and packed their coffee with a wrapped peppermint stick candy (the first food product to offer a premium). Previously, to make coffee you had to roast green coffee beans over a fire in a skillet or other contraption, grind them, and toss them into a pot of boiling water.

One premeasured pound of Arbuckle's made a full three-gallon pot of strong coffee. Cowboys wanted it strong enough to *float a horseshoe*. The cook could use the peppermint stick to entice the cowhands to grind coffee for him, wash dishes, or gather wood or cow chips for the fire. After WWI Arbuckle's had over 50% of coffee sales in the United States with cattle country its largest market; it wasn't unusual to see a cook's shopping list contain four hundred-pound crates of Arbuckle's Ariosa blend coffee.

Arbuckle's Ariosa brand was revived in 1974, roasted like the original. It still comes with an organic peppermint stick.

MUSIC THAT WE LISTENED TO IN THE 2010s

Tennessee Whiskey, performed by Chris Stapleton (2015)

Born in Lexington, KY, but now a resident of Nashville, TN, Stapleton swept the country music awards with his debut album "Traveler." *Tennessee Whiskey* was first recorded by David Allan Coe, then George Jones. Stapleton's version won him accolades when he sang it as a duet with Justin Timberlake at the Country Music Association Awards.

Shake it Off, performed by Taylor Swift (2014)

Swift has sold more than fifty million albums worldwide. Her album, *1989*, in which *Shake It Off* first appeared, was the best-selling album of 2014. Not your cup of tea? She don't care.

Happy, performed by Pharrell Williams (2013)

Happy topped the charts in two dozen countries. The song was on the soundtrack of the movie *Despicable Me 2* and was nominated for an Academy Award but lost to *Let It Go* (from *Frozen*).

All About That Bass, performed by Meghan Trainor (2015)

This song is a flat-out rejection of mass media depictions of the acceptable female body image. Trainor "ain't no size 2" and "don't need no magazine workin' that Photoshop."

Uptown Funk, performed by Mark Ronson (with Bruno Mars) (2015)

Uptown Funk is a resurrection of the funk music style of the 1960s. Compare this song to songs by groups like Parliament-Funkadelic and Sly and the Family Stone.

Fight Song, performed by Rachel Platten (2015)

Platten says she "wrote [this song] because I needed to remind myself that I believed in myself." Her "power is turned on." The song reached #1 on the Adult Contemporary and Adult Pop airplay charts.

Can't Stop the Feeling, performed by Justin Timberlake (2016)

Yes, Timberlake also was a Mouseketeer in 1993–94, along with Spears and Aguilera (and Ryan Gosling and Keri Russell). He's a singer, dancer, and actor. Justin (and Britney and Christina) is now approaching middle age.

Old Town Road, performed by Lil Nas X (featuring Billy Ray Cyrus) (2018)

Lil Nas X is the only openly gay artist to win a Country Music Association award. This collaboration with Billy Ray (yes, *Achy Breaky Heart*) won the Grammy for Best Pop Duo or Group Performance.

Billy Rae Cyrus and Lil Nas X perform at the 62nd Grammy Award Show, January 2020.

Bad Guy, performed by Billie Eilish (2019)

In her late teens, Eilish is the first pop star born in the twenty-first century. *Rolling Stone* magazine called her "the first invader from the next generation of pop masterminds." Eilish won the top four awards at the 2020 Grammys.

Chapter 18
CONCLUSION: TASTING NOTES FOR AMERICAN HISTORY

Color: Amber waves of grain, forest green, Union Blue and Confederate Grey, silver and gold, and of course Old Glory Red (Standard Color Reference of America #80080), white, and Old Glory Blue (#80075).

Aroma: Ocean water, fertile soil, freshly hewn oak, dust, steam, campfire smoke, gun powder, cigars.

Palate: Lobster, sweet corn, cranberries, potatoes, ham, cooking oil, fresh eggs, kale, green Jell-O.

Finish: Do not drive while intoxicated. Instead, go home in a merchantman ship, a prairie schooner, a stage-coach, a Pullman car, a Trans World Airlines turboprop. Or go real old school—let a whisk whisk you and your whiskey away.

Overall: Whiskey has played an important role in some of the most critical events that have shaped our nation's character. It has served as currency in the exchange of goods, it has provided revenue that kept the country solvent, it has been used to help alleviate (supposedly) many ailments, it has brought hard-working men together, it has rewarded soldiers for acts of bravery. It has been a stimulus for some of America's most innovative minds. But its uses have not always been positive. Whiskey has also been used to suppress the human rights of Native Americans, African Americans, and other minorities. Its prohibition has been used on immigrants from European shores to foster an unfamiliar way of life. It has been used to swindle the poor and make men rich, both those who played by the rules and those who were willing to cheat.

Also, whiskey has had personal consequences for individual Americans. Whiskey can brighten the day, relieve the pain, create comradery among good friends and strangers alike. But whiskey can be addictive, robbing it of any joy at all. It can dull the senses and impair the judgement.

How whiskey affects you is up to you. Partake of it with discipline. Understand its effects on you, personally. Savor each sip, taking time to appreciate it on your nose and in your mouth, and never drink so much you cannot clearly see the history in your glass.

THE FINAL TOAST

To the American people
To their history, their present, and their future
To the most common and uncommon among them.

REFERENCES FOR FURTHER READING

References to the websites of whiskey distilleries and whiskey tasters of the highlighted labels can be found in the text, as can references for the particular recipes.

WHISKEY HISTORY

Albala, K. (2020). *History of bourbon*. Chantilly, VA: The Great Courses.

Acitelli, T (1917) *Whiskey business*. Chicago, IL: Chicago Review press.

Carson, G. (1963). *The social history of bourbon*. Lexington, KY: University of Kentucky.

Cecil, S. (2010). *Bourbon: The evolution of Kentucky whiskey*. New York, NY: Turner.

Cheever, S. (2015). *Drinking in America: Our secret history*. New York, NY: Twelve.

Cowdery, C. K. (2004). *Bourbon, straight*. Chicago, IL: Made and Bottled in Kentucky.

Cowdery, C. K. (2014). *Bourbon, strange*. Chicago, IL: Made and Bottled in Kentucky.

Crowgey, H. G. (2008). *Kentucky bourbon: The early years of whiskey making*. Lexington, KY: University of Kentucky Press.

Devito, C. (2018). *Big whiskey and the distillers of America's premier spirits region*. Kennebunkport, ME: Cider Mill Press.

Getz, O. (1978). *Whiskey: An American pictorial history*. New York, NY: David McKay.

Green, B. A. (1967). *Jack Daniel's legacy*. Nashville, TN: Grant Sidney Publishing.

Greene, H. (2014). *Whisk(e)y Distilled*. New York, NY: Viking Studio.

Haara, B. F. (2018). *Bourbon justice*. Lincoln, NB: Potomac.

Huckelbridge, D. (2014). *Bourbon: A history of the American spirit*. New York, NY: William Morrow.

Isenberg, A. C. (2013). *Wyatt Earp: A vigilante life*. New York, NY: Hill & Wang.

Jester, T. M. (2011). *Popcorn Sutton: The making and marketing of a hillbilly hero*. Self: Tom Wilson Jester and Don Dudenbostel.

Lubbers, B. (2015). *Bourbon whiskey: Our native spirit*. Indianapolis, IN: Blue River Press.

McGirr, L. (2016). *The war on alcohol: Prohibition and the rise of the American state*. New York, NY: W. W. Norton.

Minnick, F. (2013). *Whiskey women: The untold story of how women saved bourbon, scotch, and Irish whiskey*. Lincoln, NB: University of Nebraska Press.

Minnick, F. (2016). *Bourbon: The rise, fall, and rebirth of an American whiskey*. Minneapolis, MN: Voyageur.

Mitenbuler, R. (2015) *Bourbon empire: The past and future of American whiskey*. New York, NY: Viking.

Monahan, S. & Perkins, J. (2018). *The golden elixir of the west*. Guilford, CT: Twodot

Rogers, A. (2014). *Proof: The science of booze*. New York, NY: Mariner Books.

Samuels, Jr., B. (2000). *Maker's Mark — My autobiography*. Louisville, KY: Saber.

Schlimm, J. (2018). *Moonshine*. New York, NY: Citadel Press.

Spoelman, C. & Haskell, D. (2013). *Guide to urban moonshining*. New York, NY: Abrams.

Stephensen, Jr., F. & Mulder, B. N. (2017). *North Carolina moonshine*. Charleston, SC: American Plate.

Veach, M. R. (2013). *Kentucky bourbon whiskey: An American heritage*. Lexington, KY: University of Kentucky Press.

Will-Weber, M. (2014). *Mint Juleps with Teddy Roosevelt: The complete history of presidential drinking*. Washington, DC: Regnery Publishing.

HISTORICAL FIGURES AND EVENTS

Ambrose, S. (1997). *Undaunted courage*. New York, NY: Simon & Schuster.

Black, B. (2013). *Poems worth saving*. Benson, AZ: Coyote Cowboy.

Brode, D. (2013). *Dream west: Politics and religion in cowboy movies*. Austin, TX: University of Texas Press.

Chernow, R. (2010). *Washington: A life*. New York, NY: Penguin Group.

Chernow, R. (2017). *Grant*. New York, NY: Penguin Press

Duncan, D. & Burns, K. (2019). *Country music: An illustrated history*. New York, NY: Alfred A. Knopf.

Eyman, S. (2014). *John Wayne: The life and legend*. New York, NY: Simon & Shuster.

Gardner, A. (1990). *Ava: My story*. New York, NY: Bantom.

Green, J. (2014). *Language! 500 Years of the Vulgar Tongue*. London, Eng.: Atlantic Books.

Guinn, J. (2011). *The last gunfight: The real story of the shootout at the O. K. Corral—and how it changed the American west*. New York, NY: Simon & Schuster.

Johnson, P. (1997). *A History of the American people*. New York, NY: Harper Collins.

Kaplan, J. (2019). *The rat pack: The original bad boys*. New York, NY: Meredith Corporation.

Kreck, D. (2013) *Hell on wheels*. Golden, CO: Fulcrum.

Lause, M. (2018). *The great cowboy strike: Bullets, ballots & class conflicts in the American West*. Brooklyn, NY: Verso.

Levy, S. (1998) *Rat Pack confidential*. New York, NY: Broadway.

Leyburn, J. G. (1962). *The Scotch-Irish: A social history*. Chapel Hill, NC: University of North Carolina Press.

McCullough, D. (2019). *The pioneers*. New York, NY: Simon & Schuster.

McPherson, J. M. (2003). *Battle cry of freedom*. Oxford, UK: Oxford University Press.

Meacham, J. & McGraw, T. ((2019). *Songs of America*. New York, NY: Random House.

Perry, M. (2004). *Grant and Twain: The story of a friendship that changed America*. New York, NY: Random House.

Powers, R. (2005). *Mark Twain: A life*. New York, NY: Free Press.

Reynolds, N. (2017). *Writer, sailor, soldier, spy. Ernest Hemingway's secret adventures, 1935-1961*. New York, NY: HarperCollins.

Seeger, A. (2019). *America's Musical Heritage*. Chantilly, VA: The Great Courses.

Twain, M. (1872), *Roughing it*. Hartford, CN: American Publishing.

Utley, R. M. & Ketterson, Jr., F. A. (1969). *Golden spike*. Washington, DC: Division of Publications, National Park Service.

Vestal, S. (1970). *Jim Bridger: Mountain man.* Lincoln, NB: University of Nebraska Press.

White, R. (2012). *Railroaded: The transcontinentals and the making of modern America.* New York, NY: W. W. Norton.

Whitman, W. (2007). *Franklin Evans or the inebriate.* Durham, NC: Duke University.

COOKBOOKS

Cannon, P. & Brooks, P. (1968) *The president's cookbook.* Chappaqua, NY: Funk & Wagnalls.

Lohman. S. (2016) *Eight flavors: The untold story of American cuisine.* New York: Simon & Schuster.

O'Connell L. H. (2014). *The American plate: A culinary history in 100 bites.* Naperville, IL: Sourcebooks.

Shapiro, L. (2004). *Something from the oven: Reinventing dinner in 1950s America.* New York, NY: Penguin.

Snoop Dogg, *From Crook to Cook.* P. 110. © 2018 by Snoopadelic Pictures, used with permission of Chronicle Books LLC, San Francisco, CA. Visit chroniclebooks.com.

Wallach, J. J. (2013). *How America eats.* Lanham, MD: Rowman & Littlefield.

MAGAZINES

I consulted four magazines on numerous occasions for interesting stories and facts.

American Whiskey. Norwich, England: Paragraph Publishing, Ltd. https://americanwhiskeymag.com/

Bourbon+. Alexander City, AL: Covey Rise, LLC. https://www.bourbonplus.com/

The Bourbon Review. Lexington, KY: Bourbon Review, LLL. https://www.gobourbon.com/

Whisky Advocate. New York, NY: M. Shanken Communications, Inc. http://whiskyadvocate.com/magazine/

ONLINE MEDIA

I frequently searched the following websites to help me quickly check and fill in facts:

https://www.wikipedia.org/

https://commons.wikimedia.org/wiki/Main_Page

https://www.apple.com/itunes/

ILLUSTRATION CREDITS

Chapter 1. Prerequisites

Cover photo: Courtesy of Glencairn Crystal Company

A diagram of the Glencairn whiskey glass: Courtesy of Glencairn Crystal Company

Chapter 2. A Decidedly Ambivalent Meeting of the New and Old

Cross section of a 17th century merchant ship: Public Domain.
Musphot / CC BY-SA
https://commons.wikimedia.org/wiki/File:17th-century-merchantman.jpg

"The First Thanksgiving 1621," at Plymouth Plantation painted by Jean Leon Gerome Ferris, circa 1912-1915:
Public Domain.
https://archive.org/details/TheFirstThanksgiving_932

"Indian Massacre of 1622" depicted cut in wood by Matthäus Merian, 1628: Public Domain.
By Matthäus Merian https://commons.wikimedia.org/w/index.php?curid=330485

James E. Pepper: Public Domain.
By Unknown author - The Successful American Magazine Co.
https://commons.wikimedia.org/w/index.php?curid=57090999

American Cookery by Amelia Simmons, 1796: Public Domain.
Library of Congress
https://www.loc.gov/resource/rbc0001.2015amimp26967

John Newton, Stained glass image, St Peter and Paul Church Olney, Buckinghamshire, South of London: Public Domain

https://commons.wikimedia.org/w/index.php?curid=64196634

Chapter 3. A New Nation (and Distillery) is Born

George Washington: Courtesy of the Mount Vernon Museum

A flag of the Whiskey Rebellion: Courtesy of Richard R. Gideon and the North American Vexillogical Association

A pot still: Permission granted Society of Wine Educators

A column still: Creative Commons: Public Domain
https://commons.wikimedia.org/wiki/File:Column_still.svg

Star Spangled Banner original poem: Public Domain
Francis Scott Key
https://commons.wikimedia.org/wiki/File:KeysSSB.jpg

Chapter 4. Kentucky and Its Bourbon Follow Shortly

The Missouri and Mississippi River drainage system: Public Domain
https://commons.wikimedia.org/wiki/File:Mississippiriver-new-01.png

A steamboat being loaded with whiskey: From Lexington History Museum: Public Domain

Elijah Craig: Public Domain
Unknown author: Public Domain
https://commons.wikimedia.org/wiki/File:Elijah_Craig_woodcut.png

Daniel Boone
National Portrait Gallery, Smithsonian Institution; partial gift of the William T. Kemper Foundation and of the Chapman Hanson Foundation
https://npg.si.edu/object/npg_NPG.2015.102

Chapter 5. Tennessee Whiskey: Who Taught Jack Daniel to Make Whiskey?

Jasper Newton "Jack" Daniel: Public Domain
Unknown author
https://commons.wikimedia.org/wiki/File:Jackdaniel.jpg

George Green seated next to Jack Daniel in a photograph taken in the Mid-1800s: Public Domain
Unknown author
https://commons.wikimedia.org/wiki/File:26jack-web1-superJumbo.jpg

A. P., Maybelle, and Sara Carter, 1927: Public Domain
https://commons.wikimedia.org/w/index.php?curid=19206658

Statue of W. C. Handy in Handy Park, Memphis, TN: Public Domain
https://commons.wikimedia.org/w/index.php?curid=15519827

Chapter 6. A House Divided and Reunited

A painting of the White House reception after Jackson's inauguration: Public Domain
Louis S. Glanzman, image courtesy of the White House Historical Association.

Painting of the surrender at Appomattox, April 9, 1885: Public Domain.
Thomas Nast
https://commons.wikimedia.org/wiki/File:General_Robert_E._Lee_surrenders_at_Appomattox_Court_House_1865.jpg

Going for a 3rd Term: Public Domain
Library of Congress
https://loc.gov/pictures/resource/cph.3b37019/

Whiskey Ring cartoon: Licensed by Getty Images

U. S. Grant painting from Vanity Fair magazine, June 1, 1872: Public Domain
Thomas Nast
https://commons.wikimedia.org/wiki/File:US_Grant_Vanity_Fair_1_June_1872.JPG

Harper's Weekly illustration of attack on John Brown's Fort: Public Doman.
https://commons.wikimedia.org/w/index.php?curid=260944

Chapter 7. The First Voice of the American Common Man

A visage as distinct as his writing: Licensed through Getty Images

Mark Twain: Public Domain
Library of Congress
https://www.loc.gov/item/2004678589/

The First Arrival: *Life on the Mississippi*: Public Domain
Chapter 60 illustration
https://www.gutenberg.org/files/245/245-h/245-h.htm

Twain and Rudyard Kipling in a 1950s *Old Crow* advertisement: Public Domain

Godey's Lady's book cover, October 1862: Public Domain
https://commons.wikimedia.org/w/index.php?curid=49216732

Stephen Foster: Public Domain
https://commons.wikimedia.org/w/index.php?curid=16562493

Cover of sheet music of *Maple Leaf Rag*, 3rd Edition: Public Domain
https://commons.wikimedia.org/w/index.php?curid=6568621

Chapter 8. Opening the West: Cowboys and Outlaws

The route of the Lewis and Clark Expedition: Public Domain
https://commons.wikimedia.org/wiki/File:Carte_Lewis-Clark_Expedition-en.png

Tent saloon, Laramie, WY, 1868: Public Domain
Denver Public Library, Western History Photographic Collections, photo by Arundel Hull

Judge Roy Bean's Saloon and "Hall of Justice", Langtry, TX, c. 1900: Public Domain
https://commons.wikimedia.org/wiki/File:%22Judge_Roy_Bean,_the_%60Law_West_of_the_Pecos,%27_holding_court_at_the_old_town_of_Langtry,_Texas_in_1900,_trying_a_horse_th_-_NARA_-_530985.tif

The lawman stands alone: Licensed through Getty Images

Chuck wagon dinner, c. 1908: Public Domain
https://www.loc.gov/pictures/item/2004679069/

Chapter 9. Cow Towns

The completion of the Transcontinental Railroad, Promontory, UT, May 10, 1869: Public Domain
https://commons.wikimedia.org/w/index.php?curid=41243910

Benton, Wyoming Territory, 1868: Public Domain
Denver Public Library, Western History Photographic Collections, photo by Arundel Hull

The Long Branch Saloon, Dodge City, KS, in 1874: Public Domain
https://commons.wikimedia.org/w/index.php?curid=32891645

Chester (Dennis Weaver), Miss Kitty (Amanda Blake), and Marshall Matt Dillion (James Arness), Outside the Long Branch Saloon in the television series, Gunsmoke: Licensed through Getty Images

Joseph Smith: Public Domain
https://commons.wikimedia.org/w/index.php?curid=1388993

Brigham Young: Public Domain
https://commons.wikimedia.org/w/index.php?curid=11302639

Dale Evans & Roy Rogers c. 1950: Licensed through Getty Images

Chapter 10. Banning Booze and Shunning Strangers

The Drunkards Progress a lithograph by Nathaniel Currier in 1846: Public Domain
https://commons.wikimedia.org/w/index.php?curid=4174669

Carrie Nation: Public Domain
https://cdm17228.contentdm.oclc.org/digital/collection/imc/id/20315

Four Hours in a Bar Room by Frank Beard, 1874: Public Domain
https://loc.gov/pictures/resource/pga.06355/

Billie Holiday: Public Domain
https://commons.wikimedia.org/w/index.php?curid=11181478

An old-fashioned whiskey cocktail: Public Domain
https://commons.wikimedia.org/w/index.php?curid=41774270

A real old fashioned cock's tail: Courtesy of FreeImages.com
https://www.freeimages.com/photo/gockel-2-1497132

Shrimp Cocktail: iStock paid to download image
https://www.istockphoto.com/nl/en/photo/shrimp-cocktail-gm93614144-5934653

An image of dystopia?: Courtesy the Lester S. Levy Collection of Sheet Music, Sheridan Libraries, Johns Hopkins University.

Barbra Streisand and Judy Garland: Licensed through Getty Images

Chapter 11. Bootleggers and Moonshiners, You Ain't Never Heard Of

George Remus: Licensed through Getty Images

Imogene Remus: Library of Congress, Public Domain
https://www.loc.gov/item/2016860884/

Popcorn at his still: Courtesy of Don Dubenbostel
www.x-rayarts.com

Junior Johnson gets a (legit) job: Licensed through Getty Images

George Jones: Licensed through Getty Images

Chapter 12. America (and Bourbon) Takes Flight

Hemingway (on right) and friends, likely outside the Ritz-Carlton in Paris: Licensed through Getty Images

Statue of *Barfly* Hemingway at his favorite seat at La Floridita, Havana Cub: Public Domain
https://commons.wikimedia.org/w/index.php?curid=1591475

Total per capita ethanol consumption all types, United States, 1935–2017: Public Domain
https://pubs.niaaa.nih.gov/publications/surveillance113/CONS17.htm

Margie Samuels: Courtesy of Maker's Mark Distillery

Jerry Lee Lewis, Carl Perkins, Elvis Presley, and Johnny Cash, Sun Studios, Memphis TN, December 4, 1956: Licensed through Getty Images

Monument in front of the Surf Ballroom, Clear Lake, IA: Public Domain
https://commons.wikimedia.org/w/index.php?curid=81795320

Chapter 13. "Ladies and Gentlemen, Direct from the Bar…"

The Rat Pack (Peter Lawford, Sammy Davis Jr., Frank Sinatra, Joey Bishop, Dean Martin): Licensed through Getty Images

Ava Gardner in *The Killers:* Licensed through Getty Images

Congressional Declaration 1963: Public Domain
History, Art & Archives, U. S. House of Representatives, "Designating Bourbon Whiskey."
https://history.house.gov/Records-and-Research/Listing/lfp_010/ (June 26, 2020)

Marjorie Child Husted: Licensed through Getty Images

Chapter 14. Maybe Dad was Hipper Than I Thought

Jane Fonda's Workout Book was a New York Times Best-Seller in 1981: Licensed through Getty Images

C. Everett Koop was Surgeon General from 1982 to 1989: Public Domain
https://commons.wikimedia.org/wiki/File:C._Everett_Koop,_1980s.jpg

Lillian Carter: Public Domain
https://commons.wikimedia.org/w/index.php?curid=2775942

Lillian and Jimmy Carter: Public Domain
https://commons.wikimedia.org/w/index.php?curid=16595598

Moosewood Cookbook cover, 1974: Fair Use
https://en.wikipedia.org/w/index.php?curid=17695727

Bette Davis, her eyes, and Gary Merrill: Public Domain
https://commons.wikimedia.org/w/index.php?curid=18424474

Chapter 15. Who to Drink With? Renowned Whiskey Drinkers of Yesterday and Today

Jane Meadows and Steve Allen: Licensed through Getty Images

William Faulkner: Public Domain
https://www.loc.gov/item/2004662865/

Chandler wrote the book, Faulkner wrote the screenplay, Bogart and Bacall starred: Licensed Through Getty Images

Christina Hendricks: Creative Commons, Public Domain
https://commons.wikimedia.org/w/index.php?curid=36716084

Jim Beam tasting wheel: Image provided courtesy of James B. Beam Distilling Co.

Sugarhill Gang: Licensed through Getty Images

Chapter 16. Making Friends with the Goliaths

Barbie Dolls fashioned after Betty Francis (formerly Draper), Don Draper, Joan Holloway, and Roger Sterling from *Mad Men*: Licensed through Getty Images

Waterfill & Frazier Bottle Labels: Courtesy of Allen Barteld, Lodestone Beverages

Representative ketones: Public Domain
https://commons.wikimedia.org/w/index.php?curid=7454019

Britney Spears: Licensed through Getty Images

Chapter 17. Making Room for the Davids

Kings County Distillery (right), current residence of the Paymaster Building in the old Brooklyn Navy Yard (left): Courtesy of Kings County Distillery

The Flaviar Tasting Spiral for Kings County Straight Bourbon Whiskey: Courtesy of Flaviar Tasting Club

Tasting room at Lost Spirits Distillery: Licensed through Spencer Lowell/Trunk Archive

Billy Rae Cyrus and Lil Nas X perform at the 62nd Grammy Award Show, January 2020: Licensed through Getty Images

Section divider photo credit: iStock (itakdalee)

ACKNOWLEDGEMENTS

A work like this relies on the help and kindness of many others to come to fruition.

Thanks go to those folks who dared to try something different:

- Richard and Rebecca Cottingham, for being the first to open their home for a "Beta Test" of the whiskey dinner
- Andrew Skibitsky and David Martone, for hosting a dinner at Classic Thyme Cooking School, Westfield, NJ, without the slightest idea what would happen
- Rex Schultze, Becca Simley, Kyla Bayne, and the crowd at the Hillcrest Country Club, Lincoln, NE, for also stepping into the unknown
- Robert Corey and the staff at the Seasoned American Bistro, Estes Park, CO, a creative chef with an adventurous mind

To those in the spirits business who could have ignored my pestering emails and phone calls but instead stepped up and responded with more help than I dared ask:

- Dan Burgess, Executive Vice President, Director of Public Relations, Doe-Anderson, Inc. for Maker's Mark
- Kristy Isla Nicholson, Design & Marketing Manager, Glencairn Crystal
- Samantha Santiago, Legal Specialist, Global Intellectual Property, Beam Suntory Distillers
- Colin Spoelman, Co-Founder and Distiller, Kings County Distillery

To the museum and library folks who revealed enormous enthusiasm for informal education:

- Dawn Bonner, Manager of Visual Resources, Mount Vernon, Ladies Association, Mount Vernon, VA
- Lynell Seabold, Museum Director, Ava Gardner Museum, Smithfield, NC
- Alison Kelly, Science Research Specialist, Library of Congress, Washington, DC
- Meghan Harmon, Reference Librarian, Abraham Lincoln Presidential Library and Museum, Springfield, IL
- Jo-Anne Alverez, Library Assistant, Cerritos Library, Cerritos, CA

- Coi E. Drummond-Gehrig, Digital Image Collection Administrator, Denver Public Library, Denver, CO

To Katy Sykes, the first person to read this book and comment on it who wasn't related to me and therefore obligated to be nice.

To the team at Skyhorse Publishing:
- Hector Carosso, project editor
- Kirsten Dalley, production editor
- Brian Peterson, cover designer

To my literary agent, Steve Harris, CSG Literary Partners, Cresskill, NJ. In Steve, I found someone (or did he find me?) who was supportive, patient, instructive, and enthusiastic. He "got it" from Day 1.

And finally, to my wife Beth, to whom this book is dedicated. She was my constructive critic, eagle-eyed editor, and tireless research assistant as the book took shape. More importantly, whenever I have accidently given voice to a wild idea—"You know what might be fun. . ."— her response has been, "Let's do it"!

INDEX

PEOPLE IN HISTORY

PLACES

WHISKEYS, DISTILLERIES, AND TASTERS

RECIPES AND CHEFS

SONGS AND PERFORMERS

ABOUT THE AUTHOR

HARRIS COOPER is the Hugo L. Blomquist Distinguished Professor of Psychology and Neuroscience, Emeritus, at Duke University. At Duke, he has served as chair of two departments and as the Dean of the Social Sciences for the College of Arts & Sciences, helping administer the departments of history, sociology, political science, and cultural anthropology, among others.

He is the author of four textbooks, editor of three books on social science research methods, and four books on education policy. His work on families and schools has led to appearances on numerous television and radio shows and coverage in every major American newspaper.

Dr. Cooper is a Gold Chalk Award winner for Excellence in Graduate Education from the University of Missouri-Columbia.

Dr. Cooper has been an avid reader of American history for more than four decades. He is an Executive Bourbon Steward and has visited over 60 distilleries throughout the United States.

Dr. Cooper is a fan of baseball, crossword puzzles, and fly fishing. He lives in the Research Triangle in North Carolina with his wife, Beth. His two children are both university professors.